EMOTIONAL INTELLIGENCE IN EVERYDAY LIFE

EMOTIONAL INTELLIGENCE IN EVERYDAY LIFE

A Scientific Inquiry

edited by

Joseph Ciarrochi
University of Wollongong

Joseph P. Forgas
University of New South Wales

John D. Mayer
University of New Hampshire

Ψ Psychology Press
Taylor & Francis Group

NEW YORK AND HOVE

Published by
Psychology Press, Inc.
29 West 35th Street
New York, NY 10001
www.psypress.com

Published in Great Britain by
Psychology Press, LTD.
27 Church Road
Hove, East Sussex
BN3 2FA
www.psypress.co.uk

Psychology Press, Inc., is an imprint of the Taylor & Francis Group.
Printed in the United States of America on acid-free paper.

EMOTIONAL INTELLIGENCE IN EVERYDAY LIFE: A Scientific Inquiry

2 3 4 5 6 7 8 9 0

Printed by Edwards Brothers, Lillington, NC, 2001.
Cover design by Claire C. O'Neill.
Cover: Detail from "Venus and Mars" by Sandro Botticellio © National Gallery, London.

A CIP catalog record for this book is available from the British Library.
∞ The paper in this publication meets the requirements of the ANSI Standard Z39.48-
1984 (Permanence of Paper).

Library of Congress Cataloging-in-Publication Data
Emotional intelligence in everyday life : a scientific inquiry / edited by Joseph Ciarrochi,
Joseph P. Forgas, John D. Mayer.
        p. cm
    Includes bibliographical references and index.
    ISBN 1-84169-027-9 (case ; alk. paper) — ISBN 1-84169-028-7 (pbk : alk. paper)
    1. Emotional intelligence. I. Ciarrochi, Joseph. II. Forgas, Joseph P. III. Mayer,
John D., 1953–

BF576 .E465 2001
152.4—dc21   2001018160

ISBN (case) 1-84169-027-9
ISBN (paper) 1-84169-028-7

CONTENTS

ABOUT THE EDITORS

Joseph Ciarrochi received his Ph.D. degree from the University of Pittsburgh, a postdoctoral fellowship in emotion research from the University of New South Wales, and currently has a position as lecturer in psychology at the Unversity of Wollongong. He has been conducting cutting-edge research in how emotions influence thinking and behavior and how enotional intelligence can best be measured and used. His findings have been published in the top journals in psychology and have been presented at numerous international conferences. In addition to conducting research, Dr. Ciarrochi has been developing training programs that are designed to increase people's social and emotional intelligence.

Joseph P. Forgas is a Scientia Professor of Psychology at the University of New South Wales, Sydney. He received his DPhil degree from the University of Oxford and subsequently was awarded a DSc degree from the same university. He has written or edited 14 books and is the author of more than 120 scholarly articles and chapters. He is a fellow at the Academy of Social Sciences, Australia; the American Psychological Society; and the Society of Personality and Social Psychology. His current research focuses on the role of affect in social thinking and interpersonal behavior. This work has received international recognition, including the Research Prize from the Alexander von Humboldt foundation (Germany) and a Special Investgator Award from the Australian Research Council.

John (Jack) D. Mayer pioneered research in emotional intelligence. Since the late 1970s, he has studied the interaction of emotion and thought. Between 1990 and 1993, Dr. Mayer coauthored the first peer-reviewed scientific articles on emotional intelligence, with his colleague Dr. Peter Salovey of Yale University. Since then Dr. Mayer has further examined how to measure and use emotional intelligence. At the same time, he has developed a conceptual model for the more general study of human personality. He has published more than 70 scientific articles, book chapters, and tests. Dr. Mayer is currently a professor of psychology at the University of New Hampshire. he has served on the editorial boards of

Psychological Bulletin and the *Journal of Personality* and has been a National Institute of Mental Health Postdoctoral Scholar at Stanford University. Dr. Mayer received his Ph.D. and M.A. degrees in psychology at Case Western Reserve University and his B.A. degree from the University of Michigan. Dr. Mayer's current work on emotional intelligence has been featured widely in the media. He has spoken on the topic in academic, business, and government forums, both nationally and internationally.

CONTRIBUTORS

Reuven Bar-On
Institute of Applied Intelligence
Israel

Peter Caputi
Department of Psychology
University of Wollongong, Australia

David R. Caruso
Moodware, USA

Amy Chan
Department of Psychology
University of Wollongong, Australia

Joseph Ciarrochi
Department of Psychology
University of Wollongong, Australia

Maurice Elias
Department of Psychology
Rutgers University, USA

Julie Fitness
Psychology Department
Macquarie University, Australia

Judith M. Flury
Department of Psychology
University of Texas at Arlington, USA

Joseph P. Forgas
Department of Psychology
University of New South Wales, Australia

Lisa Hunter
Department of Psychology
Rutgers University, USA

William J. Ickes
Department of Psychology
University of Texas at Arlington, USA

Jeffrey S. Kress
William Davidson School of Jewish Education
Jewish Theological Seminary, USA

John D. Mayer
Department of Psychology
University of New Hampshire, USA

Richard Roberts
Department of Psychology
University of Sydney, Australia

Peter Salovey
Department of Psychology
Yale University, USA

Robert J. Sternberg
Department of Psychology
Yale University, USA

Graeme John Taylor
Department of Psychiatry
University of Toronto
and
Mount Sinai Hospital, Canada

Charles J. Wolfe
Charles J. Wolfe and Associates, USA

EMOTIONAL INTELLIGENCE IN EVERYDAY LIFE: AN INTRODUCTION

John D. Mayer
Joseph Ciarrochi
Joseph P. Forgas

Few areas of psychology have generated so much popular interest as emotional intelligence (EI). In the last five years, EI has been a topic of best-selling books, magazines, and newspaper articles. It has also been the topic of considerable scientific research. There are several explanations for the explosion of interest in EI. One explanation is that EI somehow fits the zeitgeist—the intellectual spirit—of the times. A persistent theme of contemporary life is that we can solve technical problems far better than human problems. The promise of EI is that it might help us solve at least one aspect of human problems, namely, conflict between what one feels and what one thinks. A second, everyday explanation for the interest in EI is that the EI concept implies (to some) that people without much academic ability might still be highly successful in life if they are high in EI. Another reason for its popularity may be that the concept provides critics of traditional intelligence tests with ammunition to attack those tests (after all, one might not need traditional intelligence to succeed). And finally, journalists and writers have written lively, popular accounts of EI and its potential role in everyday life. Such accounts have challenged the view that human nature involves a continuous conflict between the head and the heart. Moreover, they have led people to believe that EI may make us healthy, rich, successful, loved, and happy. Such bold and important claims need to be evaluated scientifically. This is what our book sets out to do.

☐ A Dialogue about Human Nature

Beginning in the twentieth century, psychologists began to insert themselves into the debate on human nature. They helped inform political scientists about why people vote in certain ways; provided input to aeronautical engineers about how to compensate for human weaknesses in the cockpit of airplanes; and informed computer scientists on the ways that people think. Most relevant here, they also began to tell psychotherapists and others about how people felt, and what those feelings meant.

Pronouncements about why people do the things they do, and the nature of human nature, long predate psychology, of course. As our species evolved tens of thousands of years ago, Homo sapiens must have found themselves increasingly self-aware in a largely mysterious and unpredictable world. This self-awareness prompted them to develop language and culture to communicate information about life and existence. From the earliest times, philosophers, religious prophets, mystics, and poets have provided greatly sought (and sometimes forcibly imposed) directions on how life should be lived. From Ancient Greece came political philosophy and the invention of democracy. From China came a code of family life evolved in the form of Confucianism. From the Middle East came monotheism and the commandments of Moses.

The forms of government, the religions, and the moralities in use today are descendants of earlier systems of thought. In general, those systems that survived and flourished did so in part because they worked. Thoughts evolve as well as organisms, and only those systems of thinking survived that were useful enough to assist with daily living. When the expertise is completely wrong, it is deemphasized and eventually ignored. The conversation between the experts and audience flourishes when experts are helpful, and vanishes when they are not. We can see the process today: Communism's view of humanity as "economic man" was simply too restrictive, too simplistic to properly channel human energy. Its followers finally brought about its demise. On a smaller scale, the members of isolated suicide cults die off because their own self-destruction makes it finally impossible to further spread their message. Likewise, the belief that emotions are irrational may be destined for extinction. Emotional intelligence has attracted the attention of the public because it suggests that emotions convey sensible meaning, which requires understanding.

☐ Dialogue about Feeling

To add to the larger debates on governance, religion, and morality, experts also developed theories of how people should feel. The ancient Greek Stoics argued that thinking was reliable but that feelings were too subjective, idiosyncratic, and unreliable to be used in constructive ways by society. Although stoicism failed as a movement, its central tenets influenced the Judaism of the time to a slight degree and, to a greater degree, the then-emerging tenets of Christianity. The Stoic ideas were therefore conveyed through the branches of some religions. Centuries later, the rational, scholarly, and empirical emphasis of the European Enlightenment appeared to further discredit emotionality. There were some rebellions against this trend, including the European romantic movement, in which artists, writers, and philosophers argued for the importance of feeling and of following one's heart.

Just a few decades ago, when many contemporary emotions researchers were coming of age, the political rebellions of the 1960s also placed a high value on the emotions. For example, in the United States, then Secretary of Defense Robert McNamara referred to himself as a "human computer" who would not let emotion interfere with his thoughts about the War in Vietnam. In contrast, demonstrators against the war followed their feelings of sympathy toward innocent people who were dying, anger at a government that was responsible for those deaths, and, perhaps, fear at having to serve in an unpopular war. They believed that the cold, computer-like arguments of people like Robert McNamara were being used to disparage those feelings. Whatever the merits of the arguments, the debate was often characterized as one of reason against feeling. There was little recognition that thought and feeling could be integrated [41].

☐ Advent of Emotional Intelligence

Emotional intelligence is the latest development in understanding the relation between reason and emotion. Unlike earlier ideas, its unique contribution is to see thought and emotion as adaptively, *intelligently*, intertwined. Whereas Blaise Pascal wrote, famously, that "The heart has its reasons of which reason knows not" [1, p. 113], the concept of EI suggests the two may not be so far apart as supposed.

As with past developments in the view of human nature, there is interplay between the experts in the field and those who are interested in using the knowledge for more practical purposes. Today, EI spans two worlds: that of popular psychology, with its best-selling volumes on codependence, personality types, healing of the soul, and jazzy newspaper science, on the one hand, and that of careful, painstaking research science, on the other hand. This intersection creates a rather uneasy tension at times, and often misleading cross talk.

The scientist says, "Here is what I have been working on recently. . . . "

The journalist replies, "This is really important," and then jazzes up the story in a way that seems close to lunacy: "EI is twice as important as IQ!" (This often-made, often-repeated claim cannot be substantiated, as is pointed out in a number of chapters of this volume).

Readers think the idea is important and follow the journalistic reports closely. Seeing this, the scientist thinks, "People are interested in what I do (even if they don't quite get it). I'll give them more" and then proceeds to write a carefully analytic piece that might be, however, off the topic, or so advanced as to be unfathomable to nonpsychologists. (Much of EI writing really is not about EI, as several authors note in their chapters.)

At the same time, this intersection between the scientific and popular world can lead to genuine collaboration between the scientist and the public, but only if the scientist cares enough to write clearly and the interested reader is motivated to think critically.

☐ Rationale for this Book

In the past few years, people have expressed a strong desire for information about EI, as is shown by the proliferation of popular books and magazine and newspaper articles. Scientists also have become fascinated by the topic; there has been a marked increase in serious research within the area. We were motivated to develop this edited volume in response to the curiosity about the concept and the availability of new information about it in the scientific literature.

In this volume, we have invited internationally renowned scientists and scientific practitioners to present their views and scientific findings related to EI. We have asked them to write in an accessible, accurate, and informative fashion, so that people from a wide variety of disciplines and walks of life can easily understand the book. We have asked them to keep their footnotes and citations to a minimum (although you will still find the most important references you need to other important works in the area). The result is a collection of essays that are frequently worthwhile and informative, often provocative, and sometimes (we think) wonderful.

These essays address: Why are experts now saying EI exists? What is the concept, and what does it mean? What does it say about aspects of our everyday life, including our health, economic decisions, relationships, and ability to have a successful career? This book explains what is known about each of those questions.

☐ Book's Contents

People approaching the area of EI do so with different interests, needs, and agendas. The chapters of this book will no doubt appeal in different ways to different readers. To spare the reader the effort of striking out at random, we will introduce briefly the authors and chapters of this volume. This should help readers find what is closest to what they are looking for.

Part I: Fundamental Issues

The first part of the book is a general introduction to the field of EI and its study. It introduces some of the concepts, measures, and research underlying the general study of EI.

John D. Mayer, along with another contributor to this volume, Peter Salovey, have published a number of articles on EI, including what may be the first theoretical integration and measurement instrument in the field, in 1990. Dr. Mayer recounts some of that history in Chapter 1, "A Field Guide to Emotional Intelligence." He sorts out some of the interweaving of popular and scientific psychology to provide a field guide of what's what in defining EI, measuring it, and what ultimately might be the significance of the field. If you are new to the area, or unfamiliar with the different meanings or history of EI, this chapter is a good place to start.

When the first EI scales were introduced, Joseph Ciarrochi, Amy Chan, Peter Caputi, and Richard Roberts were among the first researchers to study the available scales and to publish articles on what they saw the scales as actually measuring. They served as important critics of the field of EI measurement. After all, what good is a scientific concept if it can't be measured? In Chapter 2, "Measuring EI," they examine a variety of psychological tests that have been developed to measure EI, all of which are quite different from one another. Here, they pool their collective knowledge and talents to provide a state-of-the-art look at what measures of EI tell us today. Their chapter critically evaluates the EI tests and describes the strengths and weaknesses of each.

The field of EI was influenced strongly by several related fields. One of these was the psychological study of "cognition and affect," or, how emotions and thoughts interact. Joseph Forgas has been a central contributor to that field, and his *Handbook of Affect and Social Cognition* summarized much of that field. In Chapter 3, "Affective Intelligence: The Role of Affect in Social Thinking and Behavior," Dr. Forgas describes processes that contribute to and detract from high EI. For example, he describes how emotions progress over time and how we tend to overestimate how long negative emotions last. Drawing on his knowledge of cognition and affect, he also describes an important, unexpected finding: The more we try to reason about something, the more our irrelevant moods will bias our thoughts. His chapter describes a number of other ways that emotions influence our thinking and behavior and presents a model of these influences.

Part II: Applications of Emotional Intelligence Research to Everyday Life

The second part of the book examines how EI applies to clinical psychopathology, education, interpersonal relationships, work, health and finances, and psychological well-being.

In clinical psychology and psychiatry, there are a number of scientific and clinical concepts that are closely related to EI. Among the most important of these is the clinical syndrome of alexithymia. Alexithymia means "without emotion words" ("a": without; "lexi": words; "thymia": emotions). Graeme Taylor is among the leading researchers on that condition, which overlaps, in important ways, with lower levels of EI. In Chapter 4, "Low EI and Mental Illness," Dr. Taylor provides a comprehensive review of alexithymia research and shows how it may contribute to the development of problems in interpersonal relationships and in coping with distressing emotions and stressful life events. He also provides evidence for the important link between alexithymia and psychiatric disorders (e.g., substance abuse and eating disorders).

Reuven Bar-On began his psychological career studying well-being and the many personality dimensions related to it, such as self-regard, reality perception, and stress tolerance. He developed a scale to measure those attributes, the current version of which, the Bar-On Eqi, is now a frequently used measure of the emotional quotient (EQ). His chapter 5, "EI and Self-Actualization," describes his own approach to measuring EI. He then reviews evidence that suggests that EI is essential for realizing one's full potential in life.

All of us enjoy the pleasures and suffer the pains of interpersonal relations. Julie Fitness has devoted her career to studying the role of emotions in long-term relationships and marriage. In Chapter 6, "EI and Intimate Relationships," she discusses ways in which EI may be essential to maintaining a strong, healthy relationship. She also argues, however, that EI may not be enough for a happy relationship: Such intelligence could be used to manipulate and hurt the partner. Dr. Fitness then discusses the values and beliefs that are necessary in combination with EI to create and maintain happy, long-term relationships.

Interpersonal relations begin with a "getting to know you" period. Judith Flury and William Ickes have been conducting cutting-edge research on people's ability to read the thoughts and emotions of others. In Chapter

7, "Emotional Intelligence and Empathy," they discuss the processes that are involved in accurate emotion perception and ways in which such perception can be improved. They also describe research that suggests that being emotionally intelligent sometimes means deliberately not trying to know how the other person feels. In other words, sometimes delusions may be as necessary to our happiness as realities.

Educators have expressed a tremendous interest in EI. Maurice Elias is an eminent scholar in education and a major force in bringing EI into educational contexts. In Chapter 8, "Emotional Intelligence and Education," he and his colleagues, Lisa Hunter and Jeffrey Kress, discuss the wide range of social and emotional learning (SEL) programs that have been implemented in schools and how some of these programs have brought about a number of positive changes in students' lives (better academics, less aggression and drug usage). Dr. Elias and his colleagues' chapter is essential reading for educators, parents, and anyone who is interested in how EI can be taught.

There has been a great deal of popular interest in how EI can be applied to the business world. David Caruso is not only a trained intelligence researcher and codeveloper of some central measures of EI, but he also has served as an executive coach in the business world. He and his business colleague Charles Wolfe describe the ways in which EI is essential to success in the workplace, making liberal use of examples. In Chapter 9, "Emotional Intelligence in the Workplace," they describe how EI is relevant to selecting and developing a career and how EI can help people deal effectively with coworkers. The chapter further discusses how EI assessment can be integrated with other forms of assessment to provide people with feedback about their strengths and weaknesses. The chapter concludes with a blueprint for an EI training program within the workplace.

Peter Salovey codeveloped the theory of EI with John D. Mayer in the early 1990s and has continued work in the field since that time. In Chapter 10, "Applied Emotional Intelligence: Regulating Emotions to Become Healthy, Wealthy, and Wise," he examines how EI may contribute to both our health and our wealth. He shows that the inability to manage emotions effectively can lead to health problems such as heart disease. He also shows how poor management of negative emotions can lead to disastrous financial decisions. His chapter is rich with illustrations of how using better emotional and cognitive strategies may lead us to more fulfilling lives.

Part III: Integration and Conclusions

Robert Sternberg occupies a unique position in intelligence research today, as both insider and critic. The developer of such concepts as practical intelligence and creative intelligence, he also has served as an outspoken commentator on the field of intelligence, its foibles, and its promise. In the course of doing so, he has edited the most significant volumes in intelligence research, including, perhaps most centrally, the *Handbook of Intelligence*. In the commentary chapter, Chapter 11, "Measuring the Intelligence of an Idea: How Intelligent Is the Idea of Emotional Intelligence?" Dr. Sternberg surveys the EI area and examines its contributions to traditional intelligence research. He evaluates whether the idea of EI is "correct" or is consistent with available evidence, whether EI is novel and appropriate in accomplishing what it is supposed to, and whether EI is useful in understanding important life outcomes. Dr. Sternberg's comments tie together much that is in the book. In addition, the historical and scientific perspective he lends makes his chapter an important contribution in its own right.

Together, these articles represent a diversity of approaches, disciplinary outlooks, and perspectives on the concept of EI. The field of EI is still in its early stages; nonetheless, we are confident that each of the approaches represented in this volume will inform the reader about what EI is and how it may be important to all aspects of everyday life.

FUNDAMENTAL ISSUES

CHAPTER 1

John D. Mayer

A Field Guide to Emotional Intelligence

The field of emotional intelligence (EI) began as a topic of study within academic psychology. From there, educators, psychiatrists, human resource specialists, and others became interested, and the field grew. Today, popular magazines and articles report on the field's activities, while rigorous scholarly journals publish articles in the area. The diversity of those interested in the field has led to a comparable diversity of definitions used for EI, the measures involved, and the claims for its significance. In fact, a person encountering the EI field for the first time may wonder how to make sense of it all. To provide a field guide, this chapter will briefly discuss five central questions. First, "How did the field begin (and how was it popularized)?" This question is central to understanding the diversity of constituencies and definitions employed. In fact, the field is so diverse and has so many competing interests that the second question, "Which EI are we talking about?" is critical. A closely allied question is, "How is EI best measured?" because which EI we are talking about will direct our measurement approach. The last two questions concern the significance of the area. Many astonishing claims have been made for EI. The question, "Is EI the best predictor of success in life?" addresses such claims and asks whether they could be true. The last question, "Why is EI important?" is in many ways a rejoinder to the popular claims. That is, if those claims are untrue, does EI still matter?

The discussion of the above questions will be focused on upholding reasonable conceptual standards that make a science worth studying. So, throughout the chapter I will make a concerted effort to discuss the field

3

in a critical, careful fashion. In particular, I will advocate for such matters as (a) a history of the field based on a reasonable understanding of the areas that led up to it, (b) terminology that is consistent with existing research in psychology, (c) measures that are valid, and (d) realism concerning predictive claims. People interpret such things as consistency, validity, and realism differently, of course, and that is where the more serious and interesting controversies will arise.

☐ How Did the Field Begin (and How Was It Popularized)?

Philosophical considerations of the relations between thought and emotion in Western culture go back more than 2000 years (see [41] for an overview). Here, however, I concentrate on activities in psychology from 1900 forward, using a fivefold division of years: (1) from 1900 to 1969, during which the psychological study of intelligence and emotions were relatively separate; (2) from 1970 to 1989, when psychologists focused on how emotions and thought influenced each other; (3) from 1990 to 1993, which marked the emergence of EI as a topic of study; (4) from 1994 to 1997, when the concept was popularized, and (5) the present era of clarifying research. Table 1.1 provides an overview of the five time periods.

The period from 1900–1969 was an era that treated research in intelligence and in emotion as separate areas. Within the area of intelligence, the first tests were developed, explored, and understood. Intelligence became viewed as involving the capacity to carry out valid, abstract reasoning, and various biological explanations of intelligence were investigated. Within emotions research, early investigators focused on a chicken-and-egg problem: Would a person who encountered a stressful situation such as meeting a bear in the woods first respond physiologically (e.g., with an increased heart rate) and then feel emotion, or was the emotional feeling primary, followed by physiological changes. A second problem focused on whether emotions held universal meaning, or whether they were culturally determined and idiosyncratic. Darwin had argued that emotions evolved across animal species; this was met with skepticism by social psychologists who believed that emotions were manifested differently in different cultures (see [15] for a review).

The second era, 1970–1989, was a time when several precursors of EI were put into place. Whereas intelligence and emotion previously had been considered separate fields, they were now integrated in the new field of "cognition and affect" (i.e., thought and emotion). Within this

TABLE 1.1. The emergence of the emotional intelligence concept: An overview

1900–1969: *Intelligence and Emotions as Separate, Narrow Fields*	*Intelligence research:* The realm of psychological testing for intelligence was developed during this period and a sophisticated technology of intelligence tests arose (see [18] for a review). *Emotions research:* In the separate field of emotion, debate centered on the chicken-and-egg problem of which happens first: physiological reaction, or emotion. In other areas of work, Darwin had argued for the heritability and evolution of emotional responses, but during this time, emotion was often viewed as culturally determined, largely a product of pathology, and idiosyncratic (see [15] for a review of Darwin's work). *The search for social intelligence:* As intelligence testing emerged, the focus was on verbal and propositional intelligence. A number of psychologists sought to identify a social intelligence as well; however, efforts in this direction were apparently discouraging and conceptions of intelligence stayed exclusively cognitive.
1970–1989: *Precursors to Emotional Intelligence*	The precursors to "emotional intelligence" were put into place in this two-decade period. The field of *cognition and affect* emerged to examine how emotions interacted with thoughts. It was suggested that depressed people might be more realistic and accurate than others and that mood swings might enhance creativity [28]. The field of *nonverbal communication* developed scales devoted to perception of nonverbal information—some of it emotional—in faces and posture [6]. Those in the field of *artificial intelligence* examined how computers might understand and reason about the emotional aspects of stories [14]. Gardner's new theory of *multiple intelligences* described an "intrapersonal intelligence," which involves, among many other things, the capacity to perceive and symbolize emotions. Empirical work on *social intelligence* found that it divided into social skills, empathy skills, prosocial attitudes, social anxiety, and emotionality (sensitivity) [27]. Brain research began to separate out connections between emotion and cognition (e.g., [50]). Occasional use of the term "emotional intelligence" appeared (e.g., [52, pp. 103, 107]).
1990–1993: *The Emergence of Emotional Intelligence*	In the four-year period beginning in the 1990s, Mayer and Salovey published a series of articles on emotional intelligence. The article, "Emotional Intelligence" provided a first review of areas potentially relevant to an emotional intelligence. At the same time, a demonstration study, including the first ability measure of emotional intelligence under that name was published. An editorial in the journal *Intelligence* argued for the existence of an emotional intelligence as an actual intelligence. (See [36], [38]; [45]). During this time, further foundations of emotional intelligence were developed, particularly in the brain sciences (e.g., [12]).

(Continued)

TABLE 1.1. The emergence of the emotional intelligence concept: An overview

---

1994–1997: *The Popularization and Broadening*	Goleman, a science journalist, published the popular book, *Emotional Intelligence*, loosely modeled on the academic writings in the area (see above). The book became a worldwide best-seller and was widely copied. *Time Magazine* used the term "EQ" on its cover. A number of personality scales were published under the name of emotional intelligence. (See [2], [9], [22].)
1998–Present: *Research on and Institutionalization of Emotional Intelligence*	A number of refinements to the concept of emotional intelligence take place, along with the introduction of new measures of the concept and the first peer-reviewed research articles on the subject. (See [2], [13], [34].)

---

area, researchers sought lawful rules of what emotions meant and when they arose. Earlier philosophical writings concerning the logic of emotions were rediscovered. Researchers reasserted Darwin's idea that emotions had evolved across species, and that emotions were universal expressions of internal feelings about relationships. The influence of emotion on thought was examined in depressed individuals, as well as those suffering from bipolar disorder (manic depression). Researchers in artificial intelligence became interested in whether expert systems could be developed in the form of computer programs that could understand the feelings of story characters. To do this required drawing on some of the same basic laws of emotions and their meanings as were studied in cognition and affect. There was a small but definite interchange among researchers in artificial intelligence and those studying cognition and affect (see [41] for an overview).

Although the term "emotional intelligence" was used sporadically during this time, it was never defined or described in any definite way—probably because the foundations of the concept were still being developed. Such definitions that arose were precursor definitions, in the sense that they either referred explicitly to EI but were unclear, or were clear but failed to refer to emotional intelligence. For example, an unpublished dissertation by Dr. Wayne Payne distinguished EI from more purely cognitive forms of intelligence as follows:

> The facts, meanings, truths, relationships, etc., [of emotional intelligence] are those that exist in the realm of emotion. Thus, feelings are facts. . . . The meanings are *felt* meanings; the truths are emotional truths; the relationships are interpersonal relationships. And the problems we solve are emotional problems, that is, problems in the way we feel. [44, p. 165]

This is partway to an EI. For example, "the problems we solve are . . . problems in the way we feel" makes sense. Still, at this point much in this definition seems more rhetorical than clear. For example, the concept of *"felt* meanings" or the statement that "feelings are facts" are not explained in the text, and make sense, at best, only looking back from a better-developed field.

Another sort of precursor definition was clear but did not refer to an EI. For example, Howard Gardner wrote of intrapersonal intelligence, that the "capacity at work here is *access to one's own feeling life*—one's range of affects or emotions" [20, p. 239]. For Gardner, however, this access to feeling life did not constitute EI, but rather was part of a more general self and social knowing that were intertwined with one another [20, 240 ff.]. Gardner continues to view any separate EI as an inappropriate application of the intelligence concept [21]. A number of other areas developed precursors to EI. For example, in the literature on child development, a concept of emotional giftedness (also termed "emotional overexcitability") was proposed, which, in some ways, also anticipated the concept of EI [11, p 116].

There were several things left to be done in the late 1980s before the EI field could properly emerge. One was to draw together the various strands of research that had been performed and to recognize that they pointed to an (until then) overlooked human capacity. Another was to define the term "emotional intelligence" in an explicit, clear fashion and to connect the term to the relevant research lines that supported it. Yet another was to demonstrate some empirical evidence for the concept. In 1990, my colleague Dr. Peter Salovey and I drew together much of the above research and developed a formal theory of EI and a coordinated measurement demonstration. To do so, we examined evidence from intelligence and emotions research, as well as research in aesthetics, artificial intelligence, brain research, and clinical psychology. We applied the term "emotional intelligence," to the human capacity we believed existed and reported a study employing the first empirical test designed explicitly to measure the concept [36, 45]. In a follow-up editorial in 1993, in the journal *Intelligence,* we argued that EI was a basic, overlooked intelligence that held the promise to meet a rigorous definition of intelligence. It called for serious study in the area [38]. For these reasons, the third era, 1990 to 1993, is generally regarded as the demarcation point for the emergence of the study of EI (e.g., [16, 22], p. 43; Sternberg, this volume).

The fourth era (1994 to 1997) marked a rather unusual turn of events as the field became popularized and broadened. It was during this time that the term "emotional intelligence" was popularized in a best-selling book by a science journalist, Daniel Goleman [22]. He and others seized upon the term as a banner for a great deal of research and public policy.

In the book and the popular accounts that accompanied it, EI was said to be, possibly, the best predictor of success in life, to be accessible by virtually anyone, and to be similar to "character." The book's combination of lively writing, extraordinary claims for the concept, and loose description of the concept created an explosion of activity in a new, and now increasingly fuzzily defined, area. Tests were sold as measures of EI that were not originally defined that way, associations of educators and business people were created to teach and consult on EI—defined as nearly anything having to do with character—and many other popular books attempted to ride the coattails of the success of the 1995 popularization.

We are now in the current period, extending roughly from 1998 to the present. During this time, theoretical and research refinements in the area have taken place, new measures of EI have been developed, and serious research is taking place within the field, of which this volume is one example. The field is complicated by the fact that it possesses both scientific and popular aspects. These often-conflicting constituencies have led to definitions of EI that verge on the chaotic. This is why the next sections address the question of which EI we are talking about.

☐ Which Emotional Intelligence Are We Talking About?

Definitions

Nowadays we speak of many different kinds of intelligences. In each case, intelligence refers to the capacity to perceive, understand, and use symbols; that is, to reason abstractly. For example, we talk of verbal intelligence, spatial intelligence, social intelligence, and other interrelated intelligences. The modifier—verbal, spatial, or social—specifies the intelligence and what it refers to. So, verbal intelligence denotes the capacity to understand and use words. Spatial intelligence denotes the capacity to understand and use objects in space. Social intelligence denotes the capacity to understand, and use social information. Within psychology, EI belongs to this same group of interrelated intelligences and denotes the capacity to understand, and use emotional information. In addition, EI plausibly reflects the emotion system's capacity to enhance intelligence.

The initial ability definitions of EI arose in 1990 in working with Salovey. These early definitions used a two-part approach, speaking first of the general processing of emotional information and second specifying the skills involved in such processing. An early version of our definition follows:

A type of emotional information processing that includes accurate appraisal of emotions in oneself and others, appropriate expression of emotion, and adaptive regulation of emotion in such a way as to enhance living. [36, p. 773]

By 1999, my colleagues and I had expanded on this definition a bit, keeping its two-part form:

Emotional intelligence refers to an ability to recognize the meanings of emotions and their relationships, and to reason and problem-solve on the basis of them. Emotional intelligence is involved in the capacity to perceive emotions, assimilate emotion-related feelings, understand the information of those emotions, and manage them. [34, p. 267]

During the popularization of EI, its definition was changed quite substantially. In Goleman's [22, p. 43) treatment of our definition [22, p. 189], EI became the five areas of

knowing one's emotions . . . managing emotions . . . motivating oneself . . . recognizing emotions in others . . . [and] handling relationships. [22, p. xii]

With this small change, the emphasis was shifted toward motivation (motivating oneself) and social relationships generally speaking (handling relationships). Ability at understanding and processing emotion was mixed in with some other characteristics. A different mixed model is presented in a manual describing a test under the name of an emotional quotient:

an array of noncognitive capabilities, competencies, and skills that influence one's ability to succeed in coping with environmental demands and pressures. [2, p. 14]

Thus there emerged two lines of definitions: (a) the original approach that defined EI as an intelligence involving emotion and (b) the popularized, mixed approaches that blended EI with other skills and characteristics such as well-being, motivation, and capacities to engage in relationships.

Component Abilities and Skills

The apparently small changes in the wording of the definitions above become magnified when one examines more specific lists of characteristics said to define EI. Consider the three models of emotional intelligence presented in Table 1.2. The ability theory (updated in 1997) divides EI into four areas. The first area includes ability at emotional perception and expression, including the accurate assessment of emotions in the self and others. The second area involves the ability to use emotions to facilitate thought, including the accurate association of emotions to other sensa-

TABLE 1.2. Characteristics said to make up emotional intelligence

Ability approach	Mixed approach		
Mayer, Caruso, & Salovey [34] (revised from Salovey & Mayer [45])	Bar-On [2]	Goleman [23] (revised from Goleman [22] and Salovey & Mayer [45])	
(1) The ability to perceive emotions accurately — Emotional awareness; emotions in faces, music, and designs	Accurately perceiving (1) ... personal EQ — awareness, Assertiveness, self-regard, Self-actualization, Independence	(1) Intra-awareness	(1) Self- — Emotional self-awareness; Accurate self-assessment; Self-confidence
(2) The ability to use emotions to facilitate thought — Accurately relating emotions to other basic sensations (e.g., colors, textures); Using emotions to shift perspectives	(2) Inter-personal EQ — Empathy, Interpersonal relationships, Social responsibility	(2) Self-regulation	Self-control; Trustworthiness; Conscientiousness; Adaptability; Innovation
(3) The ability to understand emotions and their meanings — Ability to analyze emotions in parts; Ability to understand likely transitions from one feeling to another; Ability to understand; Ability to understand	(3) Adaptability EQ — Problem solving, Reality testing	(3) Motivation	Achievement drive; Commitment; Initiative; Optimism

(4) The ability to manage emotions	complex feelings in stories Ability to manage emotions in the self Ability to manage emotions in others
(4) Stress management EQ	Stress tolerance, Impulse control
(5) General mood EQ	Happiness Optimism
(4) Empathy	Understanding others Developing others Service orientation Leveraging diversity Political awareness
(5) Social Skills	Influence Communication Conflict management Leadership Change catalyst Building bonds Collaboration and cooperation Team capabilities

tions, and the ability to use emotions to enhance thought. The third area, understanding emotions, involves analyzing emotions into parts, understanding likely transitions from one feeling to another, and understanding complex feelings in social situations. Finally, the fourth area, managing emotions, involves the ability to manage feelings in oneself and others.

The mixed definition that defines EI as noncognitive competencies [2] is far broader. It starts with five categories: (1) intrapersonal, which includes such qualities as self-actualization, independence, and emotional self-awareness; (2) interpersonal, which includes such qualities as empathy and social responsibility; (3) adaptability, which includes such qualities as problem solving and reality testing; (4) stress management, which involves impulse control and stress tolerance; and (5) general mood, which includes happiness and optimism.

This can be contrasted with the five-part popular elaboration of EI proposed by Goleman. Updated to its 1998 areas, the (1) self-awareness area includes such attributes as emotional awareness and self-confidence; (2) self-regulation includes self-control, trustworthiness, and innovation; (3) motivation includes achievement drive, initiative, and optimism; (4) empathy includes such attributes as understanding others and political awareness; and (5) social skills involve such qualities as influence, conflict management, and team capabilities.

Big Divisions of Personality Inform What EI Ought to Denote

Recall that the term EI was said to most naturally describe the ability to carry out reasoning in regard to emotions, and to include emotion's enhancement of thought. These ideas are central to the ability model; they are, however, oddly de-emphasized or missing from the mixed, broadened models just reviewed. For example, why might motivation be included within a theory of EI? Motivation is often considered to be a sphere of mental functioning separate from emotions and cognition. Are persistence, optimism, political savvy, and the like parts of EI—and if not, what are they?

Personality psychology is the relevant discipline to decide, for it studies hundreds of parts of the mind. And indeed, virtually all personality parts, from EI to extroversion, can be systematically organized and classified according to their structures and functions [7], [29], [30], [42]. The above classification systems can be approximated with reasonable precision using a simpler approach, which I will refer to here as the systems set of Primary Parts. This approach divides personality into four primary parts, in a sort of updated version of the id, ego, and superego. These four parts can then be divided and subdivided until one arrives at all the commonly discussed contemporary parts of personality according to those compre-

TABLE 1.3. The systems set division of personality[a]

Major divisions or "agents" of personality	Traits describing the divisions

Energy Lattice:
Represents the coherent cooperation of the lower-level motivational and emotional systems of personality. It consists of a person's basic urges and emotional responses to those basic urges.
	* Motives
	  Need for achievement
	  Need for affiliation
	  Need for power
	*Motivational levels
	  Persistence
	  Zeal
	*Emotions
	  Happiness
	  Anger
	  Sadness/depression
	*Emotional Style
	  Emotionality—Emotional stability

Knowledge Works:
Represents the information store of personality: feelings and thoughts about the self and the world, and operates on that knowledge.
	*Abilities and achievement
	  Verbal intelligence
	  Spatial intelligence
	  Emotional intelligence
	*Cognitive styles
	  Optimism—Pessimism
	  Detail orientation

Role Player:
Responsible for expressing and projecting internal personality into the world. It plans important social activities and roles and carries those out.
	*Expressive Styles
	  Extroversion—Introversion
	  Warmth—Coldness
	*Expressive Skills
	  Politeness
	  Good eye contact
	  Role-playing ability

Conscious Executive:
The seat of consciousness contains both consciousness and the conscious will (self-control). It oversees personality and contributes high-level, creative thought when necessary.
	*Consciousness
	  Aware—Unaware
	  Self-conscious—unself-conscious
	*Will
	  High–low willpower

[a]Modifed and developed from the Relational Classification System for the Parts of Personality [29].

hensive classification systems [31]. By doing this, one can see where the proposed parts of EI, such as persistence, optimism, political savvy, and self-control, fall within the personality system.

Briefly, the four parts are as follows. The **energy lattice** includes an individual's motives and emotions, and provides a general direction to the individual in terms of doing things. The **knowledge works** contains information about the self and the world required for the individual to function, including diverse areas of knowledge such as one's life history, mathematical knowledge (e.g., how to add), and social and emotional knowledge. The third, **role player**, forms and enacts plans about how to interact socially, such as leading (or following) others, or being sympathetic, or making a good impression. Finally, there is an **executive consciousness**, which contains a person's conscious awareness, consciously managing and regulating the other parts of personality.

Now consider persistence and zeal, optimism, political savvy, and self-control, all of which have been said by popularizers to make up EI. Persistence and zeal are properties that primarily describe the energy lattice and its capacity to direct the individual in the face of obstacles. A second proposed part of EI is "optimism"—a way of envisioning the world that is embedded in an individual's knowledge works. Third, consider political savvy: Can a person publicly convey a supportive attitude toward others and take bold stands on issues? Can he or she avoid alienating those who disagree? This is surely a skill associated with the individual's role player. Finally, self-control involves the power of the conscious executive: Can the person change to become a better person? Self-control is essential to getting along in life.

The fact that these four attributes pertain to four different parts of personality suggest that they are rather unrelated to each other. The popularizers' additions (persistence, optimism, political savvy, and self-control) seem to have little to do specifically with emotions or intelligence. Perhaps they share the common fact that certain people desire to possess those qualities. Other than that, there is little or nothing to suggest that they form a unitary whole. Indeed, they may conflict with one another. Persistence toward a goal may undercut political savvy; optimism may promote a *lack* of self-control if a person thinks, "Oh, I won't get caught" or "It won't hurt."

Contrast that with EI conceived of as an ability. This EI is focused on the knowledge works and its interactions with the emotions of the energy lattice. In terms of these four primary parts, the knowledge works perceives emotion by monitoring and feeling the emotion in the energy lattice. Sometimes, emotion from the energy lattice activates (e.g., energizes) concepts in the knowledge works and reprioritizes life endeavors in a smart way. For example, a serious illness might remind a person of what is truly important in life. Additional learning occurs as the role player experiments with various emotion-laden actions. Gradually, the knowledge works builds up expert knowledge about emotions that can become quite accurate. Finally, through attempts at self-management (from the conscious executive), the best emotional reactions for the individual can be favored and encouraged. This conception of EI is unitary because it is centered in the knowledge works. And because, although it involves the other parts as well, does so only insofar as those other parts contribute to the intelligent interaction of emotion and thought. Its unifying theme is that emotion enhances thoughts and the person is intelligent about emotion.

The difference between the ability-based and mixed-list approaches to EI, therefore, are very substantial. Mixed-list approaches are of potential value in that they are studying multiple aspects of personality at once. They are not, however, particularly related to any new concept of EI, or even to emotion or intelligence. Indeed, the decades-old California Psychological Inventory (CPI) [26] is composed of a number of individual scales that sound like some of today's mixed-list emotional intelligence tests: self-acceptance, empathy, responsibility, socialization, good impression, well-being, tolerance, intellectual efficiency, flexibility, and self-control. (The CPI was originally designed to measure folk conceptions of mental health).

Seemingly in response to such issues, some mixed-concept researchers acknowledge that EI—as they see it—is "not at all new" [3, p. xi]. Perhaps more germane is that such scales of mixed qualities largely duplicate personality research under a different name. A careful connection of such mixed-list approaches to the personality field would make the tests easier to interpret and understand because of the considerable overlap between new scales and old. By contrast, EI as ability does have promise as one among a set of new intelligences, including practical intelligence and newly revised versions of social intelligence (e.g., 49).

There is one relatively new area in these long lists of mixed traits. It involves measures of the meta-experience of mood. Meta-experience refers to reflections on mood such as, "I know how I'm feeling," and "I clearly understand my mood." Scales under the name meta-experience, meta-mood, and meta-emotion, as well as similar concepts from the field of alexithymia (inability to use emotion words), were one of many precursors of EI (e.g., [37], [39], [46, p. 147], [46]). These scales measure a reflective, conscious experience of emotion that appears important to know about. Still, as my colleagues and I wrote of one of our own scales of meta-experience, "we have little interest in claiming that the measure discussed here is some kind of emotional intelligence test" [46]. That would seem to be over-claiming what they really do measure—a reflective, conscious experience of mood.

If mixed models of personality are little more than haphazard composites of personality traits, it seems worth returning to the more focused ability conception. Still, there are arguments against the ability approach. The first is that it may be more exciting (and easier) to gather together the group of positive personality qualities suggested by popularizers and use them to predict success at work or at home. There is nothing wrong with assessing such positive qualities and combining them. Still, if a researcher adds all those positive attributes together, he or she will not likely come up with a simple, powerful predictor of success. Prediction studies of important criteria, such as getting good grades in school, being happily married, or landing a good job, indicate that each type of success is a product of qualities unique to that area. These studies also regularly show that qualities that generally seem good can interfere with success in a specific area.

The problem becomes that what is "positive" depends on the how and when it is applied. The optimist's supportive comment, "Don't worry, you'll get over it," may work for some individuals. It could, however, just as easily raise the specter of death for a seriously ill person, seem cruel to the man who wants to honor his recently-deceased wife, or dismissive to a spouse who feels she isn't being heard seriously. Conversely, the seemingly negative expression of anger can have many positive consequences when used to set limits for children, warn complacent students they must work harder, and indicate that an employee has to get organized. When, in the dark days of World War II, Winston Churchill offered the British people, "Blood, sweat, and tears," he was not nice and it was not optimistic, but it was arguably quite emotionally intelligent. It is for these reasons (and the fact that a century of personality research contradicts the likelihood) that EI researchers who hope to somehow live up to popular claims about success by studying the positive aspects of personality are likely to be disappointed. The fact is that "positive attributes" can take prediction only so far. This returns the researcher to the search for new, powerful dimensions of prediction that have been overlooked. One of these, perhaps, is EI as an ability. The irksome thing about such new dimensions is that they take some time and sophistication to properly measure and assess their importance. That agenda cannot keep up with the escalating claims for EI in the popular literature (to be discussed).

The final argument for why mixed approaches might work is that they indirectly measure EI ability. This argument states that people higher in EI should become happier and more optimistic than others over time, so measuring optimism and happiness is enough. According to this argument, if one formed two groups of people, one high and one low in EI ability, but otherwise matched on their average emotional states (e.g., depression, aggression, and anxiety), the group high on EI would feel better over time because of their superior emotional understanding. This is a potentially compelling point, and it is likely true to a slight degree. Still, the relationship between EI and such positive qualities as optimism or self-esteem is not strong for several reasons. First, EI is not always highly valued or rewarded by society, and so the person with high levels of it may experience a great deal of frustration at seeing what others cannot see. Second, even if a person's EI is valued, his or her goals may not be happiness. There are many people quite willing to take on emotionally difficult roles—helper, caretaker, therapist—so as to make the world a better place. Consider Paul Britton, a leading criminal psychologist in Great Britain. Motivated by the plight of crime victims, he empathically entered into their lives to try to identify the criminals who abused and, sometimes, murdered, them. Britton valued a sense of helping and moral responsibility over happiness. Speaking of the victims and their families who he tried to help, he wrote:

> Looking back, I don't remember the victims' faces because usually the pictures I see are taken after death when the light has gone out of their eyes. What I do remember are their minds because so much of what I do involves learning the intimate details and rhythm of their lives. It's knowing them and knowing what happened to them that makes the pain and sadness of the deaths even greater. This is not enjoyable work. [5, p. 650]

A third reason EI does not inexorably lead to happiness is that emotional work and self-improvement, like any personal change, typically takes a long time. Hence, such positive differences that EI can bring about in personality may not be seen until middle age or later.

Although it would be nice, persistent, and optimistic to argue that "mixed" concepts of EI represent a unique and novel perspective on EI, it may be more realistic to view them as haphazard descriptions of desirable personality and compare them with other descriptions of desirable personalities. Such serious comparisons have not yet taken place. This book on EI must deal broadly with the field, and that means including both versions of EI: the "intelligence" version and the "mixed" version.

☐ How Is Emotional Intelligence Best Measured?

The concept of EI emerged with attempts to measure it. An experimental measure of EI was introduced along with the first theory (see [36]). As the concept became popularized, journalists expressed some ambivalence about measuring EI. In its story on EI, *Time Magazine* asked, "What's your EQ?" in big block letters across its cover. The lower-left-hand corner of the page elaborated: "It's not your IQ. It's not even a number. But emotional intelligence may be the best predictor of success in life, redefining what it means to be smart."

The statement, "It's not even a number," implied that EI might not be quantified in any usual sense. Yet the same passage made the apparently quantitative assertion that it may be "the best predictor of success in life." The present discussion examines how EI can indeed be measured (and sometimes, mismeasured). The next section returns to the issue of what EI predicts.

After the 1995 *Time Magazine* piece and other popularizations there was a rush to create scales of EI. With the popularization, the cacophany of conceptualizations and definitions began. Consequently, the first difference among measures to check is what definition of EI they are based on.

Scales Sorted by Definition of EI

For example, in the wake of the popularization, a number of quickly developed measures emerged. Some popular magazine and newspaper articles included ad hoc scales of optimism, or of delay of gratification, to measure EI. Other approaches involved relabeling already-existing tests, or tests then coming to market, as measures of the concept. Given the broad definition of EI employed in the popularizations, virtually any pre-existing personality test that measured positive attributes could be considered a relevant measure. The Bar-On EQ-i (Emotional Quotient Inventory), published in 1997, was said to be based on a 1988 scale originally intended as a measure of psychological well-being [2]. The Emotional Competencies Inventory (ECI) by Goleman and Boyatzis was based on earlier work that modeled and assessed effective managers according to general competencies [4]. Goleman [24, p. 320] stated that 14 of 16 abilities on this earlier Boyatzis scale "were emotional competencies."

Such scales of well-being or managerial effectiveness were occasionally said to have started the era of EI. Given the dozens of already existing scales of well-being and managerial effectiveness, it seems strange to single out one or another of them as starting a field. No such early scale included a theory of EI—or even a use of the term. Moreover, if EI equals persistence, zeal, optimism, empathy, and character, dozens of traditional personality scales could be said to measure EI. For example, the widely used, well-validated CPI might be considered the first measure of EI given its coverage of social strengths, dominance, and motivation—and its initial publication date of 1956—and yet this would seem to stretch matters.

New scales also were developed. Some of these used mixed models as well, such as the EQ Map (Orioli, credited in [9]). A scale by Schutte and her colleagues [47] was based on a combination of the ability theory and more popular approaches. My colleagues and I further developed our own ability line of measurement research in the area, based on our ability conceptions (e.g., [36]).

Scales Sorted by Measurement Approach

Beyond the model or definition of EI upon which the scales were based, a second chief difference among them was their measurement approach. Many of the scales described above employed self-judgments (e.g., "How emotionally smart are you?"). Self-judgments measure differently than observer ratings (e.g., asking an observer how emotionally smart you are), and both of these measure something different than ability tests with right or wrong answers (e.g., "What does 'envy' mean?"). Self-judgments work if one views EI as a collection of certain nonability-related personality traits. For example, Schutte and colleagues' scale, the EQ Map, and the EQ-i questionnaire ask many similar questions such as, "Are you clear about your emotions?" "Are you good at solving problems?" and "Is your mood positive?" Scales such as this, which correlate very highly with pleasant mood (and have negative correlations with unpleasant mood) basically measure a person's self-perceived well-being. It is exactly this quality of positivity that accounts for the fact that most of these scales have very high correlations with positive emotionality (about $r = .50$ to $.80$, depending upon the scales). Because positive emotionality predicts a lot of good things, so might a lot of these new scales, but it is a case of reinventing the wheel. There is little evidence, as of yet, that predictions from any of these mixed scales go beyond predictions that can be made from positive emotionality and the absence of negative affectivity. (For a detailed review of this issue, see Chapter 2.)

Another serious problem with self-report is that it does not relate to actual measured intelligence. In the traditional intelligence field, at least, measured IQ does not correlate well with self-reported intelligence, with correlations rarely exceeding modest levels (e.g., between $r = .00$ and $.30$). This makes sense if one thinks of a school classroom. Therein, one will find average students who think they are much brighter than they are, students who excel but are so self-critical that they don't fully grasp their own capacities, and students so limited in mental capacity that they cannot fully comprehend the question.

A real-life example of this concerns an amateur sailor who had repeatedly run aground in a homemade boat off the north coast of Wales while trying to sail across the Irish Sea from Anglesey. Upon the occasion of his eleventh rescue—at a cost to British taxpayers of more than $85,000—he was described by his rescuers as "clueless." This assessment did not coincide with the sailor's own self-judgment. He explained that any navigational training was superfluous, in his case. Referring to his lack of a skipper's license he told reporters: "I don't need one. . . . I'm far more intelligent.'" He had, however, been using a road map as his primary navigation device (Reuters, August 11, 2000). This is merely an extreme example of the disconnect between actual and self-judged ability.

A second approach to measuring EI is to use observer ratings. This makes particular sense if one considers EI to refer to effective behavior. In observer ratings, an observer—someone who knows the person—decides whether a person is emotionally intelligent or not. Within organizational settings it is sometimes the custom to measure "360 degrees of feedback" from all around the individual. So, a manager in a company would receive feedback from subordinates, colleagues, and supervisors on a number of competencies believed related to EI. An example of such a scale using a mixed definition of EI is the ECI [25].

What held true for self-report and intelligence, however, also holds true for observer ratings. That is, it is hard for observers to judge others' intelligence. A very bright mental performance may be over many an observer's head. Moreover, even very bright observers may confuse performance that is a consequence of intelligence with performance that is more a product of average intelligence mixed with hard work, luck, or creativity. In all, it is no wonder that observer reports of intelligence do not correlate well with actual intelligence either. (One exception is that teachers are fairly good estimators of their students' intelligence.)

If one adheres to a concept of EI as an intelligence, one is likely to seek out ability tests as the measure of choice. These are tests in which a person has to solve problems and there are "right" answers. This is the traditional way in which intelligence is measured and some measures of EI also use that approach. For example, one can show people a face and see if they understand the emotions expressed in the facial expression. Or, one could ask people what "anger" means, and see how well they understand its definition. Examples of such scales are the Multifactor Emotional Intelligence Scale (MEIS), and the Mayer–Salovey–Caruso Emotional Intelligence Test (MSCEIT). These tests provide the best evidence yet that EI is a true intelligence, is different from cognitive intelligence, predicts important new things, and develops with age. Because these tests have been described in great detail elsewhere, I will not repeat these descriptions here (see [34], [40]; also, Chapter 9).

The question, "Which EI are you talking about?" becomes critical here, because it is likely that these different approaches will yield quite different measurements on the same person. When two tests measure the same thing, people are supposed to obtain the same score on them. In the realm of intelligence testing, a person who scores high on the Wechsler Adult Intelligence Scale should (and usually does) score high on the Stanford Binet Intelligence Scale. Similarly, another person who scores low on a given intelligence test will score low on another [51], [53]. The same is true in the realm of testing social traits: Someone who scores high on the

Eysenck Personality Inventory Scale of Extroversion will similarly score high on the NEO-PI scale of Extroversion [10], [17]. That is, tests that measure the same entity should rank people the same way.

That is likely to be *un*true for scales in the area of EI. Scales based on an ability model will measure characteristics with only minimal relations to scales based on concepts of well-being or success. Research thus far suggests that ability measures chiefly assess the capacity to process emotional information. Self-report measures of mixed models may pick up some of that (see [46]). At the same time, however, their primary measurement is of positive mood, optimism, positive self-regard, and extroversion. In fact, the overlap of the mixed scales with traditional personality traits is so high that researchers have concluded that nothing new is measured by such self-report approaches relative to existing scales (e.g., [13], [43]). Finally, the observer rating approaches appear to measure some combination of a person's social impact or social dominance, as perceived by others, along with issues surrounding the person's reputation at work (see also Chapter 2 for a further discussion of these perspectives).

The clear distinction between ability scales and self-report measures is an important one in the intelligence literature, and yet there are areas where intelligence as an ability and other personality traits do overlap modestly. For example, traditional intelligence has low but definite relations to other traits such as intellectual flow and intellectual curiosity [33]. In the case of EI, there is a correlation between ability scales and self-reported empathy of about $r = .00$ to 30 and a lower relationship with meta-experiences of mood. As test-to-test correlations go, these are very low and indicate the essential independence of the measures. By way of contrast self-report scales have very high correlations with each other and with positive mood ($r = .50$ to .80). Because mood state is highly predictive of many outcomes (e.g., rated job satisfaction, rated well-being, and so on), it is important to control for current mood in empirical work done with self-judgment scales. Regrettably, most research in this area does *not* do this.

Although all of the above attributes are potentially important, they are related unequally to notions of what EI really concerns. It may turn out that as the field develops more attention is paid to these discrepancies.

☐ Is Emotional Intelligence the Best Predictor of Success in Life?

The first theory of EI made only the claim—controversial enough at the time—that such an intelligence might exist. Ten years later, that claim is still somewhat disputed, despite a groundswell of support for the idea. In addition to the claim that EI might exist was some discussion of what EI might predict: social sensitivity, persistence, and general well-being.

Claims for EI escalated markedly in popularizations of the concept. Emotional intelligence was said to be as or more important than IQ in predicting success in life (e.g., [22, p. 34]). My colleagues and I never made such claims. Indeed, the claim was astonishing, as intelligence has long been considered the benchmark predictor of academic success, and, sometimes, of professional success. Walter Mischel's brutal critique of personality assessment in 1967 carefully left aside intelligence as too powerful to criticize. Why? Intelligence regularly predicts academic grade point average at $r = .50$ level; moreover, the prestige of an occupation (as rated by independent observers) correlates about $r = .80$ with the average IQ of people in the occupation.

To claim that EI outpredicts intelligence means that it should have correlations above those $r = .50$ and $r = .80$—a stiff hurdle. Those searching for documented evidence for the 1995 claim in the popular book were disappointed. For example, a widely reported Bell Labs study of engineers was said to indicate that emotionally intelligent engineers outperformed others at work. The study in question, however, involved no psychological measurements at all, and emotion was barely mentioned in the study, which was focused instead on the fact that successful engineers shared information with their peers. Although such sharing of information *might* be a matter of EI, it could as easily have been a matter of extroversion, political savvy, expediency, or common decency. The article does not say.

It was perhaps popular claims such as this, along with the opportunistic relabeling of self-report measures as measures of EI, that led some psychologists to dismiss the area entirely. That dismissive position is, perhaps, equally extreme in a negative way. For example, writing in the *Journal of Personality and Social Psychology,* Davies, Stankov, and Roberts [13] wrote, "as presently postulated, little remains of emotional intelligence that is unique and psychometrically sound."

Rather than retreat from such claims, however, the popular claims escalated—doubled, in fact. For example, EI became "twice as important as IQ and other technical skills," in Goleman's [23, p. 31] book, and this claim was repeated by him in a much-read article in the *Harvard Business Review* [24]. This time, documentation was produced: The figure was based on a survey of job descriptions that indicated that "emotionally-intelligence-related criteria appeared twice as often as technical requirements." Basing such an extreme claim on such a study is worrisome. Job performance is, of course, not best measured by the study of job descriptions. What *is* measured is merely the words used in job advertisements. It is unsurprising that so many of those words would fall within the EI category employed by Goleman. As noted, by 1998, Goleman had expanded his list of emotionally intelligent attributes to 25 characteristics so broad that almost anything not explicitly labeled IQ, from political savvy to tolerance for diversity, were included in EI. To return to the first issue: The content of job advertisements does not necessarily reflect actual success. Such content rather may be affected as much by how many adjectives it takes to communicate an impression as by anything else. Understanding what actually predicts success requires employing actual measures of personality and predicting actual on-the-job performance.

So, there is little or no evidence thus far that EI is the best predictor of success in life, let alone twice as important as IQ. This lead us to the last question, "Why is emotional intelligence important?"

☐ Why Is Emotional Intelligence Important?

Why is EI important? The answer depends on which EI one is talking about. The more general, popular, "mixed" versions of EI have generated a renewed excitement over general scales of personality—lurking under the label "emotional intelligence." Emotional intelligence has, in other words, served to interest organizations in predicting good performance through traditional personality assessment. Given the potential value of personality measures, that cannot be all bad. When the dust settles, self-report measures of EI will probably be found to be composed—mostly—of standard personality traits: extroversion, sociability, self-esteem, optimism, and so forth, and a few of the newish qualities such as metamood experience. Although the greater part of such scales do not have much to do with either emotion or intelligence, or even EI, as understood here, they possess the same predictive powers as the original personality traits that they measure under a new name. As those original personality traits have been underemphasized in the recent past, that is not all bad.

In fact, a host of relationships have been found between self-report instruments of EI and on-the-job satisfaction and, sometimes, performance. None of these are on the scale of being more important than intelligence; still, they are promising. For example, one self-report scale, the EQ-i, apparently distinguished successful Air Force recruiters from unsuccessful recruiters [48]. Such findings, if able to withstand the rigors of peer review, and if replicable, are of pragmatic value. Their scientific interpretation, however, is another matter. The particular self-report measure used correlated very highly with measures of positivity such as extroversion and very negatively with measures of negativity such as neuroticism and the Beck Depression Inventory. So it is likely telling us that more positive people make better recruiters for the Air Force. That is, the study is likely replicating Martin Seligman's well-known finding that optimism predicts success among salespeople. Future studies with such self-report measures will need to control for overall levels of pleasant–unpleasant affect, introversion–extroversion, optimism and the like to be clearly interpreted.

If one now turns to the ability conception of EI, the implications appear clearer, stronger, and less subject to alternative explanation. First, the ability conception identifies a new ability trait, with little overlap with any traits of any sort in the past. As a new trait, EI may predict important outcomes that have been unpredictable (or less predictable) before. For example, it appears that higher EI predicts lower levels of violence and other problem behaviors. This occurs even after the effects of intelligence, gender, and self-reported empathy are statistically controlled for (e.g., [8]). If this is the case, it will have important pragmatic uses.

Even more importantly, however, may be the theoretical and cultural implications. If emotions convey information, and if there are rules for processing that information, then the "interruption" and "bother" of emotion are neither; rather, emotions will often convey important information. Put another way, if EI satisfies traditional standards for an intelligence then that is a persuasive reason to discuss emotions and the information they convey.

On an individual level, the existence of EI means that among some of those called "bleeding-hearts" or "hopeless romantics," sophisticated information processing is going on. Recognizing this sort of ability-based EI legitimizes its discussion at an organizational level—in schools, businesses, and other institutions that heretofore have been indifferent or even hostile to feeling life. After all, if emotions convey information, then dismissing such information is done at the organization's risk. Finally, on a societal level, the ability conception of EI marks a transcendence between two opposites: the stoic's idea that emotions are unreliable guides to life and the romantic's position that one should follow one's heart. It may be that the concept of EI marks a turning point in the long battle between the head and the heart. Perhaps those two warring parties can, through EI, attain a higher level of understanding and live at peace more often.

Joseph Ciarrochi
Amy Chan
Peter Caputi
Richard Roberts

CHAPTER 2

Measuring Emotional Intelligence

☐ EI: Fact or Fiction?

Many people believe that emotional intelligence (EI) is important to everyday life (e.g., [69], [78], [92], [106]). It seems reasonable to assume that people who are poor at dealing with emotions will have worse relationships, poor mental health, and less career success. For example, if you cannot control your anger in the workplace, you might upset your coworkers, alienate your boss, and maybe even lose your job. Similarly, if you do not know what other people are feeling, you may have trouble establishing meaningful social interactions, becoming romantically involved, or maintaining a close circle of friends.

These intuitions seem reasonable, but they are not sufficient to prove that EI is important, either practically or scientifically. Indeed, some researchers and philosophers are beginning to argue against the value of EI. Some say that we have simply given a new name to an old concept. Perhaps EI is what the philosophers have termed wisdom [54]. Maybe it is nothing more than temperament [72]. It is even possible that EI does not exist, but rather is an invention of the mass media or big business.

How can we address these issues and determine the value of EI? We must start by examining how EI is assessed. If we cannot adequately measure EI, then we must admit that it might not exist as a meaningful scientific construct [84]. This chapter will review a range of psychological measures that have been designed to assess EI. We will present evidence that EI can be assessed reliably, that it is distinct from traditional intelligence and other related concepts, and that it predicts behavior and important life outcomes. We conclude that although much more work needs to be done to validate EI measures, the current scientific evidence does suggest that EI is important for success in life.

☐ EI and Everyday Life

Figure 2.1 presents a model of the potential roles of EI in aspects of everyday life. Before discussing this model, we need to describe a few concepts. *Emotional Intelligence* has been defined formally in Chapter 1 as the ability to perceive, express, understand, and manage emotions (see also [84]). *Life events* can be positive or negative and range from major events (marriage, the death of family member, or a job promotion) to everyday events (losing things, rejection, or being visited by a friend). *Life outcomes* refer to the potential ways that people can adapt to these myriad life events. For example, if a person experiences a series of stressful life events at work, they may experience a number of adverse outcomes. They could become depressed and suicidal (mental health outcome), they might handle their aversive emotions poorly and alienate friends and family (relationship quality outcome), they might be too stressed to perform creatively at work (work success outcome), and they might become sick (physical health outcome).

Figure 2.1 illustrates how EI might impact on everyday life. In general, we expect that people low in EI will adapt poorly to stressful life events

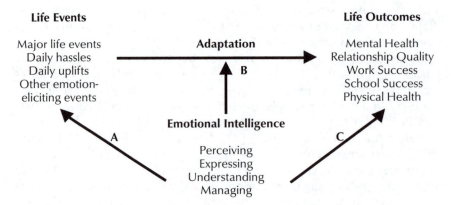

FIGURE 2.1. The potential roles of emotional intelligence in everyday life.

(Link B), responding with more depression, hopelessness, and other negative life outcomes. In contrast, those individuals with high EI should show more adaptive responses to negative life outcomes. We also expect that EI will be directly related to life events and life outcomes. For example, we expect that people high in EI will arrange their lives in such a way that they experience fewer negative life events (Link A). They may also be more skilled at establishing and maintaining high-quality relationships (Link C).

It is worth noting that the hypotheses described above are just that: hypotheses. They have not yet been sufficiently tested, largely because EI is a relatively new concept. The main point of Figure 2.1 is to illustrate what EI is and what EI likely is not. EI is not stress (or life events), it is not adaptation, and it is not mental health, relationship quality, work success, or physical health. Rather, EI may be something that helps us to understand and predict these aspects of everyday life.

☐ How Do We Know if We Have a Good Measure of EI?

Now that we have some sense of what EI is, and is not, we need to establish some scientific bases for what constitutes a good measure of EI. Fortunately, the field of psychological assessment has a rich research history. Moreover, it is relatively uncontroversial in that a good deal of consensus has been reached on how to establish the worthiness of a psychological test. Using expert opinion from this field (e.g., [55]), the ideal EI test should satisfy each of four criteria:

1. *Adequate coverage of content domain.* A scientifically valid test of EI is required to cover a representative sample of the domain that it was designed to assess. If, for example, a test is to serve as a measure of emotion management, then its developers need to ensure that all major aspects of emotion management are covered by the test items (and in the correct proportions). The test should probably cover both managing self-relevant emotions and managing others' emotions, and should not focus exclusively on one management strategy (e.g., using alcohol or drugs) to the exclusion of other management strategies (e.g., seeking professional help, meditation, distracting oneself with leisure time activities, and so forth).
2. *Reliability.* If EI exists as a scientifically meaningful individual differences construct, then people ought to reliably differ along its main dimensions. In particular, if a person taking an EI test gets a below-average score on one occasion, then he or she should get a below-

average score when given the same test again (sometime in the future). In assessing what is termed the test–retest reliability of a measure, an individual's performance should be similar from one test session to the next. If this performance is inconsistent, then what is being measured is unstable, likely not an enduring disposition, and therefore of questionable value. Another form of reliability involves determining the extent to which responses that people give on items, within the same test, relate to each other (i.e., internal consistency reliability). For example, if each item in an emotion perception test is measuring emotion perception, then responses to each item should relate (or correlate) with responses to all the other items of this test.

3. *Usefulness.* If an EI test has no productive power, then it does not matter whether other criteria are satisfied. EI measures should predict important practical outcomes, such as how well people deal with stress, how effective they are at maintaining relationships, and how accepted they are by their peers (see Figure 2.1).

4. *Similarity and distinctiveness.* Suppose you have a measure that adequately covers the content domain, is reliable, and is useful in predicting important outcomes. Ideally, this EI measure should also relate to other similar, EI measures (similarity) but should not relate too highly with non-EI measures (distinctiveness). Two tests are said to "relate" or "overlap" if they have similar items and a person scoring high on one test also tends to score high on the second test. A test of multiplication ability and a test of addition skill should overlap; a test of multiplication ability and a test of sporting ability probably should not overlap much.

Whenever an EI measure has large overlap with another non-EI measure (say, optimism) then it might be argued that the EI measure in question is really just another measure of the non-EI construct (in this case, optimism). Generally, we should not make up a test and call it EI when really it is a measure of some other, well-established personality trait. If we did this repeatedly, we would end up inventing thousands of new (but redundant) tests each year. Even worse, two scientists might be studying exactly the same thing and not realize it, because they have given different names to the same test.

Distinctiveness is not always a necessary condition for an EI measure to be considered scientifically valid. A researcher might create a new measure by building on past measures that relate to EI. For example, it might be argued that people high in self-esteem have more resources to manage aversive affect [99] and therefore are more emotionally intelligent. It may make sense, therefore, for an EI test to contain a subtest that measures self-esteem. We must be careful, however, to identify how our EI measures overlap with preexisting measures. This way we can acknowledge what has been found in past research and relate it to investigations that are carried out in the future.

To evaluate the distinctiveness of EI, we need to see how much EI overlaps with measures of intelligence. We also need to assess how much EI overlaps with the well-established, "Big Five" personality dimensions: neuroticism, extroversion, openness, agreeableness, and conscientiousness (see, e.g., [70]). Because the extent of overlap between these personality dimensions has proven to be an important aspect of EI research [72], a brief description of these constructs follows.

People high in *neuroticism* (sometimes referred to as negative affectivity in some models; e.g., [103]) tend to experience psychological distress, such as anxiety, anger, and depression. *Extroverts* (sometimes termed positive affectivity in the aforementioned model) tend to be sociable, active, and experience positive emotions such as joy and pleasure. People high in *openness to experience* are imaginative and sensitive to art and beauty and have a rich and complex social life. Those high in *agreeableness* tend to be trusting, sympathetic, and cooperative. And, finally, those high in *conscientiousness* tend to be scrupulous, well-organized, and diligent.

In our review of EI tests, we will describe the amount of overlap (or correlation) between EI and other measures as either nonexistent, small (absolute value of correlation between 0.10–0.29), medium (0.30–0.49), large (0.50–0.69), or very large (0.70–0.99). If an EI test has small to medium overlap with another test, then we can be reasonably comfortable in concluding that the two tests are different from each other. However, should the tests show small to medium overlap, we must still be concerned that the EI test may not have predictive power over and above the other tests it relates to. For example, let's say that an EI test has medium overlap with self-esteem. If we find that the EI test predicts school success, we might want to conclude that it is EI that causes school success. However, someone might argue that because EI relates to self-esteem, it is self-esteem that causes school success, not EI. We will discuss this issue in more detail later in this chapter.

☐ Overview of EI Tests

There are two types of EI measures: performance tests and self-report questionnaires. A performance test has responses that can be evaluated against objective, predetermined scoring criteria, whereas a self-report questionnaire asks people to report their own level of EI. For example, to assess emotion perception, you can either have people identify emotions in faces (performance) or you can ask them how good they are at recognizing emotions in faces (self-report). There are five key differences between performance and self-report measures, which we discuss below.

1. Performance tests assess actual EI, whereas self-report measures assess perceived EI. Both perceived and actual EI may be important (and sometimes independent) predictors of how well people adapt to life difficulties. In other words, what people believe to be true can be as important as what is actually true.
2. Performance measures are generally more time consuming to administer than self-report measures. This occurs because self-report measures allow people to summarize their level of EI in a few, concise statements (e.g., "I am good at perceiving emotions"), whereas performance measures require a substantial number of observations before EI level can be ascertained.
3. Unlike performance measures, self-report measures require people to have insight into their own level of EI. Unfortunately, people may not have an accurate understanding of their own intelligence (let alone EI) and, indeed, past research has found only modest correlations between self-rated and actual ability measures (see, e.g., [88]). Similarly, we [68] found that self-reported emotion perception is unrelated to how people actually perform in recognizing emotions.
4. A major difficulty with self-report measures is that people can distort their responses to appear better (or worse) than they actually are. To combat these types of problems, self-report measures can include scales that measure the amount people are distorting their responses (e.g., [58]).
5. Self-report measures of EI tend to be related to well-established personality traits and in particular the various factors comprising the Big Five factor model (see, e.g., [72], [73]). Performance measures of EI, on the other hand, tend to be less related to personality measures, sharing overlap instead with traditional intelligence measures (see, e.g., [65], [91]).

☐ Performance Measures of EI

Multifactor Emotional Intelligence Scale (MEIS)

The MEIS is designed to measure four major components (i.e., branches) that are hypothesized to underlie EI [84]. Branch 1 consists of four tests that assess the perception and appraisal of emotion in stories, designs, music, and faces. Branch 2 consists of two tasks that assess the ability to assimilate emotions into perceptual and cognitive processes, whereas Branch 3 consists of four tests that assess the ability to reason about and understand emotions. Finally, Branch 4 consists of two tests that assess how skilled participants are at managing their own emotions and the emotions of others.

Many of the Branch 2, 3, and 4 tests are composed of short vignettes, depicting real-life episodes that are specially selected to invoke emotional responses. For instance, the Relativity Test (Branch 3) measures people's ability to estimate the feelings of two characters in conflict. One test item describes a car hitting a dog and asks the participant to rate the dog owner's feelings and the driver's feelings. For example, participants must decide how likely it is that the dog's owner felt "ashamed about not being able to have better trained the dog."

Because EI remains in its infancy, the authors of the MEIS currently recommend that the subtests be scored in one of three different ways. The first, which is favored by the authors (see [84]), involves determining how closely a participant's answer matches a consensus answer. For example, if most people think a particular face is expressing a great deal of anger, then it is assumed that the face does indeed express a great deal of anger. People who do not judge the face to express anger are "less correct" than others. A second scoring criterion is based on judgments made by a panel of experts. Test takers who agree with the expert judgments tend to get higher scores than those that do not agree. The third scoring criterion is based on the extent to which the test taker guesses how a target (photographer, artist, musician, and so on) was feeling at the time he or she was engaged in an activity (taking a photograph, drawing a design, playing music, and so on) that ultimately created the test item.

Test Evaluation

The MEIS yields a reliable measure of overall EI (which is based on all the subtests), emotional perception, and of understanding and managing emotions (based on all the nonperception subtests). A number of the subtests, especially those related to perception, are also reliable in their own right. Other subtests (e.g., those related to managing emotions) have less satisfactory reliabilities.

Perhaps one of the greatest strengths underlying the MEIS is its distinctiveness. It has only small to medium overlap with positive and negative affectivity and other, well-established personality measures [65], [66], [91]. It has small to medium (positive) overlap with verbal intelligence [84], which is precisely what one would expect if the MEIS is measuring a type of cognitive ability. The MEIS also has been shown to be useful.

People who score high on the MEIS tend to report greater life happiness, relationship success, and parental warmth. They also engage in behavior that tends to maintain or increase their positive moods [65].

In a recent study, researchers investigating the role of emotion perception in people's ability to deal effectively with life stress found further evidence for the distinctiveness and usefulness of subtests making up this particular branch of the MEIS [68]. In particular, emotional perception was found to be unrelated to life stress and to measures of mental health, which is consistent with a view that EI is different from these variables (see Figure 2.1). A second important finding was that people high and low in emotion perception responded differently to stress. Emotionally perceptive people appeared to be more strongly impacted by stress than their less perceptive counterparts, expressing higher levels of depression, hopelessness, and suicidal ideation.

Why did emotionally perceptive people appear to respond less adaptively to stress than others? There are at least two hypotheses. The *insensitivity hypothesis* suggests that unperceptive people successfully repress stressful thoughts or else ignore them altogether [68]. This hypothesis implies that being unperceptive may be beneficial to the individual because it can help to protect them from stress. In contrast, the *confusion hypothesis* suggests that people who are low in emotion perception are indeed sensitive to stress but simply do not realize that it is impacting on them adversely [68]. By definition, low perceptive people should be more confused about what they are feeling and should show less understanding of how it is impacting upon their life. This second hypothesis suggests that being unperceptive is detrimental to the individual because he or she does not know that he or she is feeling bad and thus probably will not do anything to change the situation. In general, research in EI (particularly that focusing on the construct of alexithymia [lack of emotionality; see below]) is consistent with the second hypothesis (e.g., [100]; see Chapter 4, this volume).

In contrast to these positive findings, a study conducted by Roberts, Zeidner, and Matthews [91] points to certain limitations to the scoring protocols currently making up the MEIS. These authors found a series of inconsistent (indeed contradictory) trends that were dependent on how the tests were scored. For example, using expert scoring, males were shown to have higher EI than females, with the effect reversed for consensual scoring. In addition to gender, different findings were evidenced between consensus and expert scoring for ethnicity, intelligence, personality, and even the structure of the MEIS itself.

In summary, the MEIS has been shown to be reliable, distinctive, and related to important life outcomes. However, it does have some weaknesses: It takes a while to administer the whole test, some subscales do not have satisfactory levels of reliability, and there are some questions about the scoring methods. On the whole, however, the MEIS shows promise as a viable and valid index of EI.

Mayer–Salovey–Caruso Emotional Intelligence Test, MSCEIT V.1.1 and V.2.0

The MSCEIT (pronounced "Mes - keet") was designed to resolve some of the problems associated with the MEIS [83]. The MSCEIT V.2.0 is a shorter version of MSCEIT V.1.1. and may be more useful to professionals and reseachers who have a limited time to administer the test.

Performance on the MSCEIT can be described roughly by a single overall performance level. At the same time, this can be divided into subareas of experiential and strategic EI. The emotional experience EI score assesses a person's ability to perceive, respond to, and manipulate emotional information, without necessarily understanding it. It indexes how accurately a person can read and express emotion and how well a person can compare that emotional stimulation with other sorts of sensory experiences (e.g., colors or sounds). It may also indicate how a person functions under the influence of different emotions.

The emotional strategies EI score assesses a person's ability to understand and manage emotions, without necessarily perceiving them well or fully experiencing feelings. It indexes how accurately a person understands what emotions signify (e.g., that sadness typically signals a loss) and how emotions in oneself and others can be managed. The two general areas, experiential and strategic EI, can be further divided into four subscales that measure, respectively, the ability to (1) accurately perceive emotions; (2) use emotions to facilitate thinking, problem solving, and creativity; (3) understand emotions; and (4) manage emotions for personal growth. These four branches are made up of two tasks each (e.g., perceiving emotions is assessed by having people identify emotions in faces and pictures).

The MSCEIT yields two scores for each of the dimensions, factors, and tasks. That is, each person receives *two* overall EI scores, two scores for emotional experience EI, two scores for perceiving emotions, and so forth. One set of scores indicates a person's correctness on the test as judged by a consensus. The second set of scores indicates a person's correctness on the test as judged by an expert criterion. (See discussion of these scoring methods in the MEIS section.)

Test Evaluation

The MSCEIT appears to be an improvement over its predecessor, the MEIS. It is shorter and quicker to administer, with the MSCEIT V.2.0 requiring only about 30 minutes to perform. Despite being shorter, the MSCEIT appears to measure more dimensions of EI than the MEIS, and its subscales have been shown to be more reliable [83]. There are also extensive norms available for the test. Overall, then, the MSCEIT V.2.0 shows substantial promise. However, because the test is so new, further research is still needed to fully explore its potential.

Levels of Emotional Awareness Scale (LEAS)

The LEAS consists of 20 scenes that involve two people, which have been constructed to elicit four types of emotion: anger, fear, happiness, and sadness [80]. Each scene is followed by two questions: "How would you feel?" and "How would the other person feel?" Corresponding to these questions, each person's answer receives two separate scores for the emotion described: one for the self and one for others. One scenario is as follows:

> You and your best friend are in the same line of work. There is a prize given annually to the best performance of the year. The two of you work hard to win the prize. One night the winner is announced: your friend. How would you feel? How would your friend feel?

Each scene receives a score of 0 to 5, corresponding to Lane and colleague's [80] theory of the five levels of emotional awareness. A glossary of words at each level is available to guide interpretation and scoring. The lowest, Level (0), reflects nonemotional responses, where the word "feel" is used to describe a thought rather than a feeling (e.g., "I'd feel stupid"). Level 1 reflects an awareness of physiological cues (e.g., "I'd feel sick"). Level 2 consists of words that are typically used in other contexts but are frequently used to convey relatively undifferentiated emotions (e.g., "I'd feel bad"). Level 3 responses involve use of one word conveying typical, differentiated emotion (e.g., "happy," "sad," "angry"). A Level 4 score is given when two or more Level 3 words are used to convey greater emotional differentiation than any word alone.

In addition to receiving a score for the *self* and *other*, participants also receive a total score. This score equals the higher of these two scores, except in those instances where both self and other receive Level 4 scores. Under these circumstances, a total score of Level 5 is given. An example of a Level 5 response for the scenario presented above is as follows:

I'd feel *disappointed* that I didn't win but *glad* that if someone else did, that person was my friend. My friend probably deserved it! My friend would feel *happy* and *proud* but slightly *worried* that my feelings might be hurt." ([80], italics added)

Test Evaluation

The LEAS has been shown to be reliable and has only small to medium overlap with the theoretically relevant measures of maturity, openness, empathy, and intelligence. It also shares moderate correlation with the MEIS and other EI measures [66], [80], [82]. Importantly, it is not related to temperament and other major personality traits. In overlapping only modestly with things that it ought to overlap with, yet not too much with established psychological measures, the LEAS appears a potentially good measure of EI.

How useful is the LEAS? Lane and colleagues [81] have shown that, when processing emotional stimuli, people who score high on the LEAS differ from others in terms of blood flow in particular parts of the brain, which suggests that people high and low in emotional awareness do indeed differ in how they process emotional information. In addition, Lane and colleagues [81] have found that the LEAS predicts actual emotion recognition, regardless of whether the recognition task is verbal or nonverbal.

Recently, we [66] attempted to evaluate whether the LEAS is useful in predicting emotionally intelligent behavior. Previous research has found that when people are aware of their mood, they try to prevent that mood from biasing how they think [98]. For example, if someone is sad because it is a rainy day, they will tend to say they are less satisfied with their life. However, if you make these people aware of the source of their mood, they will try to prevent the mood from influencing their life-satisfaction judgments. They may even overcorrect and say they are more satisfied with their life when in a sad mood.

We reasoned that this same effect would occur for people who are chronically, highly aware of their emotions (i.e., those who score high on the LEAS). In one study, we measured people's level of emotional awareness and then showed them a video that put them into a positive, neutral, or negative mood [66]. We then had them evaluate their satisfaction with life. People who scored low on the LEAS showed the expected pattern: When in a sad mood, they reported being less happy with life, whereas when in a happy mood, they reported being happier with life. In contrast, people high in emotional awareness showed the opposite pattern. When in a sad mood, they reported higher life satisfaction, whereas in a happy mood, they reported lower life satisfaction. This finding is consistent with the idea that people who score high on the LEAS are more aware of their moods and try to prevent those moods from biasing their judgments.

In summary, the LEAS has been shown to relate to emotional processing in particular parts of the brain, to predict the accuracy of emotion recognition, and to predict how people respond to their moods. This provides some evidence for the usefulness of this measure.

Other Performance Measures of EI

Measuring Emotion Expression Skill

Researchers have attempted to measure people's skill at expressing emotions, which is one aspect of EI. One method asks people to pose basic emotion expressions on cue (e.g., "Now make an angry face"). The expressions are photographed and groups of judges view the expressions and attempt to recognize them. An emotionally intelligent person, it is argued, should be capable of expressing basic emotions in a way that judges can easily identify. A second method of measuring expression skill involves examining how people spontaneously express emotions. For example, one study examined how skilled people were at concealing inappropriate happiness [75]. People were led to believe that they had won a competition and were filmed in the presence or absence of the person whom they had beaten. Judges later rated the videos in terms of the emotions they expressed after winning. This type of design allows one to assess the amount of expression (e.g., "How much did the participant smile in general?"), as well as expression skill (e.g., "Did the participant smile at the wrong times, for example, when the defeated peer was in the room?").

There is evidence that emotion expression skill can be measured reliably and that it is moderately related to theoretically relevant variables such as exhibitionism and the tendency to monitor one's own behavior [75], [76]. There is also evidence that expressive individuals tend to be evaluated more favorably in social situations [77]. Further research is needed to examine the extent that performance measures of expression predict important life outcomes.

Measuring EI in Children

Research has shown that components appearing to make up EI (often referred to as "emotional competence" in developmental approaches) can generally be measured reliably and validly in children [93]. For example,

Cassidy, Parke, Butkobsky, and Braungart [63] measured emotional understanding by showing children (in kindergarten) photographs of people experiencing a discrete emotion (e.g., anger or sadness). These children were then asked a series of questions about the pictures. These questions included, "How do you think this kid is feeling?" "What kinds of things make you feel this way?" and "If your Mom saw you feeling this way, what would she do?" Responses were scored for the presence or absence of emotional understanding. A highly emotionally intelligent child would be able to identify the emotion, acknowledge experiencing the emotion, understand what caused the emotion, acknowledge expressing the emotion, and reveal understanding of the appropriate responses to others' expression of the emotion. This measure of EI was shown to have good interitem reliability and to be related to how accepted children were by their peers. No information was provided in this study about the distinctiveness of the measure.

In another study, Barth and Bastiani [61] presented young children (aged 4 to 5 years) with facial expressions of classmates and had them identify the emotion being expressed. The researchers then calculated an accuracy score based on the congruence between the judged expression and the expression the classmate was intending to produce. A bias score was also calculated, which was based on the number of times a child identified a particular type of emotion. For example, some children were biased to see anger in every face. The researchers found that bias scores were reliable across time, whereas accuracy scores were not. Importantly, children who were biased and saw high levels of anger in faces also tended to have poorer relationships with their classmates. In general, bias scores were better predictors than accuracy scores of peer acceptance. No information was provided in this study about the distinctiveness of the EI measure. However, a study employing similar measures suggests that emotionally perceptive children tend to have moderately higher intelligence test scores [74].

☐ Self-Report Tests

Bar-On Emotional Quotient Inventory (EQ-i)

It is claimed that the EQ-i is the most comprehensive self-report measure of EI available [58], [59], [73]. It consists of 12 EI subscales, which include emotional self-awareness ("It is hard for me to understand the way I feel"), assertiveness ("It's difficult for me to stand up for my right"), self-regard (e.g., "I don't feel good about myself"), independence (e.g., "I prefer others to make decisions for me"), empathy (e.g., "I am sensitive to the feelings of others"), interpersonal relationship (e.g., "People think that I'm sociable"), social responsibility (e.g., "I like helping people"), problem solving (e.g., "My approach in overcoming difficulties is to move step by step"), reality testing (e.g., "It's hard for me to keep things in the right perspective"), flexibility (e.g., "It's easy for me to adjust to new conditions"), stress tolerance (e.g., "I know how to deal with upsetting problems"), and impulse control (e.g., "It's a problem controlling my anger"). In addition to the subscales, the EQ-i contains three factors that are considered "facilitators" of emotional intelligence [59], which include happiness (e.g., "It's hard for me to enjoy life"), optimism (e.g., "I believe that I can stay on top of tough situations"), and self-actualization (e.g., "I try to make my life as meaningful as I can"). The EQ-i yields a measure of overall EI as well as scores on each of the subfactors. The Bar-On inventory also contains four validity indicators that measure the extent to which people are responding randomly or distorting their responses to appear favorably or unfavorably to the person administering the test.

Test Evaluation

According to Bar-On [58], (see also [73]), the EQ-i and its subscales have been shown to have high levels of internal consistency (across a wide variety of cultures) as well as high test–retest reliability. It would also appear that the EQ-i is useful. It has, for example, been related to people's employment status (employed versus unemployed), academic success, success at fitting into a culture, prison status (in prison versus not in prison), and skill at coping with stress ([58]; see also [60]).

How distinctive is the EQ-i? The measure is meant to be a continuation and expansion of past research in the field of individual differences [58]. Consequently, it is not surprising that the overall EI score and each of the subscales are very highly related to other measures. For example, high total EI is very strongly related to high trait anxiety, depression, borderline personality, and emotional instability [58], and is highly related to each of the Big Five personality traits [73]. The EI subscales show moderate to very strong relationships with high positive and low negative affectivity [58]. In addition, each of the subscales is highly related to other measures. For example, self-regard is highly related to other measures of self-esteem and low empathy is highly related to a measure of antisocial personality.

It is important to bear in mind the ways that the EQ-i is related to established measures. Such relationships suggest that EI, as assessed by the EQ-i, actually has been under investigation for decades. Therefore, to fully understand the importance of the EQ-i, it is essential to understand not only research directly related to the measure, but also the research related to the earlier measures to which it is highly related. An important additional question is how different the EQ-i is from traditional personality measures. If the EQ-i is similar to the traditional personality measures, we might want to know the additional predictive value the EQ-i delivers in organizational settings. This could be particularly important for those organizations that use it in hiring personnel because, as demonstrated by Schmidt and Hunter [96], personality measures add little incremental validity (over general intelligence measures) in the selection context.

Trait Meta-Mood Scale (TMMS)

The TMMS assesses attention to emotion (e.g., "I don't think it's worth paying attention to your emotions or moods"), emotional clarity (e.g., "Sometimes I can't tell what my feelings are"), and emotion repair (e.g., "I try to think good thoughts no matter how badly I feel"; [94]). The scales have been shown to possess adequate reliability and the emotional clarity scale is useful in predicting how much people seem to dwell unproductively on sad thoughts [95]. Recent evidence suggests that the emotion repair scale is not distinct from measures of negative affectivity or neuroticism. The attention and clarity scales, however, do appear to be reasonably distinct from negative affectivity and from a wide variety of other personality and intelligence measures [72].

Schutte Self-Report Inventory (SSRI)

The SSRI is based on the most recent theorizing of John Mayer and his colleagues [97]. The scale assesses overall EI, as well as four EI subfactors: emotion perception (e.g., "I find it hard to understand the nonverbal messages of other people"), managing self-relevant emotions (e.g., "I seek out activities that make me happy"), managing others' emotions (e.g., "I arrange events others enjoy"), and utilizing emotions (e.g., "When I feel a change in emotion, I tend to come up with new ideas").

Test Evaluation

The overall EI score and the perception and managing emotion scores tend to be reliable in both adults and adolescents, whereas the utilizing emotions subscale exhibits relatively poor reliability [64]. Regarding the distinctiveness of the SSRI, people who score high on the general EI scale also tend to score low on measures of negative affectivity and high on measures of positive affectivity (or extroversion), openness to feelings, and empathy. With individual subscales, the managing-self-emotions scale seems to be the least distinctive, having large overlap with positive and negative affectivity. In contrast, the other subscales have only small to medium overlap with affectivity and other personality variables. Moreover, the SSRI has been shown to be useful in predicting school success [97]. These positive features aside, the SSRI may be a more problematic instrument than its creators had envisaged. Thus, a study examining it with powerful statistical techniques failed to provide evidence for a general EI factor, indicating its match to theory was less than perfect [89].

Toronto Alexithymia Scale (TAS-20)

The TAS-20 is one of the most commonly used EI measures, although in truth it was not designed explicitly for this purpose, instead originally intended as a measure of the clinical syndrome known as alexithymia. It consists of 20 items and three scales [56]. It assesses difficulty in identifying feelings (e.g., "I am often confused about what emotion I am feeling"), difficulty describing feelings (e.g., "It is difficult for me to find the right words for my feelings"), and externally oriented thinking (e.g., "Being in touch with emotions is essential"). The TAS-20 yields an overall alexithymia score, as well as a score for each of the three scales.

Test Evaluation

The overall alexithymia score and the first two scale scores tend to be highly reliable. However, the third scale has sometimes been found to be somewhat less reliable than is desirable [56]. Importantly, the TAS-20 has been shown to be a valid instrument across disparate cultures and different types of populations (e.g., students and psychiatric patients) (see, e.g., [100].

As predicted by Bagby and his colleagues [57], the TAS-20 has large overlap with other theoretically relevant scales (e.g., openness to feelings), which suggests that the scale is measuring what it is expected to measure. People who score high on the TAS-20 also tend to score high on measures of negative emotionality and low on positive emotionality, but this overlap is only small to medium in magnitude [57]. In addition, the TAS-20 tends not to overlap too highly with either conscientiousness or agreeableness.

The TAS-20 has been shown to be related to a number of important life outcomes. For example, people high in alexithymia are more prone to drug addiction, eating disorders, and experiencing physical symptoms (e.g., feeling sick). The scale also predicts the ability to process and manage emotional states and the ability to recognize faces [101]. In short, the TAS-20 appears to be a reliable, useful, and distinctive measure. Nevertheless, as alluded to in the introduction of this scale, the fact that the TAS-20 was never intended to explicitly assess EI renders it a rather notional measure that cannot encompass the many facets thought to make up EI.

Other Self-Report Measures Related to EI

There are numerous other self-report measures that are related to EI, but because of a lack of space we can only mention them briefly here. The *Emotional Control Questionnaire* [90] measures people's ability to control emotion in trying circumstances and consists of scales for measuring "aggression control," "rehearsal," "benign control," and "emotional inhibition." Goleman's [78] *Emotional Quotient (EQ) Test* measures emotional abilities, general social competencies, and "character." The test contains such subscales as "knowing one's emotions," "motivating oneself," and "handling relationships." The *Repression-Sensitization Scale* assesses the extent that people defensively avoid aversive emotions and stimuli [105]. Repression tendency has predicted how accurate people are at identifying emotions [82], [105]. The *Response Styles Questionnaire* [87] measures the tendency to experience behaviors and thoughts that focus on one's depressive symptoms. Such a focus appears to be emotionally unintelligent in that it increases (rather than decreases) depressive symptoms.

A substantial number of other scales measure how people cope with aversive affect and may relate to the managing emotions component of EI. For example, the *Monitoring-Blunting Scale* [86] measures the extent that people seek out (or avoid) information when faced with a stressful situation. The *COPE* Inventory [62] measures how people generally cope with stressful events and includes subscales that measure active coping, denial, turning to religion, and seeking social support.

It is worth noting that the vast majority of self-report measures discussed in this passage at best measure one or two components of emotionality that would appear to be related to EI. Indeed, because many of these measures were constructed before the concept of EI came into vogue they are likely to serve as instruments by which new tests of EI are validated (rather than serving to define this concept in all its complexity). Caution should also be exercised when using some of these tests. Goleman's [78] EQ Test, for example, appears to possess very poor measurement properties [72].

☐ Disentangling EI from Other Measures

The preceding review of self-report measures consistently has revealed that EI relates to two broad components of temperament, negative and positive affectivity. An explicit definition of these components is as follows. *Negative affectivity* ("NA" or neuroticism) is a trait sensitivity to negative events, causing high trait scorers to experience a broad range of negative moods, including not only anxiety and sadness but also such emotions as guilt, hostility, and self-dissatisfaction. Negative affectivity tends to be highly related to low trait self-esteem [66]. *Positive affectivity* ("PA" or extroversion) is defined as a trait sensitivity to positive events, causing high scorers to feel joyful, enthusiastic, energetic, friendly, bold, assertive, proud, and confident, whereas those low in positive affectivity tend to feel dull, flat, disinterested, and unenthusiastic [102], [103]. Positive affectivity tends to have a small to moderate relationship with high self-esteem.

Figure 2.2 illustrates hypothetical relationships between self-reported EI, temperament, and positive life outcomes. There are three potential explanations for the link between temperament and EI. First, people who experience a large number of negative emotions would require more skill to control these emotions. For example, one item on a measure of managing self-relevant emotions might be, "I have trouble controlling my anger." If people endorse this item, is it because they have an "angry temperament" or because they lack basic skills in managing their anger? It is likely to be influenced by both factors.

Second, people high in NA may tend to have less stable emotional experiences [71]. At one moment they may feel angry, and at another moment, sad. Such instability may make it difficult for them to have a clear understanding of what they are feeling and why they are feeling it. A third reason for the relationship between EI and temperament is that people with a good temperament (low NA, high PA, and high self-esteem) tend to be optimistic about their abilities in general. Thus, when

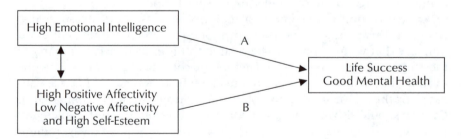

FIGURE 2.2. The relationship between some measures of emotional intelligence, affectivity, and life success.

you ask them to evaluate how emotionally intelligent they are, they confidently say they are very emotionally intelligent, even though they might not be so.

Given that self-report EI measures show moderate to strong overlap with temperament, we must be careful in making conclusions. For example, if we find that people high in EI tend to have good mental health, we might want to conclude that it is EI that leads to superior mental health (Link A, Figure 2.2). However, it might be just as reasonable to argue that people high in EI have a good temperament, and it is good temperament that predicts superior mental health (Link B). There is certainly strong evidence that people with a good temperament and high self-esteem tend to do better in life [104].

How can the effects of EI and temperament be distinguished? One way is to design an EI test that has little overlap with temperament, as has been accomplished by a number of the performance measures described in this chapter. A second method involves looking at the effect of EI on outcomes while statistically controlling for temperament and/or self-esteem. "Statistical control," in this case, means essentially eliminating Link B in Figure 2.2. This method already has been used with certain self-report measures, with some level of success. For example, Salovey, Mayer, and their colleagues [95] found that a measure of emotional clarity successfully predicted ruminative thinking, even after controlling for aspects of temperament. Similarly, using the SSRI, Ciarrochi and colleagues have examined the impact of EI on various outcomes while controlling for aspects of PA and NA. In one study they found that adolescents who scored high in EI tended to have better social support, to be better at recognizing facial expressions, and to engage in behavior that would maintain good (and reduce aversive) moods [64]. In a second study, Ciarrochi, Deane, and Anderson [68] found that people who were good at managing others' emotions tended to adapt better to stress, responding with less suicidal ideation. Finally, Ciarrochi and Deane [67] found that people high in EI had better experiences in getting help from mental health professionals and were more willing to seek help in the future. Taken together, these findings demonstrate that self-reported EI may have predictive power over and above temperament.

Performance measures of EI tend not to overlap with temperament, but do have small to medium overlap with traditional measures of intelligence. Thus, it is important to statistically control for intelligence when examining the effects of performance EI. Using this statistical approach, Lane and his colleagues [80], [81] have demonstrated that the LEAS predicts individual differences in emotional processing, whereas we [66] have shown that the MEIS predicts mood management behavior. Although further research is clearly needed, it would appear that performance measures do have some predictive power over and above intelligence measures.

☐ Conclusions

The preceding review indicates that there are many unresolved issues in EI research. For example, should EI really be considered a type of intelligence? Jack Mayer and his colleagues have argued that in order for EI to be a "true" intelligence, it should (1) reflect performance rather than preferred ways of behaving, (2) correlate, but not too highly, with currently existing IQ measures, and (3) improve during childhood to middle adulthood. It is worth noting that models that fail to consider the ways in which EI might rightfully constitute an intelligence render the concept a euphemism rather than a precise scientific term (see [85]).

Only the MEIS has been shown to satisfy all three of the criteria [84], although there may still be other criteria that need to be satisfied before it should be considered a legitimate measure of intelligence [91]. The LEAS has been shown to satisfy criteria 1 and 2, but no research has established whether it satisfies the third criterion, let alone still other criteria for an intelligence. It is probable that the MSCEIT satisfies the three criteria, given that it is closely related to, and derived from, the MEIS. However, research is still needed to confirm this possibility.

In general, the self-report measures do not reflect actual performance and do not correlate with general intelligence, so it might be argued that they do not measure a type of intelligence. Perhaps it might be better to say that these measures assess emotional "competence" rather than intelligence [93]. The very least we can conclude is that the self-report measures do relate to emotionally intelligent behavior, even if they do not formally satisfy the criteria for an intelligence.

Another issue involves the causal role of EI in everyday life. Many of the studies reviewed in this chapter have shown that EI relates to important behavior, but these studies do not necessarily prove that EI is *causing* the behavior in question. For example, does EI lead to higher-quality friendships, or do good-quality friendships lead to higher EI? The best way to determine if EI functions as a causal variable is to train people to be more emotionally intelligent and to observe the impact of such training on behavior. This type of research already has been undertaken and generally has suggested that training young people in EI leads to more adaptive behavior and improved mental health ([107]; see Chapter 8 this volume). One limitation of this research is that it tends to teach people a number of skills other than EI, so that we cannot be certain whether it is the EI or the other skills that are leading to improvement. Still, the results are encouraging.

In summary then, evidence presented in this chapter suggests that EI can be measured reliably; is different from older, well-established measures of intelligence and temperament; and predicts important behavior and life outcomes. Despite this encouraging initial evidence, EI research is still in its infancy and much more research needs to done to fully establish the validity of EI measures. We hope that EI research will continue to flourish. It has the potential to show us how we can deal effectively with emotions and use them to enrich our lives.

CHAPTER 3

Joseph P. Forgas

Affective Intelligence: The Role of Affect in Social Thinking and Behavior

☐ Introduction

It is a bright sunny day outside, and you are in an excellent mood. As you stop for a cappuccino on your way to work, a person in the bar reminds you of a childhood friend, and happy memories about your school years come flooding back. At work, you are on a selection committee, and as you interview the first applicant, you notice with delight what a pleasant person he is. As you discuss your decision with your colleagues, you act in a cooperative and friendly way. What role does mood play in the way people think and act in such everyday situations? How and why do mild affective states influence our thoughts, memories, and behaviors? This chapter reviews recent evidence documenting the pervasive influence of affect on social thinking and behavior and argues that emotional intelligence (EI) necessarily involves knowing how, when, and why such effects occur.

Arguably, affect remains perhaps the last frontier in our quest to understand the dynamics of human behavior [127]. Although most of us intuitively know that our feelings and moods can have a crucial influence on our mental life and actions, until recently we did not fully understand how and why these influences occur. A critical—and so far rather neglected—component of EI is to be aware of how affective states will influence our thoughts and behaviors. Most of these effects are subtle, subconscious, and difficult to detect introspectively. It is only as a result of the recent impressive growth of experimental research on affect that we begin to understand the multifaceted influence of feelings on everything that we think and do. An important aspect of EI is to know how these affective influences function, and to know how to control and manage them.

The issues covered here are not only of interest to psychologists, but also to everyone who wants to understand the complex role that affect plays in human affairs. This chapter presents an integrative review of past and present ideas about the role of subconscious mood states in how we think and behave in everyday social situations. Moods, unlike emotions, are relatively low-intensity, diffuse, and enduring affective states that are often subconscious and have no salient cause. Because moods tend to be less subject to conscious monitoring than more intense emotions, paradoxically, their effects on social thinking and behavior tend to be potentially more insidious, enduring, and subtle. The main message of this chapter is simple. Although affect *may* color everything we think and do, it only does so in certain circumstances that require us to think in an open, constructive way. It is only this kind of thinking style that invites incidental affect infusion. The chapter surveys recent empirical evidence for affect infusion into thoughts, judgments, and behaviors, and highlights the conditions that facilitate or inhibit these effects.

Surprisingly, most of what we know about the role of affect in social cognition and behavior has only been discovered during the past two decades [127]. Recent studies showed that affect and cognition are not separate, independent faculties of the mind as often assumed by philosophers and psychologists. Rather, there is a fundamental interdependence between feeling and thinking in human social life. Our affective experiences are integrally linked with the way information about the world is stored and represented. In turn, experiences of even mild moods have a profound influence on the memories we retrieve, the information we notice and learn, and the way we respond to social situations. Affect can influence both the *process* of thinking (*how* we deal with social information) and the *content* of thinking, judgments, and behavior (*what* we think and do). It is these effects we want to explore in this chapter. However, we will first take a brief look at some historical ideas about the role of affect in human affairs.

□ Emotional Thought: Sometimes Intelligent, Sometimes Not?

Since the dawn of human civilization, philosophers such as Aristotle, Socrates, Plato, St. Augustine, Descartes, Pascal, and Kant have been fascinated by the role of affect in thinking and behavior. Plato was among the first who thought that affect constitutes a more primitive, animal aspect of human nature that is incompatible with reason. The idea that affect subverts rational thinking survives to this day thanks to the speculative ideas of Freud and others. Writers such as Arthur Koestler [137] even suggested that our inability to know and control our violent affective reactions is because of a fatal flaw in the way our central nervous system developed, an evolutionary mistake that threatens the very survival of our species.

However, recent research in psychology and neuroanatomy suggests a radically different picture. According to these views, affect is often a useful and even essential component of an adaptive response to a social situation. Research with brain damaged patients shows that people who cannot experience affective reactions because of isolated frontal lobe damage also tend to make disastrous social decisions and their social relationships suffer accordingly, even though intellectual abilities remain unimpaired. Indeed, Adolphs and Damasio [108] believe "affective processing to be an evolutionary antecedent to more complex forms of information processing; . . . higher cognition requires the guidance provided by affective processing" (p. 45). Thus, we have two diametrically opposed views of the role of affect in human affairs: as an essential component of effective responses to social situations, or as a dangerous, invasive influence on rational thinking that contributes to judgmental errors and produces maladaptive responses. Neither of these positions is entirely true. Rather, affect may either facilitate or impair effective thinking and responses depending on the circumstances involved. Thus emotional thought can be either intelligent or unintelligent, adaptive or maladaptive. A key task of contemporary research—and this chapter—is to help us to understand how, when, and why such affective influences occur.

☐ Affect and Predicting the Future

How happy would you be, and for how long, if you won the lottery? And how devastated would you feel if your current romantic relationship ended? Many of our everyday choices are made on the basis of expected emotional reactions to possible future events. However, such "affective forecasting" can be subject to serious distortions. Winning the lottery may not make you as happy and for as long as you expected, and the end of a relationship may not be as traumatic as anticipated. Most people overestimate the intensity and duration of their positive and negative reactions to future events. Daniel Gilbert at Harvard University coined the term "miswanting" to describe the common mistake of wanting things that will not make us nearly as happy as we hope and avoiding things that will not be as bad as we fear [136]. Why do these mistakes of affective forecasting occur?

We can go wrong because we often focus on the wrong (nonrepresentative) details when imagining a future event and then misunderstand and misread our own likely reactions. When thinking about winning the lottery, we focus on having all that money, but we don't think about the difficult investment decisions we'll have to make, how our relatives might react, and what being much richer than our friends might do to our relationships. Such *focalism* (focusing on the salient features of emotional events and ignoring the rest) produces unrealistic expectations and subsequent disappointment. Many fervently desired consumer acquisitions leave us less happy than we expected. It is for such reasons that people keep on buying goods they will never use such as exercise equipment or dieting products. They focus on the positive feelings linked to having a beautiful body, but they fail to forecast the pain, exhaustion, and hunger that necessarily goes with the purchase.

Similarly, negative events often are less traumatic than we expect. We have many spontaneous and subconscious cognitive strategies—a psychological "immune system"—for coping with problems, and people typically underestimate and neglect to consider this when anticipating adversity. Distraction, self-affirmation, and rationalization are just some of the highly effective and spontaneous strategies that make up the psychological immune system. "Immune neglect"—ignoring the immune system—leads to an overestimation of negative affective reactions. Numerous experiments now confirm that actual emotional reactions to both positive and negative events are far less intense and enduring than people expect [136]. How can we avoid these mistakes? Emotional intelligence requires that we consider *all* features of a future event and not just its focal aspects, and take into account the proven efficacy of our psychological immune system. As consumers, our purchases should always be based on a skeptical assessment of our real needs, rather than the superficial feelings and emotions that advertisers always try to appeal to.

☐ Affect Infusion: Feeling Good and Thinking Good

Perhaps the most universal influence of affect is that it colors our thoughts and responses. When we feel good, we tend to see the world through rose-colored glasses. When depressed, everything appears bleak and gloomy. Some 60 years ago Razran [141] found that people who were made to feel bad by an aversive smell also made more negative judgments about unrelated issues than those who felt good after receiving a free lunch. Such "affect congruence" appears to be a very common and reliable everyday phenomenon [138]. Why exactly do these effects occur, and what can we do about them?

Psychodynamic theories suggested that affective impulses will invade and infuse unrelated thoughts unless sufficient pressure is exerted to control them. Indeed, attempts to suppress affect can sometimes increase the pressure and the likelihood of affect infusion. Thus, people who feared electric shocks and were trying to suppress their fear were more likely to see fear in others [116]. Alternative conditioning theories maintained that such dynamic assumptions are not necessary. According to this view, affect will spontaneously attach itself to unrelated thoughts and judgments because of simple temporal and spatial conditioning. For example, when people are made to feel bad because of the excessive heat and humidity in a room, they will form more negative impressions of people they meet because of a conditioned association between their affect and the target people [114]. However, neither psychoanalytic theories nor theories based on "blind" conditioning principles could explain the apparent situation sensitivity and context sensitivity of affect infusion. In contrast, contemporary theories emphasize cognitive, information processing mechanisms that link affect to thinking and behavior. Affect appears to play a key role in how our memory representations about the world are organized and activated, and it is this link that drives affect infusion into thinking and behavior. When in a positive mood, we are significantly more likely to access and recall positive information and information that was first encountered in a previous happy mood state (as did the hero in our introductory paragraph while reminiscing about happy childhood memories when feeling good). In contrast, negative mood selectively facilitates the recall of negative information. According to the associative network model developed by Gordon Bower [111], affective states are closely linked to any information we store and recall. Recent neuroanatomical evidence provides strong convergent "evidence for the inseparable relation between emotion and other aspects of cognition. Our everyday experience also clearly shows that affect influences essentially all other aspects of cognitive functioning, including memory, attention, and decision making" [108].

Affective influences on memory have widespread consequences for the way people think and behave. This occurs because we can only make sense of complex events by calling on our memories and prior experiences to interpret them. Surprisingly, the more complex or unusual a social event, the more likely that we will have to search our memories to make sense of it and the greater the likelihood that affect will influence the ideas we access and the interpretations we make. In other words, affect infusion increases when an open, constructive thinking style is adopted to deal with difficult, unusual situations, because only this kind of thinking promotes the incidental use of affectively primed information [120]. Ironically, this is why people may be much more influenced by their mood when thinking extensively about difficult personal problems in their relationship. However, mood effects are much weaker when less difficult, requiring less thinking, issues are considered [119].

This is not the only way that affect infusion can occur, however. Sometimes, people respond to situations without any careful or elaborate consideration of the evidence, relying on simple and readily available cues to produce a response [115]. When this happens, instead of "computing a judgment on the basis of recalled features of a target, individuals may . . . ask themselves: 'How do I feel about it?'/and/in doing so, they may mistake feelings due to a pre-existing state as a reaction to the target" [142]. Such simplified or "heuristic" thinking is most likely when people lack sufficient interest, motivation, or resources to produce a more elaborate response. For example, in a street survey people will often give more positive responses immediately after they have just seen a happy movie, and make more negative responses after seeing a sad film [135]. This probably occurs because the simplest way to respond in such a situation is to rely on a "How do I feel about it?" heuristic, using the prevailing affective state to infer a quick reaction. As such decisions are by definition of limited importance we will devote little further attention to them, other than noting that affect can indeed function as a useful heuristic cue in some situations.

☐ Affect Infusion into Memory and Judgments

Perhaps the most fundamental influence that affective states have is on our memories. People in a happy mood remember more positive memories from their childhood, recall more happy episodes from the previous week, and have better memories for words, they have learned in a similar mood state [111]. This is why when we are in a good mood all seems well with the world and we predominantly think about and remember happy, joyful experiences. When we are in a bad mood, in contrast, we tend to think negatively, which depresses us even further. Becoming aware of these subtle memory effects is an important component of EI. However, these effects are not universal. They are most likely to occur when people think in an open, constructive manner. Mood effects can be quite easily eliminated and even reversed. For example, when people's attention is directed toward themselves they become more aware of their own affective states, and this simple manipulation often seems sufficient to reduce affect congruency [109]. Thus, simply becoming aware of such mood effects is in itself an important step toward increasing our EI. Once we know how and why these effects occur, we are in a much better position to predict and manage their consequences.

Affective states can also influence many other tasks that require the use of memory-based ideas. For example, when people are asked to look at pictures depicting ambiguous social scenes (such as two people having an animated conversation), happy persons construct more cheerful, positive stories, and those in a sad mood respond by constructing negative stories [111]. Ultimately, affect can also impact on real social judgments about people.

For example, observing others and interpreting what their actions mean is one of the most fundamental judgmental tasks we face in everyday life. Affect seems to have a profound influence even on such very basic judgments. We looked at this possibility by asking happy or sad participants to observe and rate their own and their partner's behaviors on a videotaped social encounter [130]. As predicted, happy people "saw" significantly more positive, skilled behaviors and fewer negative, unskilled behaviors both in themselves and in their partners than did sad subjects. These effects occur because affect directly influences the kinds of thoughts and memories that come to mind as observers try to interpret complex and inherently ambiguous social behaviors.

In other words, the same smile that is seen as warm and friendly by a person in a good mood can easily can be judged as condescending or awkward by somebody in a bad mood. These kinds of mood effects also influence how we interpret our own behaviors and our successes and failures in real-life tasks such as passing an exam [131]. Part of the reason for these judgmental effects may be that people also tend to selectively focus on mood-consistent rather than mood-inconsistent information [129]. Thus, affect appears to influence what we notice, what we learn, what we remember, and, ultimately, the kinds of judgments and decisions we make. However, this kind of spontaneous affect infusion is rather a fragile process and can be reversed easily once people become aware of their mood states. An important aspect of EI is thus to know how, when, and why these effects occur.

☐ A Paradoxical Effect: Thinking More Increases Affect Infusion?

A surprising result confirmed in recent research is that affect infusion is significantly greater when people engage in more extensive and elaborate thinking that increases the opportunity of using memory-based information. In fact, it was a real-life episode that first suggested the idea for experiments testing this prediction. While sitting in a restaurant on one occasion, I found myself noticing an unusual couple: a young, beautiful woman and a rather old and not-so-attractive man were showing all the usual signs of intense romantic involvement at a neighboring table. As I surreptitiously observed them, I found myself wondering about their relationship. It occurred to me that the more I tried to make sense of this unusual couple, the more I was forced to rely on my own memory-based ideas and associations to interpret what I saw, and the greater the likelihood that my mood could influence the ideas I came up with and the kind of judgments I formed.

I decided to test this prediction in a series of experiments. For example, in a controlled replication of the above restaurant scenario, we made participants feel happy or sad after showing them standard mood induction films and then presented them with images of well-matched or badly matched couples. Their judgments showed significant affect infusion: happy participants formed more positive impressions than did sad participants. Critically, when the couples were unusual and badly matched, affect had a much greater effect on judgments than for couples that were typical and well matched [118], [121]. When we looked at just how long people took to deal with this information, we found that badly matched couples indeed required more lengthy and extensive thinking. Paradoxically, it was precisely this more elaborate thinking that increased affect infusion. The conclusion is clear: The more we need to think about something, the more likely that our affective state may influence our thoughts, memories, and, eventually, our responses.

This pattern has been confirmed in a number of other studies. For example, affect had a greater influence on judgments about more unusual, mixed-race rather than same-race couples. In other studies, we simultaneously manipulated *both* the physical attractiveness and the racial match of observed couples, and so created well-matched (same race, same attractiveness), partly matched (either race, or physical attractiveness matched), and mismatched, unusual couples (different race, different attractiveness). Affect had the greatest influence on judgments about mismatched couples, had a weaker effect when they were partly matched, and the smallest effect when they were well matched [121]. The same kind of results also are obtained when people make judgments about themselves: Affect has a greater influence when judging less familiar, peripheral aspects of the self, but these effects are reduced when central, familiar features are judged [144].

What happens when we are thinking about our intimate partners and relationships? Common sense suggests that such personal and highly familiar judgments should be more resistant to affective biases. In fact, the opposite seems to be the case. Surprisingly, when we asked people who were feeling happy or sad to think about their own intimate relationships, mood effects were consistently greater when more extensive thinking was required to deal with more complex and serious rather than simple, everyday interpersonal issues [119]. In a way, the more we know about a person or an issue, the richer and more extensive the number of relevant memories we can call upon, and the more likely that affect may have a strong selective influence on what comes to mind and the kind of judgments we make.

This might explain the remarkable effect where people may make extremely positive or extremely negative judgments about the same personal relationship at different times, despite having very detailed and extensive knowledge about their intimate partners. When feeling good, we selectively access memories about happy, positive events and the relationship seems fabulous. When in a negative mood, all that comes to mind is problems and difficulties, and the same relationship seems hardly worth having. Such affective biases in relationship judgments can be very dangerous, especially if couples get caught up in each other's affective states (see also Chapter 6). It is an important component of EI to know that affect can have a profound influence on memories and judgments. Becoming aware of these effects is a helpful first step in controlling and eliminating the cycle of negative affectivity that otherwise often can spiral out of control.

☐ Affect and Thinking Styles

Affect influences not only the content of cognition and behavior (what we think and do), but also the *process* of cognition, that is, *how* individuals think. It was initially thought that positive mood simply produces a more lazy, relaxed, and superficial thinking style, as if good mood "informed" us that no particular effort is required and bad mood was a warning to be more careful and attentive. However, more recent evidence suggests that positive affect does not just make people "lazy" thinkers. Rather, feeling good seems to produce a thinking style that gives greater rein to our internal thoughts, dispositions, and ideas. In this mode of thinking individuals tend to pay less attention to external information and tend to assimilate situational details into their preexisting knowledge about the world. Negative affect in contrast produces a more externally focused thinking style where accommodation to the demands of the external world takes precedence over internal ideas [110], [117].

These differences in thinking style are consistent with evolutionary ideas that suggest that affect signals appropriate ways of responding to different situations. Positive affect tells us that the environment is benign and that we can rely on our existing knowledge in responding. Negative affect is more like an alarm signal, alerting us that the environment is potentially dangerous and that we need to pay close attention to external information. Understanding these subtle processing consequences of affect is again likely to be an important feature of EI. We now know that feeling good or feeling bad does make us deal very differently with the same social situation, as the studies below show.

☐ Feeling Bad, but Thinking Carefully?

Not only can negative moods take over our thoughts and preoccupy us with a negative outlook, but they can also influence how we deal with social information. For example, when responding to persuasive messages, happy people seem to be more influenced by superficial details such as the attractiveness or status of the communicator. In contrast, those in a negative mood tend to scrutinize the message more carefully and respond more in terms of message quality [140]. Feeling bad may also help us to see things more accurately. Some clinical research suggests that those feeling depressed are actually more realistic in how they see the world and themselves, and it is "normal" people who tend to distort reality in a positive direction.

There is also some experimental evidence suggesting that negative mood may help us to avoid certain judgmental mistakes, such as the fundamental attribution error (FAE). The FAE occurs because people mistakenly assume that most actions are internally caused and ignore external influences on behavior. In several studies we asked happy or sad people to judge others based on an essay written by them that advocated either desirable or undesirable attitudes on topical issues such as student fees. Judges were also told that this topic was either freely chosen or was assigned to the writer [124]. Happy persons tended to ignore this information and simply assumed that the essay reflected the writer's attitudes, thus committing the FAE. Negative mood reduced this bias. Those feeling bad paid better attention to the available information and tended to discount coerced essays as indicative of the writer's real views.

Emotional intelligence should clearly include some attention to and awareness of these effects. Many decisions in everyday life, including important organizational decisions, are made in similar circumstances. For example, in a series of recent studies Stephanie Moylan [139] showed that positive mood tends to increase and negative mood tends to decrease the incidence of a variety of errors and distortions in performance assessment judgments. To be emotionally intelligent means knowing about these effects and knowing how to avoid or correct them.

☐ Affect and Eyewitness Memory

Eyewitness memories play an important role in everyday social behavior and are even accorded special evidential status in the legal system. How-

ever, remembering observed social events also may be influenced by affect [128]. To evaluate this, we asked people to witness complex social
events presented on videotapes (such as a wedding scene or a robbery). A
week later, we used films to induce good or bad mood and then questioned subjects about what they saw; the questions either included or did
not include "planted," misleading information about the scenes. When
subjects' memory for the incidents was later tested, those in a positive
mood when the misleading information was presented were much more
likely to incorporate this "false" information into their memories as correct. Negative mood reduced this memory distortion. The same effects
also were observed in a field study where students were asked to observe
and later recall a staged incident during a lecture [128]. Knowing that
mild mood states can produce such memory biases is an important component of EI.

☐ Coping with Stress and the "Neurotic Cascade"

However, more intense negative affect can also have debilitating consequences for our thinking. In certain individuals, extreme stress and anxiety
can produce a dangerous "neurotic cascade" of reverberating negative
affect and negative thinking [145]. In such a state, even minor problems
tend to be magnified out of all proportion. "Awfulisation" refers to the tendency to overdramatize negative outcomes by highly stressed persons,
leading to thoughts such as "I wouldn't cope if I lost this deal" or "I couldn't
survive for a week without my girlfriend." Overgeneralization is another
faulty thought pattern often found in this negative state. For example,
the loss of a partner ("She doesn't love me") will be overgeneralized to
indicate that "Nobody loves me." In such a state, people sometimes set unrealistic and unreasonable goals for themselves, show decreased flexibility in
adjusting their goals, and so inadvertently produce more negative experiences. To break this cycle of negative affectivity, it is important to make a
conscious effort to become aware of and analyze our thoughts, determine
whether they are rational or not, and to discard irrational ones. It may be
useful also to question how others might respond to the same situation
and ask ourselves whether it is helpful to maintain such negative ideas.

☐ Affect Infusion and Behavior

So far we have focused on affective influences on thinking. In social interactions we must make many rapid, constructive but largely subconscious cognitive decisions about alternative actions. In these social situa-

tions affect will usually influence the way we behave. We may expect that people in a positive mood may behave in a more friendly, skilled, and constructive way than do those in a negative mood. This prediction was confirmed when we asked female undergraduates to interact with a confederate, or researcher, immediately after they were made to feel good or bad as a result of watching a mood induction film [134]. The interaction subsequently was rated by trained observers who were not aware of the mood manipulation. Happy students communicated more and did so more effectively, used more engaging nonverbal signals, were more talkative, and disclosed more about themselves. They were seen as acting in a more poised, skilled, and rewarding manner. Sad participants in contrast were seen as being less friendly, confident, and relaxed than were happy participants. It seems then that affect will infuse not only people's thoughts and judgments, but also their real-life social interactions. Again, there are clear implications for our understanding of EI: To be emotionally intelligent means realizing that even mild mood states can fundamentally alter the way we behave and appear to others. People usually are not aware of these effects. When questioned, students in this study did not realize that their behavior was in any way influenced by their moods. It requires a conscious effort and awareness to correct for these effects if we want to increase our EI.

In real life, we often have to respond almost instantaneously to social situations, yet affect can still have a major influence on how we behave. Such a pattern was observed [124] when people had to respond to an unexpected request in a university library. Affect was manipulated by leaving pictures (or text) designed to induce positive or negative mood on unoccupied library desks. A few minutes after students read these materials, they were approached by another student (in fact, a confederate) who made an unexpected polite or impolite request for several sheets of paper. Soon afterward, a second confederate explained that the situation was in fact staged and asked them to complete a brief questionnaire about the request and the requester. The mood induction had a strong influence on responses. Students who felt bad responded with a critical, negative evaluation of the request and the requester and complied less than did those in a positive mood. Interestingly, these mood effects were greater when the request was unusual and impolite. As unusual and impolite requests violate normal expectations, they should elicit a more elaborate and open thinking style and increase the chances for affectively primed ideas to influence the response. In fact, impolite requests were considered in greater detail and were remembered better than conventional requests. Do these effects also occur when people carefully and extensively think about their social moves, such as when they formulate an interpersonal request?

☐ Asking Nicely? Affective Influences on Requesting

Asking people to do something for us—requesting—is one of the more difficult and problematic tasks we all face in everyday life. Requesting usually involves psychological conflict, because people must phrase their request so as to maximize the chances of compliance (by being direct), yet avoid the danger of giving offense (by not being *too* direct). Affect may influence request strategies, as the greater availability of positive thoughts in a happy mood may produce a more confident, direct requesting style. This prediction was confirmed in a number of experiments that found that happy persons used more direct, impolite requests, whereas sad persons used more cautious, polite request forms. Further, these mood effects on requesting were much stronger when the request situation was demanding and difficult, and required more extensive thinking [123], [125]. Again, these effects also occur in real-life tasks. In one study, we recorded the requests made by subjects who were asked to get a file from a neighboring office after receiving a mood induction [126, Exp. 2]. Even in this "real" situation, negative mood produced more polite, cautious, and hedging requests than did positive mood.

The implications of such studies clearly extend to many commonplace real-life situations. Imagine that you are planning to ask for a raise from your boss and are thinking about how to phrase your request. The particular form of words used—and their success—will partly depend on the current mood state: When happy, people might prefer more confident and direct approaches. When feeling down, more cautious and polite forms will be used. Emotional intelligence requires that we know about these effects if we want to increase our interpersonal effectiveness.

☐ Affect and Persuasion

Requesting is not the only strategy we can use to influence others. Mild everyday mood states may also influence how well we do when we try to persuade others. Imagine that you are trying to produce persuasive arguments either for or against propositions such as (a) increasing student fees or (b) nuclear testing in the Pacific. When we asked subjects to do this immediately after a mood induction [132], those in a negative mood came up with higher-quality persuasive arguments than did happy persons. The same effects were also obtained in a second study, when happy or sad people were asked to persuade a friend for or against Australia becoming a republic or for or against the populist Australia First party. In a further experiment, individuals produced their persuasive arguments in interacting with a "partner" through a computer keyboard as if exchanging electronic mail. Half the participants were promised a significant reward (movie passes) if they were successful. Those in a negative mood again thought of higher-quality arguments. However, the provision of a reward reduced the size of mood effects by imposing a strong motivational influence on how the task was approached. These results suggest that mild negative mood promotes a more careful, systematic processing style that is more attuned to the requirements of a given situation. However, a strong motivation to do well will override these mood effects. The implications for EI are obvious. If a task is performed without any thought or awareness of mood effects, then affect is likely to influence our thinking style and the quality of the response. However, becoming aware that these effects occur and being motivated to overcome them is likely to be a highly effective control strategy.

☐ Feeling Good and Getting Your Way? Affect Infusion into Bargaining Behaviors

Bargaining and negotiation by definition involve a degree of unpredictability and require careful planning and preparation. We found in several studies that happy persons set themselves higher and more ambitious negotiating goals, expect to succeed more, and make plans and use strategies that are more optimistic, cooperative, and integrative than do neutral or negative mood people [122]. Most interesting was the finding that positive affect actually helped people to do better. They were more successful and achieved better outcomes for themselves than did sad participants. These findings have striking implications for our understanding of EI. They suggest that even small changes in affective state because of a completely unrelated prior event can have a marked influence on the way people plan and execute strategic interpersonal encounters.

Why do these effects occur? Uncertain and unpredictable social encounters such as bargaining require open, constructive thinking. Positive affect may selectively bring to mind (prime) more positive thoughts and ideas that lead to more optimistic expectations and the adoption of more cooperative and integrative bargaining strategies. Negative affect in turn seems to bring to mind more negative and pessimistic memories and leads to the less cooperative and, ultimately, leads to less cooperative bargaining. These effects are largely automatic and subconscious, and few people realize that they occur at all. Being emotionally intelligent by definition involves being aware of and being able to control and manage these subtle mood effects on our thinking and actions.

☐ Individual Differences in Affect Infusion

Not all people are equally influenced by their affective states, however. For example, personality traits such as neuroticism seem to increase the intensity and duration of negative affective reactions in particular [145]. Other traits are also important. We found that people who scored high on personality measures such as machiavellianism (indicating a highly manipulative approach to people) and need for approval were less influenced by their moods when bargaining. Affect infusion was reduced for these people, because they habitually approach tasks such as bargaining from a highly motivated, predetermined perspective. It is almost as if high machiavellians and those high in need for approval had their minds made up about what to do and how to behave even before they started. As they did not rely on open, memory-based thinking, affect had much less of an opportunity to influence their plans and behaviors.

Perhaps predictably, individuals who score high on personality tests measuring openness to feelings are much more influenced by mood when making consumer judgments than are low scorers [113]. Trait anxiety can also influence affect infusion. Low trait anxious people when feeling bad respond more negatively to a threatening out-group. High trait anxious individuals seem to do exactly the opposite [112]. In general, it seems clear that differences in personality or "temperament" do play an important role in how people deal with affect.

Indeed, the very concept of EI refers to such enduring differences between people in terms of affective style (see Chapter 1 and [138]). Much of the evidence considered here suggests that individual differences in affectivity operate through a habitual preference for different ways of thinking. People who score high on measures such as self-esteem, machiavellianism, social desirability, or trait anxiety seem to respond to social situations in a motivated, controlled, and highly directed fashion that makes it less likely that they openly search for and use affectively loaded information from their memory.

☐ Toward an Integration: The Affect Infusion Model

As this necessarily brief review suggests, EI requires an awareness that affect can have a powerful influence on the way people think and behave in social situations. Two major kinds of influences have been identified. Informational effects occur because affect informs the content of memories, thoughts, and judgments. Processing effects occur because affect also influences how people deal with social information. However, it is also clear that affective influences on judgments and behavior are highly context specific. A comprehensive understanding of these effects—that is, being emotionally intelligent—requires that we can specify the circumstances that promote or inhibit affect congruence and also define the conditions that lead to affect infusion or its absence.

A recent integrative theory, the Affect Infusion Model (AIM) [120] sought to accomplish this task by specifying the circumstances that promote an open, constructive processing style that leads to affect infusion [121]. According to this model, the thinking strategies people can use in social situations differ in terms of two basic features: (1) the degree of *effort* invested, and (2) the degree of *openness* and *constructiveness* of the thinking strategy. The combination of these two features, quantity (effort) and quality (openness) of thinking, defines four distinct processing styles: *direct access processing* (low effort/closed), *motivated processing* (high effort/closed), *heuristic processing* (low effort/open, constructive), and *substantive processing* (high effort/open, constructive).

Many social responses are based on the low effort *direct access strategy*, or the simple and direct retrieval of a preexisting response. This is most likely when the task is highly familiar and there is no reason to engage in more elaborate thinking. For example, if asked in a street survey to rate a well-known political leader, reproducing a previously computed and stored evaluation will be sufficient. People possess a rich store of preformed attitudes and judgments. Retrieving them requires no constructive thinking and affect infusion should not occur. The second *motivated processing strategy* involves highly selective and targeted thinking that is dominated by a particular motivational objective. This strategy also precludes open information search and should be impervious to affect infusion. For example, if in a job interview you are asked about your attitude toward the company you want to join, the response will be dominated by the motivation to produce an acceptable response. Open, constructive processing is inhibited, and affect infusion is unlikely. Depending on the particular goal, motivated processing may also produce mood-incongruent responses and a reversal of affect infusion.

The third strategy, *heuristic processing,* is most likely when the task is simple, familiar, and has little personal relevance, and there is no reason for more detailed processing. This kind of superficial, quick processing is likely when we need to respond to an unexpected question, say, in a telephone survey [143] or a street survey [135]. Heuristic processing can sometimes lead to affect infusion if people adopt the simple "How do I feel about it" strategy. Finally, *substantive processing* is used when people need to fully and constructively deal with a social situation. This is an inherently open and constructive thinking style that characterizes most of our most personally relevant and important decisions. This kind of thinking should be used whenever the task is demanding, atypical, complex or involving, and there are no ready-made direct access responses or motivational goals available to guide the response.

The AIM predicts greater affect infusion whenever more substantive thinking is required to deal with a more demanding task. This paradoxical effect has been confirmed in a number of studies, as we have seen above. Unfamiliar, complex, and atypical tasks should recruit more substantive thinking. Affect itself also can influence processing choices; as we have seen, positive affect promotes a more internally driven, top-down thinking style, and negative affect triggers more externally focused, bottom-up thinking. An integrative model such as the AIM makes a useful contribution to our understanding of EI because it helps to specify the circumstances leading to the *absence* of affect infusion when direct access or motivated processing is used and the *presence* of affect infusion during heuristic and substantive processing.

Two of the thinking styles identified by the model may also be involved in how we manage our everyday moods. We have seen that substantive processing typically facilitates affect infusion and the maintenance and accentuation of an existing affective state. In contrast, motivated processing may produce affect-incongruent responses and the attenuation of the affective state. Affect management can thus be achieved as people spontaneously switch their information processing strategies between substantive and motivated processing so as to calibrate their prevailing moods. In other words, these two thinking styles may jointly constitute a dynamic, self-correcting mood management system. Several studies support this account. When responses by happy and sad people are monitored over time, initial mood congruence spontaneously gives way to mood incongruent responses [133]. This switch from "first congruent, then incongruent" responses suggests the existence of a spontaneous affect regulation system, and EI is likely to involve a ready ability to switch from substantive to motivated thinking.

☐ Summary and Conclusions

This chapter argued that EI necessarily includes a degree of awareness of how affective states infuse our memories, thoughts, judgments, and interpersonal behaviors. The research reviewed here suggests that different information processing strategies play a key role in explaining these effects. Theories such as the AIM [120] seek to explain when and how affect influences everyday judgments and behaviors. A number of studies showed that more constructive, substantive thinking reliably increases affect infusion into thinking. Further, affect infusion also impacts on a range of interpersonal behaviors, such as the use of requests, persuasive communication, and strategic bargaining. We also have seen that positive and negative mood produce different thinking strategies, and, as a result, positive mood often increases and negative mood decreases memory and judgmental errors.

In contrast, affect infusion is reduced or absent whenever a social task can be performed using a simple, well-rehearsed direct access strategy or a highly motivated strategy. Frequently, the social situations we face impose strong motivational demands to act in required ways that override these subtle mood effects. Sometimes the pressures to act in a particular manner come from within. We have seen that certain personality traits can strongly predict how people will act. When people do not rely on open, constructive thinking to figure out what to do, mood states are much less likely to influence their responses. These general principles have important consequences in many real-life situations, and our understanding of EI must include an appreciation of these effects.

Affect is thus likely to influence many relationship behaviors, group behaviors, organizational decisions, consumer preferences, and health-related behaviors, and EI necessarily involves knowing when and how these effects occur (see Chapters 6 and 7). Individuals who experience negative moods report more severe physical symptoms and more negative attitudes and beliefs about their ability to manage their health (see Chapter 10). Recent studies also confirm that affect has a highly significant influence on many organizational behaviors and decisions (see Chapter 9). The evidence we discussed clearly illustrates the multiple influences that affect has on interpersonal behavior. Being emotionally intelligent requires a degree of awareness of how and when these processes operate, as a first step toward controlling our emotional responses. I hope the work described here will contribute to a greater understanding of the role of affect in social life.

☐ Acknowledgment

This work was supported by a Special Investigator award from the Australian Research Council and the Research Prize by the Alexander von Humboldt Foundation. I gratefully acknowledge the contributions of Joseph Ciarrochi, Stephanie Moylan, Patrick Vargas, and Joan Webb to this project.

II

APPLICATIONS OF EMOTIONAL INTELLIGENCE RESEARCH TO EVERYDAY LIFE

CHAPTER

Graeme J. Taylor

Low Emotional Intelligence and Mental Illness

Today we believe that if you are emotionally intelligent then you can cope better with life's challenges and control your emotions more effectively, both of which contribute to good mental health. We might wonder, on the other hand, whether low emotional intelligence (EI) is a risk factor for mental illness. Because EI is a relatively new idea, there is not much empirical research that explores its relationships with coping styles and mental health. Since Peter Salovey and John Mayer formulated a definition of EI at the beginning of the 1990s, several competing models of EI have been proposed. Within the fields of psychiatry and psychosomatic medicine, however, clinicians and researchers have used a closely related construct for almost 30 years, that of alexithymia (difficulty identifying and communicating emotion), which preceded even Howard Gardner's idea of the personal intelligences from which the concept of EI is partly derived. In contrast to EI, alexithymia has been precisely defined, well-validated, and much data from studies have shown how it affects our everyday lives. Based on studies, the common belief is that people with alexithymia do not relate well to other people or cope well, and are prone to several common mental illnesses that involve disturbances in the regulation of emotions.

In this chapter we look at alexithymia and show how it overlaps with low levels of EI. Then I review the findings from studies showing how alexithymia and low EI may contribute to problems in interpersonal relationships and in coping with stress. Finally, I review empirical evidence of associations between alexithymia and various mental illnesses. We will

67

conclude with a brief discussion of some implications for the treatment and prevention of mental illness.

☐ What Is Alexithymia?

Whereas EI came out of research findings on how people appraise, express, and use emotion, alexithymia was derived from clinical observations. As early as 1948 the psychiatrist Jurgen Ruesch saw that many of his patients who had classic psychosomatic diseases (essential hypertension, bronchial asthma, duodenal ulcer, ulcerative colitis, thyrotoxicosis, rheumatoid arthritis, and nonallergic dermatitis) or posttraumatic syndromes lacked imagination and had a difficult time saying how they were feeling. A few years later, the psychoanalyst Karen Horney described the same situation in some of her patients who were not responding well to psychoanalytic psychotherapy because they were not aware emotionally and had few inner experiences. These psychiatric patients often showed "psychosomatic" symptoms, and, to reduce their tension and distress, often abused alcohol or engaged in binge eating or other compulsive behaviors. Because they could not verbalize how they were feeling, such patients were sometimes referred to as "emotional illiterates" [163], [165].

In the early 1970s the psychoanalyst Peter Sifneos coined the term *alexithymia* (from the Greek *a* meaning lack, *lexis* meaning word, *thymos* meaning emotion) to refer to the difficulty in identifying and describing subjective feelings that he also had seen in patients with classic psychosomatic diseases. Sifneos and his colleague John Nemiah recognized that the difficulty was associated with several other characteristics, so they created a definition of alexithymia that encompasses four important features: difficulty identifying feelings and distinguishing between feelings and the bodily sensations of emotional arousal, difficulty describing feelings to others, a poor fantasy life, and a cognitive style that is literal and focuses on the minute details of external events. Independent of Sifneos and Nemiah, several other investigators reported seeing similar characteristics among drug addicts and patients with posttraumatic states or eating disorders. It was not that the patients were without emotion—they spontaneously used words such as "sad," "nervous," or "frightened"—but they could not say what it was like to feel sad, nervous, or scared. They would talk about the events that surrounded the emotions, but because their inner resources were limited, they could not get to the meaning below the surface of the experience [158].

Although they are not part of the definition of the alexithymia construct, several additional characteristics have been reported by clinicians that also point to difficulties in emotional processing. These include an inability to separate emotional feelings from physical states, being impulsive, expressing global feelings (such as "I feel bad" or "I feel mad"), and only being able to feel pleasant emotions such as joy, happiness, and love to a limited degree. Indeed, people who are highly alexithymic are sometimes unable to feel much pleasure at all (anhedonic). Because they do not understand their own feelings, they also are unable to read others' emotions. Often they are seen as unempathic and cannot deal with others who are distressed. For example, sometimes they seek counseling because their spouse has insisted, as the following clinical vignette shows.

Richard, a 44-year-old bank manager, consulted a psychiatrist because his wife and children complained that he was insensitive to their feelings and did not express his own feelings. Although he was aware when he had global feeling such as anger and depression, Richard said that he was often confused by his emotions and generally was unaware of other people's emotions except when they showed huge changes in their moods. When the psychiatrist asked Richard about his mother's death a few years ago, he said that he had felt some sadness, but was unable to elaborate on this feeling. He believed that he loved his wife and children, but did not feel this emotion very strongly. Sex was physically pleasurable, he said, but he couldn't describe any tender or intimate feelings for his wife or previous girlfriends. Moreover, he had few interests, no close friends, and said that he never felt very happy. He gave a detailed and somewhat boring account, however, of his daily activities at the bank.

During the 1980s the alexithymia construct came under fire because there was very little scientific support for its validity. In addition, often the studies that examined the association between alexithymia and various medical and psychiatric disorders measured alexithymia with instruments that were put together hastily and subsequently were found to be not very reliable. Beginning in the mid-1980s, however, and extending for a period of almost 10 years, my colleagues and I conducted a program of research to evaluate the validity of the construct by developing a reliable and valid instrument for measuring it. This method of construct validation is widely used in personality research. We initially developed the 26-item self-report Toronto Alexithymia Scale (TAS) and later introduced a revised and improved 20-item version, which we named the Twenty-Item Toronto Alexithymia Scale (TAS-20). Although the TAS-20 has become the most widely used measure of alexithymia, it correlates highly with the TAS and both versions are reliable and valid.

The TAS-20 uses three factor scales (or subscales) to assess three of the four key features of the alexithymia construct: difficulty identifying feelings, difficulty describing feelings, and externally oriented thinking. We assess the part of the alexithymia construct that relates to low imagination indirectly by using the externally oriented thinking factor, which has been shown to correlate negatively with a measure of fantasy. There is evidence also that the TAS-20 and its three factor scales converge and diverge in theoretically meaningful ways with measures of related and unrelated constructs. For example, studies show that high scorers on the TAS-20 are unlikely to think in an analytical way and are not psychologically minded; they rarely see and reflect upon relationships among thoughts, feelings, and actions. Even though we cannot look at a personality construct without considering the tests that claim to measure it, the psychometric properties of the TAS-20 strongly support the validity of the alexithymia construct itself [165].

Some researchers don't believe that self-report scales (where one judges one's own ability) are effective for seeing how aware we are of our emotional states. Instead, they advocate using tests that measure actual ability. Studies have shown, however, that the scores people obtain on the TAS-20 and its factors show moderate to high levels of agreement with the alexithymia ratings they receive during interviews designed to assess emotional awareness and imaginal activity [164]. Moreover, in an experimental study, Richard Lane and his colleagues at the University of Arizona found that when they asked subjects to match verbal or nonverbal stimuli with verbal or nonverbal emotional responses, individuals with high TAS-20 scores did significantly worse than did those with low TAS-20 scores. The subjects matched emotion words with photographs of faces showing an emotion; matched photographs of facial expressions with photographs of scenes (without human faces) depicting different emotions; and matched emotion words with sentences that depict specific emotions but do not include words that denote emotion [155]. These tasks are similar to some of those in the Multifactor Emotional Intelligence Scale (MEIS), which was developed recently by Mayer and Salovey to assess EI on the basis of actual, rather than self-reported, performance (see Chapter 1).

People are not either alexithymic or nonalexithymic; rather, as with EI, they show the trait to varying degrees. On the TAS-20, for example, scores range between 20 and 100 and follow a bell-shaped curve distribution in the general population. Nonetheless, because we want to compare degrees of alexithymia across different clinical and nonclinical populations, we have established cutoff scores for both the TAS and the TAS-20 that identify people with high and low alexithymia. For example, high alexithymia rates for psychiatric patients ranged between 33% and 42%, in contrast to rates ranging between 4% and 16% in different groups of healthy individuals. Men tend to be more alexithymic than women [162], [165].

Although the TAS-20 is a useful screening test for alexithymia, when a patient is entering therapy it is better to interview him or her to explore the patient's ability to describe feelings and fantasies. In our own clinical work, we also have patients complete the Revised NEO Personality Inventory (NEO PI-R) [150], which provides scores for the five basic dimensions of personality (neuroticism, extraversion, openness to experience, agreeableness, and conscientiousness) and for five lower-order facets or traits within each of these dimensions. Although there is no one single facet of the NEO PI-R that represents alexithymia, individuals who score high on the TAS-20 usually also score low on the receptivity to feelings subscale and the fantasy subscale of the openness to experience dimension. Because high alexithymia people cannot fully experience joy and pleasure and differentiate negative emotions from one another, they also commonly score high on neuroticism (proneness to negative emotion) and low on the positive emotions subscale of extraversion [165]. Although in some studies the TAS-20 has shown an inverse relationship with educational level, many individuals who are highly alexithymic are high in general intelligence. Richard, for example, scored in the high alexithymia range on the TAS-20, and in terms of intelligence he rated within the top 5–10% of the population according to the Wechsler Adult Intelligence Scale.

☐ Alexithymia as Low Emotional Intelligence

In his well-known book, *Frames of Mind: The Theory of Multiple Intelligences*, Howard Gardner [152] proposed that a number of intelligences exist, including two forms of personal intelligence, which he labeled *intrapersonal intelligence* and *interpersonal intelligence*. Intrapersonal intelligence, the ability to access one's own feeling life, overlaps conceptually with two facets of the alexithymia construct (difficulty identifying feelings and describing them to others) and also with emotional self-awareness, which is what Salovey and Mayer defined as one of the core capacities of EI. Another core capacity in their definition is the ability to read the feelings and emotions of others, which is usually referred to as empathy and is part of what Gardner describes as interpersonal intelligence [161]. Although the definition of alexithymia does not include difficulty monitoring the feelings and emotions of other people, clinicians report that high alexithymia individuals do not empathize well with others. This is probably because, in part, they have a difficult time identifying emotions in the facial expressions of others, as has been found in several experimental studies [165], [166].

Two recent studies examining the relationship between the TAS-20 and the Bar-On Emotional Quotient Inventory (EQ-i) [146] showed empirical evidence that alexithymia and EI are strongly, albeit inversely, related [160]. As outlined by Reuven Bar-On (see Chapter 5), the EQ-i is based on a broad idea of EI that encompasses a variety of emotionally and so-cially competent behaviors, including the intrapersonal and interpersonal intelligences. In addition to a total EQ score, the EQ-i gives five compos-ite scale scores (intrapersonal, interpersonal, adaptability, stress manage-ment, and general mood), including 15 subscale scores. Whereas subscales within the intrapersonal and interpersonal scales assess the core compo-nents of EI, namely, emotional self-awareness and empathy, the subscales within the adaptability, stress management, and general mood scales seem to look at some outcomes of EI.

My colleagues James Parker and Michael Bagby and I collected data from 734 adults from small towns and rural communities in central Ontario. We found that their TAS-20 scores correlated negatively and sig-nificantly with the total score of the EQ-i (r was $-.72$) and also with its five composite scale scores (r was $-.66$ with the intrapersonal scale, $-.54$ with the interpersonal scale, $-.62$ with the adaptability scale, $-.47$ with the stress management scale, and $-.51$ with the general mood scale). We also saw that these adults' scores of all three factors of the TAS-20 corre-lated negatively and significantly with the five composite scales of the EQ-i and with all 15 subscale scores [160], [163].

Derek Dawda and Stephen Hart [151] conducted another study with a group of 243 university students at Simon Fraser University in British Columbia. Although the students' scores did not show as strong a corre-lation as those obtained with the community population, the TAS-20 again correlated negatively and significantly with the total score of the EQ-i and also with its five composite scale scores.

A critical aspect of high EI is that you can use what you see in your own and others' emotions to guide your thinking and behavior. Mayer and Salovey [157] recently revised their definition of EI to include the ability to understand and interpret the meanings that emotions convey and the ability to regulate your own and others' emotions. High alexithymia indi-viduals cannot use emotions as information about their internal or exter-nal worlds, because they cannot identify and give a name to the emo-tions. Also, when you can know your own feelings, you have a better sense of self. High alexithymia individuals do not feel good about them-selves. Data from our study with a community population also supports this. People who scored high on the TAS-20 obtained low scores on the self-regard scale of the EQ-i, which shows that they feel inadequate and do not respect or accept themselves (r was $-.43$) [163]. In other research, people who scored high on the TAS-20 showed low affective orientation (r was $-.37$), a construct that also overlaps with EI and is defined as the degree to which people are aware of their emotions, see them as impor-tant, and actively consider their feelings in guiding their behavior [165].

☐ Alexithymia and Maladaptive Coping

How well you react to stress is an important index of your EI level. It is commonly believed that if you are emotionally intelligent, you will be able to effectively contain and balance your emotional responses and thereby protect yourself from any adverse effects of stress. Those with low EI, on the other hand, are thought to be frequently overwhelmed and act out in unhealthy ways or become mentally or physically ill. As we mentioned already, Bar-On included stress management as one of the composite scales within the EQ-i. This scale comprises two subscales: (1) stress tolerance, which assesses your ability to withstand adverse events and strong emotions by actively and positively coping with stress; and (2) impulse control, which assesses your ability to resist or delay an impulse to act, and to control your emotions. Our Ontario community study data show that those who are highly alexithymic usually have a hard time controlling their emotions and impulses to act and in coping positively with stressful situations [160], [163].

More studies were conducted to look at how people cope in stressful situations. The three general coping styles usually identified in the psychology literature are problem-focused or task-oriented coping, emotion-oriented coping, and avoidance-oriented coping. If you are task-oriented, you cope by, for example, thinking about how you have solved similar problems in the past, analyzing the problem before you react, and considering several different solutions to the problem. If you use emotion-oriented coping strategies, then you will probably tell yourself that the situation is really not happening and become preoccupied with aches and pains, and become angry. If avoidance-oriented coping is your style, you would try to distract yourself by watching television, buying yourself something, going out for a snack or meal, or socializing with others. My colleagues and I conducted a study with a group of undergraduate university students and found that high alexithymia students generally used more emotion-oriented coping (quickly becoming angry or experiencing denial, for example) than task-oriented coping (thinking through the problem and acting rationally) than did low alexithymia students. High alexithymia students were more avoidance oriented than low alexithymia students, but both groups were as likely to go out with a friend [159]. Although going out with friends can reduce stress, avoiding stress by watching television or snacking may lead to psychological and somatic symptoms and can be a poor choice of coping strategy.

As part of her doctoral dissertation at Yale University, Carrie Schaffer developed an Affect Regulation Scale to assess the strategies people use to cope with distressing emotional states that might be evoked by various situations. She found that in a group of adult psychiatric patients, those with high alexithymia used poor methods to regulate their emotions. They tended to binge on food or develop a headache, for example, whereas those with low alexithymia used adaptive behaviors, such as thinking about and trying to understand distressing feelings or talking to a caring person. The same instrument was used in a later study by Carol Beckendam for her doctoral dissertation at the Fielding Institute in California; in a group of male parolees, those with high alexithymia had sexual and aggressive fantasies and behavior, and engaged in reckless activities and drank alcohol [162].

We try to cope with stress using conscious strategies, but our defense mechanisms are often at work in our unconscious. Each of us uses a cluster of these psychological mechanisms, which researchers categorize in order of low to high adaptiveness: immature or maladaptive defenses (including denying, splitting, projecting, acting out, and somatizing), neurotic defenses (including undoing, creating reaction formation, and idealizing), and mature or adaptive defenses (including sublimating, using humor, and suppressing). Whichever cluster we use the most characterizes our defensive style. When studied, both psychiatric and nonclinical populations have shown that those with high alexithymia use an immature defense style rather than an adaptive style. These study populations show only a weak, positive association with a neurotic style [154], [159]. Just because we have adaptive defenses does not mean we are mentally healthy. But those with more serious forms of psychopathology (such as psychotic disorders, borderline personality disorder, and some of the somatoform disorders, which we discuss later) usually use maladaptive defenses.

High alexithymia individuals usually cannot use adaptive coping strategies, including talking to and seeking emotional support from family members or close friends, because they find it difficult to become emotionally close and share feelings with others. Bar-On considers this ability to be a critical aspect of EI, and assesses it with the interpersonal relationship subscale of the EQ-i. Remember the Ontario community population? People who scored low on this subscale had high scores on the TAS-20, especially on the difficulty describing feelings factor [163].

Real trouble can happen when a high alexithymic individual marries an emotionally aware and expressive partner:

Mrs. Kennedy, a middle-aged mother of two children in their late teens, sought psychiatric counseling because she was anxious, angry, and depressed, which she attributed to chronic discontent with her marriage. Although she described her husband as a generous man and a good provider, their relationship lacked intimacy and passion, and she always felt emotionally empty. Moreover, for the past several years, she had observed that her husband seemed somewhat depressed and was drinking too much and not taking care of his health. Whenever she tried to discuss her feelings and concerns with him, her husband merely acknowledged that *she* was not feeling well; he seemed incapable of comforting her or considering that he might be contributing to her emotional distress.

In a psychiatric interview, it was obvious that Mr. Kennedy was highly alexithymic; he was unattuned to his own feelings and those of his wife and seemed to have minimal access to any inner psychological life. Using a maladaptive defense style, he denied being depressed, downplayed his consumption of alcohol, and declared that because alcoholism is inherited there was nothing he could do about his drinking. In his job as president of a small computer software company, he was under a great deal of stress from policy disagreements with his staff, daily concerns about financial markets, and frequent traveling about the country. His usual ways of coping with this stress were to drink alcohol, eat too much, and take frequent vacations. Even though he had suffered a small heart attack a few years ago and was prone to migraine headaches and attacks of irritable bowel syndrome, Mr. Kennedy saw no reason to modify his lifestyle. He seemed unable to reflect on the issues raised by his wife and claimed that his relationships with her and his children were excellent. Mrs. Kennedy and the clinician's descriptions were right: Mr. Kennedy scored in the high alexithymia range on the TAS-20, and in the low range on the fantasy and receptivity to feelings subscales of the NEO PI-R. His overall score on the EQ-i placed him in the lower 2% of the population for EI. Very low scores on most EQ-i subscales confirmed that he has difficulty properly recognizing and understanding both his own feelings and the feelings of others, has a poor self-image and self-respect, and finds it difficult to cope with stress and to form intimate relationships.

☐ Alexithymia and Psychiatric Disorders

Since the mid-1980s research studies have generated a lot of data to support earlier clinical reports of a strong association between alexithymia and certain psychiatric disorders. Because most of the studies were conducted at a particular time (cross sectional in design) and after the subjects became ill, it is impossible to determine whether high alexithymia is a cause or result of psychiatric illness. As I discuss below, however, there is clinical evidence and research that suggest that when a person is emotionally unaware and has difficulty regulating emotions, which corresponds with low EI, some mental disorders can occur or get worse.

Substance Use Disorders

Becoming addicted to drugs or alcohol depends on many factors, including one's constitution, personality, and sociocultural situation, but one thing is clear—addicts have difficulty managing their emotions. This may be because the drugs or alcohol cause a chronic inability to be emotionally aware in some people, or it may just be temporary. Once the drugs are out of his or her system, more emotional abilities return. Overall, though, evidence is showing that many people who rely on drugs or alcohol do not see, understand, or modulate their emotions well.

Even before the alexithymia construct was introduced the psychoanalyst Henry Krystal observed that many drug addicts are unable to talk about their feelings or use feelings as signals to themselves. Leon Wurmser, also a psychoanalyst with a special interest in addiction, similarly observed that individuals prone to substance use disorders do not understand their own emotions well and cannot empathize with the feelings of others. In his view, people crave drugs when they cannot deal with old and disturbing emotions that they cannot label; at other times, they take drugs to alleviate vague discomfort and tension, which they can only dimly perceive as an emotional feeling, and more usually they attribute it to something wrong either with their body or the environment.

Dr. Edward Khantzian, who has extensive experience treating narcotics addicts, also concluded that many individuals turn to drugs because of enormous difficulties in modulating, regulating, and expressing their emotions. He emphasized that substance-dependent individuals vary, however, in the degree to which their emotions are differentiated. Whereas some addicts may be aware of feelings such as depression or rage and use drugs primarily to try to alleviate their suffering, other addicts may experience their feelings as vague or diffuse and blame the painful effects or aftereffects on something concrete they can point to, like the drugs. In both instances, these individuals are self-medicating painful emotional states and related psychiatric disorders.

Consistent with these clinical impressions, studies in Canada, Poland, and the United States have found that about half of male alcoholics and/or drug addicts have high alexithymia. A recent American study reported that this rate was also true of women substance abusers, but found a lower rate of 36% of high alexithymia among men. All of these studies investigated clinical populations; however, a study with a large community population of middle-aged men in Finland found that both binge drinkers and long-term heavy alcohol users tended to be alexithymic (for a review, see [165]).

Whereas the above studies took place at one point in time (cross sectional), others have been carried out over time (longitudinal). In one such study, a group of substance-dependent patients were tested at the time they presented at a treatment center and again after they had been treated and were clean for four to six weeks. Although they were much less depressed, they did not change the alexithymia score significantly. Another study found similar results. A group of cocaine abusers were observed during a 12-week period of treatment with psychotherapy alone or in combination with pharmacotherapy. Their depression levels dropped markedly, but their mean alexithymia score stayed the same. Although it seems from these studies that addicts tend to remain alexithymic, we need to perform much longer studies and include adolescents and young adults before they start abusing alcohol or drugs [165].

Eating Disorders

During the early 1960s Hilde Bruch, an expert in the field of eating disorders, observed that not only did people with anorexia nervosa have trouble with body image and understanding what their bodies were telling them, they were confused by their emotions and often could not describe them. Over the following decades, other clinicians and researchers suggested that some of the symptoms of eating disorders, such as starvation, bingeing, vomiting, and hyperactivity, are attempts to regulate their distressing and undifferentiated emotions. Often people with eating disorders are substance abusers, promiscuous, and have shoplifted, again as defensive tactics to manage their emotions.

Since the early 1980s researchers have been able to test emotional awareness and regulation in patients with eating disorders using the interoceptive awareness and interpersonal distrust subscales of the Eating Disorder Inventory [153]. Whereas the former subscale detects the amount of confusion and apprehension in recognizing and accurately responding to emotional states, the latter subscale captures the person's reluctance to form close relationships and to express thoughts and feelings to other people. Eating disorder patients typically score significantly higher on these scales than do healthy people. In our own research with a group of anorexic patients, both subscales also correlated significantly with the TAS-20, again showing that these patients are low in important aspects of EI [167].

Studies show rates of high alexithymia ranging from 48% to 77% for patients with anorexia nervosa and from 40% to 61% for patients with bulimia nervosa. Although long-term studies have yet to be conducted to determine whether alexithymia is a permanent personality characteristic or whether it depends on their eating-disorder state, one researcher followed a group of women who had recovered from restricting anorexia nervosa for 8 to 10 years and found that even though their outcome was good, these women were more emotionally constrained and less psychologically minded than a group of same-age healthy women [149]. As noted earlier, there is an inverse relationship between psychological mindedness and alexithymia.

Somatoform Disorders

When a patient is diagnosed with a somatoform disorder, it means that he or she is having physical symptoms, but neither doctors nor mental health professionals can explain it. The names of the diagnoses include somatization disorder, hypochondriasis, somatoform pain disorder, and conversion disorder. Generally the symptoms show up as a result of what is called the defense mechanism of conversion, whereby emotional conflicts are expressed symbolically in the body, or called the defense mechanisms of somatization, whereby emotional distress is experienced primarily as sensations in the body. Researchers disagree about the concept of somatization and about the validity of some of the diagnostic categories within the broad group of somatoform disorders. Indeed, many researchers now see that hypochondriasis and somatization are a continuum, with the relatively rare somatization disorder at one end of the spectrum and most somatizing patients who go to physicians with much milder symptoms at the other end. Although there are no studies of alexithymia among patients who meet diagnostic criteria for hypochondriasis or somatization disorder, several studies have reported significant correlations between dimensional measures of somatization or hypochondriasis and the TAS or TAS-20. Researchers think this is because high alexithymia individuals cannot recognize and understand their emotional feelings, and instead, focus on, amplify, and misinterpret the bodily sensations that come with states of emotional arousal. There is preliminary evidence also of an association between alexithymia and somatoform pain disorder. In a study of survivors of motor vehicle accidents who met the criteria for this diagnosis and had complained of pain for two years, 53% had high alexithymia [165].

Anxiety and Depressive Disorders

As we said earlier, because high alexithymia individuals do not process and regulate emotions well, they seem to be prone to high levels of poorly differentiated negative emotion. Although alexithymic individuals typically score high when tested for anxiety, depression, and neuroticism, researchers note that they tend to develop those anxiety disorders in which they cannot use their emotions to help activate their psychological defenses to help modulate and contain intense emotions. Because they cannot mobilize defenses, they can be prone to panic attacks that characterize panic disorder and posttraumatic stress disorder (PTSD). Indeed, some clinicians regard panic attacks as overwhelming floods of undifferentiated emotions that have not been contained by mental representations and are expressed as profound autonomic disturbances. As the trauma expert Bessel van der Kolk has pointed out, patients with PTSD fail to use feelings as cues to attend to incoming information; instead, emotional arousal is likely to precipitate a fight-or-flight response.

Consistent with these clinical observations, studies of patients with panic disorders have reported rates of 47% and 67% of high alexithymia, compared with 12.5% in patients with simple phobia and 13% in patients with obsessive-compulsive disorder. Vietnam war veterans with PTSD had a rate of 60% of high alexithymia. Although PTSD patients may become highly alexithymic because their capacity to monitor and regulate emotions has been damaged as a result of serious psychological trauma, only about 25% of people exposed to catastrophic stress develop PTSD-like reactions, which suggests there may be predisposing personality traits. We need to further study whether low EI is a risk factor for PTSD, perhaps because it makes a person susceptible to traumatic events as well as because it limits his or her ability to handle the resulting intense emotions [162], [165].

Although depressed patients generally score high on the TAS-20, those who complain of primarily physical symptoms are the ones who are particularly low in EI [147], [165]. Their type of depression is sometimes called "masked depression." Because they cannot understand and label their emotions, they may be unaware of having a depressed mood; they may become hypochondriacally concerned about their somatic symptoms, and sometimes their doctors are compelled to overinvestigate. If these patients are aware of and able to say they are anxious or depressed, they usually blame it on their perceived physical problem. Most researchers do not use a separate category for classifying depressions with somatic presentations, so there are no empirical studies exploring the association between alexithymia and this type of depressive illness.

Borderline Personality Disorders

Individuals with borderline personality disorders are well known for their difficulties in managing emotions, especially anxiety and anger, their impulsive self-destructive behavior, their lack of empathy, and their excessive use of maladaptive ego defense mechanisms. These characteristics are all suggestive of low EI, an impression that is supported by Bar-On [147], who found that if you scored low on the EQ-i, then you would probably score high on a borderline personality feature scale.

Although there are no reports of rates of high alexithymia among patients with borderline personality disorder, a team of Canadian investigators found that a group of patients who met *Diagnostic and Statistical Manual of Mental Disorders* (DSM-III-R) criteria for this diagnosis were significantly less able to recognize facial expressions of emotion than a nonpsychiatric comparison group and had lower levels of emotional awareness in themselves and others, as measured by the Levels of Emotion Awareness Scale developed by Richard Lane and his colleagues. Other tests used in this study revealed that the patients with borderline personality disorders also had less capacity to coordinate mixed positive and negative emotions, and more intense responses to negative emotions, than the nonborderline individuals. This means that patients with borderline personality disorder are likely to misread both their own and others' emotions and to experience difficulties with integrating and modulating emotions, characteristics that are consistent with the concept of low EI [156].

☐ Implications for Treatment and Prevention

It is important for clinicians to know about whether psychiatric patients are highly alexithymic or have low EI when they put together a treatment plan. They would not respond well to insight-oriented forms of psychotherapy, for example, because they don't know their own emotions well. It would be better to focus on treatment that helps the patients to increase emotional self-awareness and the ability to tolerate distressing emotional states and to look at and use emotions as sources of information for managing stressful situations. Clinicians must teach their patients how to become more attuned to the feelings of others, along with ways to enhance their own creative imaginations that will further help them contain and regulate their emotions. Although experienced clinicians have recommended these modified psychotherapeutic approaches for more than two decades, not much has been done to see if they work. Cardiac patients took part in a preliminary study of these methods in group psychotherapy and were able to reduce their level of alexithymia and maintain it throughout a two-year period [148]. Until more outcome studies are conducted, however, most therapists will rely on drugs or supportive psychotherapies to treat the psychiatric symptoms of patients with low EI. The patients are likely to have residual symptoms and to be prone to recurrent illnesses, which sometimes lead to frequent trips to the doctor's office or mental health clinics.

We are now looking at the way children develop to see what contributes to the development of EI; we believe that understanding this will help us prevent certain mental illnesses. We have seen that the development of emotional awareness and a capacity to talk about and reflect on emotions has a lot to do with how parents respond to the emotional states of their infants and young children, and also by the patterns of attachment that are established between them. Children with secure attachments know that they will be comforted when they are emotionally distressed, but those with an insecure attachment style have become used to either suppressing outward displays of negative emotion (and even pretend to show positive emotion), or become increasingly hysterical, for example, to make sure others respond. Theorists believe that children learn attachment and affect regulation, and operate automatically, much like when we perform any learned skill such as riding a bike or playing the piano. Researchers have shown that among studies of both clinical and nonclinical adults, people high in alexithymia tend to have insecure attachment styles [162], [163]. Programs that educate parents about emotional development and the types of interactions that help secure attachment can potentially help children get the core components of EI, and, in turn, help them become more resilient to everyday stress and thereby help protect them against mental illness.

CHAPTER **5**

Reuven Bar-On

Emotional Intelligence and Self-Actualization

In this chapter, I will focus on the relationship between emotional intelligence (EI) and self-actualization and examine the extent to which the former construct influences the latter. Although many of us have heard of these concepts before, we could still benefit from learning more about how they developed so that we can better understand what they are, how they are related to one another, and why they are so important in our daily lives. Therefore, I will begin the chapter by presenting a brief historical overview of EI and self-actualization.

☐ Historical Roots of Emotional Intelligence and Self-Actualization

Since the latter part of 1995, EI has become a *hot topic*. Despite this current, reawakened interest, scientists have been studying this construct for the greater part of the twentieth century, and the actual historical roots of this wider area can be found in the nineteenth century. Although some contemporary scholars absurdly claim that they were "the first to scientifically study" EI, we should humbly give credit to great scientists like Charles Darwin who began studying this topic as early as 1837 and published the first known work in the field in 1872 [182]. In addition to our humility in acknowledging these early researchers, the magnitude of their contributions is overwhelming when we consider the conditions under which they worked. Long before the advent of sophisticated statistical methodology and without the aid of high-speed computers, Darwin demonstrated that emotional expression plays a major role in adaptive behavior, which remains an important axiom of EI to the present day.

In spite of the current flurry of activity surrounding the desire to learn more about EI, scientific publications began to appear in the twentieth century when Thorndike defined what he called "social intelligence" in 1920 [235]. Many of the early studies focused on developing ways to describe and assess socially competent behavior [178], [179], [185], [186], [187], [214], [215], [236]. Scholarly activity in the area of social intelligence continued uninterrupted from the early 1920s to the present and included scientific studies conducted by prominent psychologists like Kelly [197], Rogers [220], Rotter [221], and Cantor and Kihlstrom [176], [177]. Researchers in this area began to shift their attention from assessment and eventually focused more on understanding the purpose of interpersonal behavior and the role it plays in effective adaptability within the social context [240]. Not only did this line of research help define human effectiveness from the social perspective, it empirically strengthened one very important aspect of David Wechsler's definition of general intelligence: "The capacity of the individual to act purposefully" [239, p. 7]. This clearly positioned social intelligence as an important part of general intelligence.

It is important to point out that the early definitions of social intelligence influenced the way EI was later conceptualized. For example, some contemporary theorists viewed emotional intelligence as part of social intelligence [225, p. 189], meaning, of course, that social intelligence is part of emotional intelligence. This suggests that both concepts are closely related and may even represent major interrelated components of the same construct. In other words, we could very well be talking about the same construct rather than two separate constructs, which I am convinced is the case.

We will now take a closer look at what I think is the second major component of this wider construct. At the same time that scientists were focusing on the *social* or *interpersonal* component, others began looking at the *intrapersonal* and, primarily, *emotional* component of this construct. At approximately the same time that researchers began exploring various ways to define, describe, and assess social intelligence, scientific inquiry began to center around "alexithymia," which can be considered the essence of EI in that it focuses specifically on the ability to identify, understand, regulate, and express emotions [234, pp. 27–29]. Alexithymia grew out of clinical observations that were first published in the late 1940s and was initially intended to scientifically explain why some people develop psychosomatic disorders [203], [222]. Paul Sifneos continued to empirically develop this new idea in medicine and called it "alexithymia" [228],

Greek for "being unable to describe feelings" which he thought was at the heart of psychosomatic problems. Others [217] including Graeme Taylor and his colleagues [232], [233], [234] continued to study many different aspects of this construct with a very active research agenda. Today, there are more than 800 publications related to alexithymia and how it affects physical and psychological health.

Two new directions that paralleled and possibly grew out of alexithymia were "emotional awareness" [199] and "psychological mindedness" [211], [212]. Practitioners evaluate the psychological mindedness of patients to see the extent to which they are suitable for psychotherapy; this type of evaluation assesses the patient's ability to understand and express emotions, which is a good example of the clinical application of EI [212]. Research related to emotional awareness [198] and to the neurological basis of this wider construct [175, 200] provides us with evidence of the perceptual and cognitive foundations of EI. Emotional awareness [198], like alexithymia [234] as well as social intelligence [240], is based on a cognitive schemata. This means that what we perceive has to then be evaluated and understood (cognitively processed) to effectively guide our behavior. That which is perceived can come from within (the *intrapersonal*) as well as from outside ourselves (the *interpersonal*).

Peter Salovey and John Mayer's present conceptualization of EI [208] is also very much like that of alexithymia and has apparently grown out of a similar way of viewing this construct. However, it is interesting to point out that they first viewed EI as being part of social intelligence and traced the roots of their conceptualization back to Thorndike's early definition of this construct [225, p. 189]. It is also interesting to note that the term they chose to describe their definition of this construct ("emotional intelligence") became a media *buzzword* in 1996 but was first used as early as 1966 [201], at a time when the media and general public showed no interest at all in this topic.

Scientific work related to the intrapersonal component of this wider construct has continued in other interesting directions like Robert Sternberg's research of what he calls "practical intelligence" [230] and "successful intelligence" [229].

It is important to stress that a reoccurring theme in the EI literature is that interpersonal competence (how well we understand others and relate with them) depends on intrapersonal intelligence (the ability to understand our emotions and have them work for us and not against us). Both of these important EI components combine to help us deal with everyday life and adapt to a constantly changing environment; the more developed these two components are, the better is our chance to succeed in life. The way in which these components combine to cope with environmental demands indicates a connection between them, suggesting that both may actually be two interrelated parts of the same construct.

Also, there are clear attempts in the literature to more directly combine the intrapersonal and emotional with the interpersonal and social components of this wider construct. For example, Howard Gardner explains that his theory of "personal intelligences" is based on "intrapersonal intelligence" and "interpersonal intelligence" [191], [192]. And Carolyn Saarni describes "emotional competence" as including eight interrelated emotional and social factors [223], [224]. Lastly, I have shown that "emotional and social intelligence" is composed of 15 intrapersonal and interpersonal components that combine to determine effective human behavior [171], [172].

Based on what I have already said, it is probably more accurate for us to refer to this wider construct as "emotional and social intelligence." But in light of the title and spirit of this book, I will use the more popular term *emotional intelligence* (EI).

The historical roots of self-actualization can be traced directly to the pioneering work of Abraham Maslow in the mid-1930s [204], [205], [206], [207]. Maslow argued that we can only achieve self-actualization after we have satisfied basic survival, safety, social, and personal needs. He defined self-actualization as the process of developing your talents, capacities, and potential to the fullest. In other words, you can actualize your potential capacity for personal growth only after you are socially and emotionally effective in meeting your needs and dealing with life in general. This means that self-actualization is most likely the next, and ultimate, step after EI in the complex process of personal development. While emotional intelligence relates to being effective, self-actualization relates to doing the best you can possibly do. Or put another way, when we are self-actualized, we have gone beyond EI to achieve a higher level of human effectiveness. And this is one of the reasons why emotional intelligence and self-actualization have become such popular concepts in our generation (*the era of the self*). Never before in the history of human existence have there been so many opportunities for personal development; never before have we been exposed to so many possibilities to set, pursue, and achieve our personal goals and life dreams. And if this is a correct assessment, the next question is quite obvious: Who wouldn't like to learn more about these important concepts and how to become more emotionally intelligent and self-actualizing?

Maslow originally began his study of self-actualizing people in 1935 by screening 3,000 university students. When he came up with only *one* suitable subject who met his criteria for self-actualization, he abandoned the study. He tried again fifteen years later by selecting 60 personal acquaintances, friends, and public and historical figures who he thought had obtained self-actualization in their lifetime. He examined their personality structure in depth and arrived at what he called "composite impressions" (the essential characteristics) of self-actualizing people. Even though his methodology is questionable [180], [195], Maslow has given us one of the clearest and most comprehensive pictures of the self-actualizing person to date. Based on his findings [205, pp. 8–27), self-actualizers are characterized as individuals who:

1. are efficient in perceiving reality and are comfortable in relation with it;
2. accept themselves, others, and nature;
3. are spontaneous;
4. are problem-centered rather than ego-centered (i.e., strongly focused on problems outside of themselves and have some mission in life or some task to fulfill);
5. need privacy and are able to detach themselves to achieve this;
6. are autonomous;
7. demonstrate continued freshness of appreciation (i.e., the capacity to appreciate again and again, freshly and naively, the basic goods of life with awe, pleasure, wonder, and ecstasy);
8. have had peak or mystic experiences;
9. exhibit *gemeinschaftsgefuhl* (German for feelings for mankind);
10. have deep and profound interpersonal relations;
11. have a democratic character structure (i.e., not authoritarian);
12. can discriminate between good and evil and between means and ends;
13. possess a philosophical and unhostile sense of humor;
14. are original, creative, or inventive; and
15. resist enculturation

Fifty years later, researchers are still confirming Maslow's findings using sophisticated research methodology [169], [181], [226], [227]. When we take into account when and how this research was conducted, we are astounded by Maslow's perceptive powers and intuitive genius.

Even though many researchers have indicated a link between EI and effectiveness in coping with daily demands [171], [173], [174], [190], [194], [229], [237], [238] no one has looked at the relationship between EI and self-actualization. It is this lack of published empirical findings that prompted me to write this chapter, to examine the relationship between these two important concepts. More specifically, I want to show that emotional intelligence plays an important role in self-actualization, which in turn is related to our well-being and health.

First, I will define emotional intelligence and self-actualization so that we will have a clear idea of what we are talking about. Then, I will discuss studies that have examined the relationship between these two constructs. Finally, I will explain what the results of these studies mean and suggest how you can apply them. Because we need more research in this area, I will also recommend general guidelines for conducting such studies.

☐ Definitions of Emotional Intelligence and Self-Actualization

Emotional Intelligence

Emotional intelligence is a multifactorial array of interrelated emotional, personal, and social abilities that help us cope with daily demands. The key emotional, personal, and social abilities that make up the factorial structure of this construct are the following:

- *Self-regard*: The ability to accurately perceive and appraise ourselves
- *Emotional self-awareness*: The ability to be aware of and understand our emotions
- *Assertiveness*: The ability to constructively express our emotions and ourselves
- *Stress tolerance*: The ability to effectively manage our emotions
- *Impulse control*: The ability to control our emotions
- *Reality testing*: The ability to objectively validate our feelings and thoughts
- *Flexibility*: The ability to adapt and adjust our feelings and thoughts to new situations
- *Problem-solving*: The ability to solve our personal and interpersonal problems
- *Empathy*: The ability to be aware of and understand others' emotions
- *Interpersonal relationship*: The ability to relate well with others

In addition to these 10 key factorial components of EI, the Bar-On model includes five facilitators of emotionally and socially intelligent behavior:

- *Optimism*: The ability to be positive and to look at the brighter side of life
- *Self-actualization*: The ability and drive to achieve goals and actualize our potential
- *Happiness*: The ability to feel content with ourselves, others, and life in general
- *Independence*: The ability to be self-reliant and free of emotional dependency on others
- *Social responsibility*: The ability to identify with and feel part of our social group

I developed the Bar-On Emotional Quotient Inventory (EQ-i) to measure the above determinants and facilitators of emotionally and socially intelligent behavior [170]. You are referred to other sources [171], [172] for a more detailed description of how I developed and validated the Bar-On model and measure of emotional intelligence.

Self-Actualization

To more fully understand the definition of self-actualization I am using here, let us first look at how this specific definition was created. I wanted the definition to be comprehensive and to include the reoccurring themes used in describing this construct from Maslow onward. I found that four major themes continuously appear in the self-actualization literature:

- the ability and drive to set and achieve goals
- being committed to and involved with our interests
- actualizing our potential
- enriching our life

Mayman [210] approached the first above-mentioned theme like Maslow did [205], focusing on *growing toward goals* after satisfying basic needs. We have to be innovative and creative to set these goals, which is one of the 15 characteristics Maslow gave to describe the self-actualizing person.

Jahoda [196] views self-actualizers as people who pursue more than what is needed for mere survival, the second theme described above. These people *commit themselves* to goals and interests at home and at work, which is based on another characteristic of self-actualization that Maslow described (actively being devoted to a mission in life).

Maslow saw that once we satisfied our basic survival, safety, social, and personal needs, then we could move on to *the realization of our potential capacities* [205]. Jahoda [196] agreed with Maslow on this third theme that appears throughout the self-actualization literature; she described self-actualization as *a permanent striving to actualize our potential*. And English and English define this inner drive to develop ourselves simply as "an on-going process of developing one's capacities and talents" [189, p. 485]. Here we see that an additional characteristic of Maslow's self-actualizing person plays an important role: These people are autonomous and rely on themselves to actualize their potential capacity to the fullest [205].

Jahoda [196] characterizes self-actualizers as those who are able to lead *an enriched life*, which is the fourth reoccurring theme that appears in the literature. Mayman [210] also viewed self-actualization as the desire for a richer life, which he describes as *an investment in living*. Strupp and Hadley

[231] suggest that striving to find meaning in life is the key element in this definition. And Lindner considered it to be *a profound and complete participation in living* [202]. As Maslow similarly described, self-actualizing people are able "to experience the freshness of living" and "to achieve peak experiences in life" [205, pp. 8–27].

The definition of self-actualization used in this chapter is based on the four themes described above, which also provided the basis for developing the EQ-i self-actualization scale: Self-actualization is the process of striving to actualize one's potential capacity, abilities, and talents. It requires the ability and drive to set and achieve goals. It is characterized by being involved in and feeling committed to various interests and pursuits. Self-actualization is a life-long effort leading to the enrichment of life.

☐ Method Used to Study the Relationship between Emotional Intelligence and Self-Actualization

To help us understand the relationship between emotional intelligence and self-actualization, we will look at three different studies conducted in North America (3,831 adults; [171]), Israel (2,702 late adolescents; [190]), and the Netherlands (1,639 adults; [184]). I will also discuss additional studies to help us better understand the connection between self-actualization and successful performance in the workplace, well-being, and health.

All studies presented here used the EQ-i to assess EI. Although the EQ-i is recognized as a "test of emotional intelligence" [170], [171], [218], it is, more accurate to say that it is a self-report measure of emotional and social competence, which provides an estimate of emotional and social intelligence. There are 133 brief items in the EQ-i, and it uses a five-point Likert scale ranging from "Very seldom or Not true of me" to "Very often true of me or True of me." Responses to the EQ-i items generate a total EQ score and the following five EQ composite scale scores containing 15 subscale scores:

1. intrapersonal EQ (comprising self-regard, emotional self-awareness, assertiveness, independence, and self-actualization),
2. interpersonal EQ (comprising empathy, social responsibility, and interpersonal relationship),
3. stress management EQ (comprising stress tolerance and impulse control),
4. adaptability EQ (comprising reality testing, flexibility, and problem-solving), and
5. general mood EQ (comprising optimism and happiness).

The inventory includes the following four validity indicators: omission rate (the number of omitted responses), inconsistency index (the degree of inconsistency between similar types of items), positive impression (the tendency to give an exaggerated positive response), and negative impression (the tendency to give an exaggerated negative response). The EQ-i has a built-in correction factor that automatically adjusts the scale scores based on the positive impression and negative impression scores. You can find a list of the items, together with a detailed description of the inventory's psychometric properties, in the *EQ-i Technical Manual* [171].

Cognitive intelligence was measured by the Standard Progressive Matrices [219] in the Israeli sample and by the General Ability Measure for Adults [216] in the Dutch sample. The participants in the North American sample were the only ones whose cognitive capacity (IQ) was not examined in the three studies reviewed below.

The EQ-i self-actualization scale was used to measure self-actualization in all three studies. This scale contains nine items that tap the four basic aspects of self-actualization I described earlier. The reliability and validity of this scale has been well established and may be examined in other sources [171], [172], [183], [218]. To prevent an artificial increase in the correlation between EI and self-actualization, the self-actualization scores were not included in calculating the total EQ scale scores on the EQ-i.

☐ Findings

The results presented below show the degree of correlation between EI and self-actualization, indicate how EI distinguishes between people who are more and less self-actualizing, and suggest how EI can predict self-actualization. After presenting the results from the three main studies, I will discuss findings from additional sources suggesting how important self-actualization is in influencing your effectiveness at work, general well-being, and health.

How Related is Emotional Intelligence to Self-Actualization?

The results from the three studies clearly show that EI and self-actualization are very much related, as can be seen in the consistently high correlations between the total EQ scale and the self-actualization scale for the North American (.75), Israeli (.72), and Dutch (.71) samples. On the other hand, it is equally important for us to note that the connection between cognitive intelligence (IQ) and self-actualization for the Israeli sample (.02) and the Dutch sample (.08) is not statistically significant. This means that

TABLE 5.1. Comparison of self-actualization scale scores between individuals with high and low emotional intelligence (EQ) in the North American, Israeli, and Dutch samples

	North American sample				Israeli sample				Dutch sample			
EQ-i Scale	High EQ	Low EQ	*t* value	*p* level	High EQ	Low EQ	*t* value	*p* level	High EQ	Low EQ	*t* value	*p* level
Self-actualization	40.7	34.7	43.6	<.00	40.5	34.7	40.3	<.00	38.5	33.6	40.8	<.00

it is emotional intelligence more than cognitive intelligence that influences our ability to do our best, to accomplish our goals, and to actualize our potential. These findings strongly suggest that how well we do in school (predicted by IQ) does not predict how well we will do after we leave school.

Can We Tell Who is More Self-Actualized Based on EQ?

Based on additional findings from the three studies examined here, the answer is *yes*. This becomes obvious by looking at the results presented in Table 5.1. Those with above-average EQ scores have self-actualization scores that are significantly higher than individuals with below-average EQ for the North American, Israeli, and Dutch samples. These findings clearly indicate that people with higher EI are much better when it comes to self-actualization than those with lower EI. On the other hand, it is much more difficult to distinguish between people with higher and lower levels of self-actualization based on their cognitive intelligence (measured by IQ), as we can see from Table 5.2. In other words, emotional intelligence is a better indicator of self-actualization than cognitive intelligence.

TABLE 5.2. Comparison of self-actualization scale scores between individuals with high and low cognitive intelligence (IQ) in the Israeli and Dutch samples

	Israeli sample				Dutch sample			
EQ-i Scale	High IQ	Low IQ	*t* value	*p* level	High IQ	Low IQ	*t* value	*p* level
Self-actualization	37.8	37.7	00.2	.86	36.4	35.8	01.9	.06

Can Emotional Intelligence Predict Self-Actualization?

To estimate the degree to which EI is able to predict self-actualization and the specific way in which it contributes to our ability to self-actualize, a Multiple Regression Analysis was performed on the EQ-i scores from the North American, Israeli, and Dutch samples. The EQ-i self-actualization subscale was used as the dependent variable and the remaining 14 subscales were used as the independent variables. The results in Table 5.3 show that a very similar EI model appears in each of the samples that is able to predict self-actualization. These cross-cultural findings strongly suggest that the best predictors of self-actualization are the following EI factors and facilitators (listed in the order of their importance):

- Happiness
- Optimism
- Self-regard
- Independence
- Problem-solving
- Social responsibility
- Assertiveness
- Emotional self-awareness

The above eight components appeared in all three models and account for an average of 60% of the variance. This percentage is high and means that most (60%) of self-actualization is based on these particular factors in this specific order. Cognitive intelligence, education, and experience, for example, probably account for the remaining 40%.

We can see from the above findings that in order to predict self-actualization, we have to first look at self-motivation, which is based on a combination of happiness and optimism, factors that energize and motivate us. If we are not motivated enough, it is extremely difficult to work toward and achieve goals. But self-motivation is not enough in and of itself. We have to know who we are to know what we want to accomplish in life. This is why self-regard, the next factor, is so important. Not only do we have to know what we want to accomplish in life, we have to know how best to take advantage of our strengths and compensate for our weaknesses if we want to successfully actualize our potential and achieve our goals. It also makes sense that the self-actualization process is supported by our ability to rely on ourselves to make the right decisions (independence) and confidently come up with the best solutions (problem-solving) once we know what we want from ourselves. We also need to be committed to doing something meaningful in life and to contribute something of value, which comes from social responsibility as defined in the Bar-On model. Finally, self-actualization is the ultimate act of self-ex-

TABLE 5.3. Emotional intelligence models for predicting self-actualization based on a Multiple Regression Analysis of the North American, Israeli and Dutch samples

No. American sample (n = 3,831)	Statistical properties	Israeli sample (n = 2,702)	Statistical properties	Dutch sample (n = 1,639)	Statistical properties
	Multiple R = .80 F = 601.54 p-level <.000		Multiple R = .75 F = 345.30 p-level <.000		Multiple R = .78 F = 259.28 p-level <.000
Happiness	β = .310, t = 19.37, $p < .01$	Happiness	β = .195, t = 10.02, $p < .01$	Happiness	β = .366, t = 15.44, $p < .01$
Optimism	β = .244, t = 11.96, $p < .01$	Optimism	β = .150, t = 05.91, $p < .01$	Optimism	β = .167, t = 06.51, $p < .01$
Self-regard	β = .132, t = 07.16, $p < .01$	Problem-solving	β = .142, t = 08.08, $p < .01$	Independence	β = .157, t = 07.38, $p < .01$
Social responsibility	β = .097, t = 07.73, $p < .01$	Independence	β = .124, t = 07.65, $p < .01$	Self-regard	β = .157, t = 05.80, $p < .01$
Independence	β = .094, t = 06.53, $p < .01$	Social responsibility	β = .105, t = 06.39, $p < .01$	Assertiveness	β = .111, t = 05.02, $p < .01$
Emotional self-awareness	β = .091, t = 06.53, $p < .01$	Self-regard	β = .101, t = 04.60, $p < .01$	Problem-solving	β = .101, t = 05.53, $p < .01$
Problem-solving	β = .090, t = 06.22, $p < .01$	Assertiveness	β = .067, t = 03.68, $p < .01$	Flexibility	β = .082, t = 04.23, $p < .01$
Assertiveness	β = .063, t = 04.16, $p < .01$	Emotional self-awareness	β = .065, t = 03.93, $p < .01$	Emotional self-awareness	β = .062, t = 03.08, $p < .01$
Flexibility	β = .043, t = 03.06, $p < .01$	Reality testing	β = .049, t = 02.56, $p = .01$	Social responsibility	β = .054, t = 03.18, $p < .01$

pression (assertiveness), which strongly depends on a deep awareness of ourselves, our feelings, and needs (emotional self-awareness).

Findings from Additional Studies Indicating that Self-Actualization is Related to Occupational Performance

The results from two additional studies are presented below to demonstrate the relationship between self-actualization and occupational performance.

In the first study, the EQ-i was used to create *EQ profiles* for approximately 70 different occupations [174]. These profiles were created by asking people who completed the EQ-i to give their present occupation and to indicate how successful they felt they were at work. The highest EQ-i scale scores were then examined for each of the occupations based on a database of approximately 50,000 adults. Among other interesting findings, the results suggest a strong connection between how self-actualized you are and how well you do on the job. In 16 out of the 20 largest occupational groups studied (80%), self-actualization ranks among the top eight factors that significantly distinguish between "successful" and "less successful" employees. And within these 16 particular occupations, self-actualization ranks third regarding its ability to predict successful occupational performance.

The second study was based on an enormous survey conducted in 40 countries over a 10-year period from 1988 to 1998 [213]. Of the 100,000 managers from the private and public sector who were asked what they considered to be the most important characteristics of effective employees, the majority focused on characteristics related to self-actualization like being "goal-oriented," "committed to one's work," and "taking the initiative to develop personally and to help others develop."

Although the above two studies suggest an important relationship between self-actualization and occupational performance, we still do not know for certain if the former is a cause, an outcome of the latter, or both. Based on my experience studying factors like happiness, I believe that self-actualization both motivates us to perform and then increases when we perform well.

☐ What is the Connection between Self-Actualization, Well-Being, and Health?

There is a strong connection between the level of our self-actualization and our general well-being and health. In the three major studies reviewed in this chapter, the correlation between the EQ-i self-actualization and happiness scales was .69 for the North American sample, .60 for the Israeli sample, and .68 for the Dutch sample. Once again, it's hard to tell whether our happiness increases motivation and, hence, strengthens our achievement drive necessary to self-actualize or if we naturally feel happy as a reaction to accomplishing our goals and actualizing our potential. Happiness could well be both a motivating and barometric factor for many people. That is, they may have a surge of emotional energy when they feel happy, which helps them get things done, and then they feel happy again as a result of accomplishing something. I think that the chain of events may be that (a) EI factors and facilitators (like happiness) contribute to self-actualization as was previously shown, and (b) self-actualization contributes, in turn, to our general degree of happiness and well-being as we will discuss later.

Many studies have shown a connection between the lack of self-actualization and the presence of emotional disorders [168]. Some people who receive low scores on the EQ-i self-actualization scale may not know what they want to achieve because they are confused about themselves in general and what they want to do in life; or they may know what they want to do but are unable to accomplish their goals for various reasons, some of which may be clinical [171], [172]. The self-actualization scale negatively correlates with the Beck Depression Inventory (–.45), the Zung Self-Rating Depression Scale (–.52), and the SCL-90 Depression scale (–.83). These are important findings for our present discussion in that these three scales tap typical symptoms of depression such as withdrawal from one's interests [168], which we think of as a temporary deficit in self-actualization. Moreover, a negative correlation (–.51) with the treatment suitability scale (TRT) on the MMPI-2 [188] suggests that people who receive low scores on the EQ-i self-actualization scale do not try to improve themselves, which is the clinical opposite of self-actualization. Additional negative correlations between the EQ-i self-actualization scale and other MMPI-2 scales indicate that these people don't try to improve themselves because they may have low motivation and a general lack of drive [188]. Based on additional findings, we have found that people with low self-actualization scores may also be uncertain about their future and uninterested in what they are doing, feel dissatisfied with their lives, and feel useless [188]. This basic lack of self-actualization is a key symptom of depression [168]. Evidently, the ability to actualize ourselves requires a certain amount of *emotional energy* to sustain the drive we need to set and achieve goals.

The relationship between self-actualization and psychological health becomes even more apparent when we look at clinical samples across cultures [171]. Findings from a cross-cultural study that I have examined show that self-actualization is one of five factorial components of my model of emotional intelligence that is able to significantly differentiate between people who suffer from psychological problems and those who do not [171]. This study also shows that this particular EI facilitator is even more important for inpatients than for outpatients, which is an important finding because inpatients typically suffer from more severe problems. These findings mean that the drive to improve ourselves is not only an important factor for our general psychological health, but becomes even more important when emotional disturbance becomes more severe.

I have also received findings from two other interesting studies confirming that self-actualization not only helps people recover from emotional problems, but may also aid in people recovering from major medical problems like myocardial infarct (based on preliminary findings) [171].

☐ Conclusions

In this chapter, we have shown that emotional intelligence plays an important role in self-actualization, is highly correlated with our ability to actualize our basic talents and skills, can distinguish between those who are more able and those who are less able to develop themselves, and can predict our overall ability to self-actualize. We have also seen that emotional intelligence is more important than cognitive intelligence for self-actualization. This means that a high IQ does not guarantee that we will actualize our potential, but a high EQ is definitely more important for self-actualization. Or when we view this from a slightly different perspective, we can see that emotionally intelligent individuals with average or even below-average cognitive capacity are able to actualize their potential in life. Although the popular literature [193] has been touting this theory for a while, the findings that I have presented here are the first to empirically demonstrate this possibility.

What else have we learned from this chapter? We have learned that in order to bring out our best, we need positive self-regard, heightened emotional self-awareness, effective problem-solving abilities, and adequate assertiveness. To aid this whole process of self-actualization and to increase our ability to succeed in life, we also need to be independent, clearly know what our goals are, and be motivated enough to accomplish these goals. All of this requires a knowledge of who we are, of our strengths, and of our weaknesses.

Not only do the above-mentioned EI components strongly influence our ability to actualize ourselves, but self-actualization, in turn, influences our effectiveness at work as well as our general well-being and health.

I hope that the findings presented in this chapter will eventually make their way into remedial and preventive work. I think that practitioners could benefit from focusing on the above-mentioned factors in assessing patients and in creating intervention strategies. Parents and educators could also make use of these findings in considering how best to strengthen both emotional intelligence and self-actualization in children. This type of application could play a powerful role in raising and educating children to not only be more effective in life, but also to bring out their best.

Although the findings presented in this chapter suggest promising directions for applying EI, they need to be reexamined on larger and more diverse population samples. It is important to continue to study these EI components in order to learn how best to apply them in parenting, education, industry, and clinical work. The goal is to help make people both emotionally and socially intelligent as well as self-actualizing. This means helping individuals to become more effective in dealing with their lives and to actualize their potential to its fullest. To meet this challenge, I would recommend that future studies use a wide variety of methods to examine emotional intelligence and self-actualization. If we use diverse approaches to collect and evaluate our findings, we will be better able to learn more about these important constructs, the relationship between them, and how best to develop them.

I would like to conclude this chapter by strongly expressing the need for continued empirical research in the area of emotional intelligence. Remaining faithful to the scientific tradition when studying this area will help us avoid misconceptions about what emotional intelligence can and cannot predict and avoid unfounded *theorizing*.

6

CHAPTER

Julie Fitness

Emotional Intelligence and Intimate Relationships

To keep your marriage brimming
With love in the marriage cup
Whenever you're wrong,
admit it
Whenever you're right,
shut up
—Ogden Nash, 1962

According to Ogden Nash, the secret to a long and happy marriage is relatively simple: Know when to say you are sorry, and do not "rub it in" when your partner is in the wrong. Like so many clever aphorisms, however, its simplicity is deceptive. In fact, the art of knowing when, why, and how to say you are sorry in marriage, and the ability to practice forbearance under even the most trying circumstances, require many sophisticated emotional skills, including empathy, self-control, and a deep understanding of human needs and feelings. The interesting point about these skills is how remarkably similar they are to the proposed ingredients of so-called emotional intelligence (EI), defined by Mayer and Salovey [258] as "the ability to perceive emotions, to access and generate emotions so as to assist thought, to understand emotions and emotion knowledge, and to reflectively regulate emotions so as to promote emotional and intellectual growth" (p. 5). Indeed, this striking congruence between the kinds of abilities involved in EI and the kinds of abilities apparently required to successfully negotiate marital ups and downs suggests that if ever there were a context in which EI might be expected to matter, it is marriage. But in what ways is EI important to marriage? And what kinds of emotional skills do spouses need to help them weather the vicissitudes of married life?

The concept of EI has been received enthusiastically in the popular press, with many espousing it as the recipe for success in every sphere of life. Despite the often-extravagant claims made for its beneficial qualities, however, scientific data on the features and outcomes of EI are only beginning to emerge in the psychological literature. Furthermore, although theorists have emphasized the importance of EI in intimate relationships and speculated that more emotionally intelligent people should have longer and happier marriages, there has been little scientific research examining emotional intelligence in the marital context. No doubt this lack of research is a function both of the newness of the construct and of difficulties in finding reliable and valid measures of it. Nonetheless, psychologists have investigated other emotional phenomena in the context of marital happiness and stability, many of which would be considered to involve aspects of EI: for example, emotional perception and expression, empathy, and emotion knowledge and understanding.

The overall aim of this chapter is to discuss some of this investigative work in light of current thinking about EI. Specifically, after a brief description of the proposed facets of EI, I will review research findings from the marital literature with regard to each of the facets, paying particular attention to gender and individual differences. I will also discuss whether EI, as currently conceived, is necessarily adaptive in marriage; and, finally, I will examine whether the construct of EI itself has anything new or useful to offer scholars with an interest in marital happiness and stability.

☐ What Is Emotional Intelligence?

According to recent work by Mayer, Caruso, and Salovey [259], the umbrella term *emotional intelligence* refers to three primary mental abilities. The first, most basic ability involves the accurate perception and recognition of both our own and others' emotions. In other words, emotionally intelligent people know when they and others are experiencing emotions and can accurately identify and discriminate among emotions like anger, fear, guilt, and love. Of course, knowing that one is experiencing an emotion may seem trivially easy, but as many emotion theorists (and poets) have noted, people can be confused about the meaning of their feelings or physiological symptoms. One person, for example, might interpret his fluttering heart, sweaty palms, and feelings of giddiness as symptoms of a panic attack, whereas another might conclude she had fallen in love. In fact, the symptoms might be the result of too much coffee or signal the onset of a bout of influenza.

Knowing the particular emotion(s) one is feeling also can be less than straightforward. For example, if Susan discovers her spouse Jim has gambled away the deposit for their new house, and her heart is pounding, her fists are clenched, and she has the urge to physically assault him, then she may accurately perceive and identify this combination of physical symptoms and feelings as signifying "I'm angry." However, if Jim hears Susan joking about his sexual anxieties to friends over dinner, and he feels hot, sick, and has urges both to disappear under the table and to throw his dinner at her, then he may not recognize this combination of symptoms and feelings as signifying "I'm embarrassed because everyone is looking at me; I'm ashamed because my friends think I'm sexually inadequate; I'm angry because I've been shamed in front of my friends; and I'm hurt that my wife would humiliate me like this." Indeed, the mix of emotions associated with this situation would be difficult for even the most emotionally intelligent person to work through, not least because shame itself tends to be associated with mental confusion and an inability to get one's thoughts together [267].

According to EI theorists, then, the emotionally intelligent person notices when he or she is feeling something and accurately recognizes the nature of the feeling. Furthermore, the emotionally intelligent person notices when others are experiencing emotions and is able to identify accurately these emotions. Again, people vary in their abilities to achieve such accurate perception and identification. Some may be completely insensitive to others' feelings and have no idea that their spouses, for example, are feeling angry, sad, or jealous. On the other hand, some people are exquisitely sensitive to other people's feelings and can detect and identify their spouses' emotions, for example, from subtle nonverbal cues such as a brief frown.

Several theorists have argued that the ability to perceive and recognize one's own and others' emotions must be, to an extent, innate or biologically "hard wired" (e.g., see [262]. Without the capacity to register, at the very least, feelings of pain and pleasure, and the capacity to recognize basic emotions like anger or fear, the human infant would not survive. However, it is the environment that plays the most critical role in how humans learn to make sense of feelings and emotions. Children learn, for example, the names given to different emotions in their culture (feeling angry, sad, happy); they also learn the typical causes and features of different emotions—what elicits them; the kinds of thoughts, urges, and behaviors that typically accompany them; and their likely consequences.

The degree to which children and adults acquire more or less sophisticated knowledge about emotions is held to constitute the second, primary factor in EI: specifically, the ability to understand emotions, to know how they unfold, and to be able to reason about them. This kind of emotion understanding, or emotion knowledge, is referred to in the social psychological literature as "emotion script" knowledge. Just as the script of a play unfolds predictably from its opening to closing acts, so too do emotions tend to unfold over time in predictable sequences. Anger, for example, typically begins with a perceived injustice or insult and is accompanied by thoughts relating to the unfairness of the situation and the culpability of the offender. The angry person may experience an urge to retaliate and typically will behave in a way that communicates anger, such as confrontation. The offender is then cued to respond, perhaps with defensive anger or perhaps with an acknowledgment of wrong behavior and an apology. This behavior, in turn, sets the scene for the injured party to respond, perhaps with punishment or forgiveness (e.g., see [249], [250]).

Research has shown that most people have a general understanding of the typical elements of the anger script described above. In particular, they can report what makes people angry, what angry people tend to do, and the likely outcomes of their behaviors. Emotionally intelligent people, however, possess highly complex and fine-grained emotion knowledge. They can distinguish the causes, features, and consequences of even the most closely related emotions, such as anger and hate, shame and guilt, jealousy and envy. Furthermore, like good chess players, they can foresee how emotion scripts may unfold in complex cascades of "if–then" sequences. Recall, for example, the incident at the dinner party described earlier. Having been humiliated in front of his friends by his wife, the emotionally intelligent spouse may reason, "if I show I'm angry, then my friends will be even more embarrassed and I will look even more foolish. If I laughingly reveal one of my wife's anxieties, then my friends may assume it's all in fun, but she will know I've taken revenge. However, that will mean she has the right to be angry with me later and we'll get into a fight. If I pretend I haven't heard her remark, or I change the subject, then the situation should resolve itself for the time being and I can take it up with my wife when I feel calmer." Later, the emotionally intelligent spouse may be aware that he still feels angry and that he would like nothing more than to attack his wife. However, he may also know that an angry reaction will escalate the conflict and prolong the drama for them both. Thus he may decide to control his anger, but to express his hurt and embarrassment (emotions that tend to evoke comforting responses, as opposed to anger, which more usually evokes anger). His wife may then feel guilty, apologize for having been so insensitive, and try hard over the next few days to make him feel better.

It is this behavioral aspect of the interaction, whereby people are able to effectively regulate and manage their own and others' emotions, that constitutes what Mayer and colleagues [259] consider to be the third, primary ability involved in EI. However, as the example discussed here makes clear, although the three primary abilities constituting EI are, to a certain extent, separate, they are also highly interrelated. In particular, the effective regulation of emotions requires sophisticated knowledge about how they work and what are their likely consequences. Furthermore, although such emotion knowledge could, in principle, be purely cognitive (in the same way that we could program a computer with knowledge about the typical causes, features, and outcomes of emotions), in practice, emotion knowledge draws heavily upon the accurate perception and recognition of our own and others' bodily emotion signals to produce emotionally intelligent behavior (see also [264]).

In summary, the EI literature suggests that individuals may be more or less "intelligent" with respect to three discrete, but interrelated, abilities: the ability to perceive and accurately recognize emotions, the ability to understand and reason about emotions, and the ability to effectively manage and regulate emotions. All three abilities would, on the face of it, appear to be important in the emotion-rich context of marriage. In the next section of this chapter I will review research findings from the marital literature that are directly relevant to the proposed facets of EI, and I will discuss their implications for marital happiness and stability.

☐ Emotion Perception and Communication in Marriage

As noted previously, Mayer et al. [259] have proposed that the most basic ability involved in EI relates to the perception and accurate identification of emotions. Over the last 20 years, a number of psychologists with an interest in marital conflict have been systematically investigating this basic ability within the context of "live" marital interactions in the laboratory (e.g., see [254]; [256]; [261]). Marital interaction research tends to involve a fairly standard set of procedures. Typically, couples come into a laboratory and discuss both low- and high-conflict marital issues in front of video cameras. Each spouse may be wired up to monitoring equipment so that various physiological measures, such as heart rate, muscular activity, and skin conductance (sweating), can be taken during the interaction. Later, couples return to the laboratory and separately watch their video-recorded interactions. While watching, spouses indicate what they were feeling and thinking at various points during the discussions; they may also try to identify what their partners were feeling and thinking. Finally, the transcripts of couples' conversations and videotapes of their nonverbal behaviors (e.g., facial expressions, tone of voice, body movements) may be coded by trained observers for their emotional content.

Overall, the results of these kinds of studies have been extremely consistent. In the first place, they have demonstrated that marriage is, indeed, an emotion-rich context, and that high-conflict marital discussions are emotionally arousing, as evidenced by physiological measures such as heart rate, skin conductance, and muscular activity. They also have demonstrated that individuals do vary in their abilities to accurately perceive and identify each others' emotions, with some spouses apparently oblivious to their partners' emotion signals, or prone to misidentify even the most obvious of them (e.g., interpreting sadness as hostility). Furthermore, individuals appear to vary considerably in their abilities to clearly express emotions, with some spouses habitually sending ambiguous emotion signals to their partners (e.g., simultaneously smiling and frowning).

Importantly, researchers have found reliable associations between these variations in people's abilities to accurately express and/or recognize emotions and marital happiness. For example, Noller and her colleagues have found that happy spouses are more empathically aware of and sensitive to each other's feeling states than unhappy spouses, who are more likely to misunderstand one another's intentions and misidentify each other's emotions. Of course, it is difficult to untangle cause and effect here, because marital unhappiness may be just as likely to decrease spouses' emotional sensitivity to one another as emotional insensitivity may be to decrease marital happiness. However, marital interaction research has clearly demonstrated how emotional misperceptions can lead directly to increased conflict as a function of what researchers call "negative affect reciprocity." This term derives from the observation that interacting spouses, whether happy or unhappy, tend to reciprocate the emotions they perceive (accurately or otherwise) are being expressed to them. In particular, it appears that unhappy spouses, who typically expect the worst from one another, perceive neutral or only mildly negative emotional messages as hostile and reciprocate with overtly hostile emotional messages. These messages are, in turn, perceived even more negatively than they were intended and so trigger even more hostile responses. In this way, destructive emotion sequences or negative escalation spirals are established, from which couples find it difficult to escape. In fact, these kinds of negative escalations and "tit-for-tat" sequences typify unhappy marriages [256].

Marital interaction studies also have revealed some striking gender differences in emotional expressiveness and perceptual accuracy. Noller and her colleagues [261], for example, have found that women are better than men at accurately expressing and identifying emotions. In part, women's greater expressive accuracy derives from the way they match their nonverbal behaviors when sending emotional messages. For example, when sending a positive message to her husband, a wife is likely to use matching nonverbal cues such as smiling and a warm tone of voice. Men, on the other hand, tend to send "mixed messages," for example, expressing positive messages with smiles plus potentially threatening cues, such as eyebrow flashes.

As might be expected, men's difficulties with accurately identifying and expressing emotions are particularly salient in unhappy marriages. For example, despite being highly emotionally aroused during marital conflict (as indicated by physiological measures such as heart rate), unhappy husbands frequently present a picture of almost complete emotional withdrawal, a phenomenon Gottman refers to as "stonewalling." Observers have noted how, faced with an obdurate, stonewalling husband, a wife tends to respond with ever-increasing demands for emotional engagement; her demands, however, only serve to aggravate her husband's withdrawal. Like the negative escalation cycle discussed previously, this "demand–withdraw" sequence is difficult to escape and also tends to characterize unhappy marriages [245].

To summarize, marital interaction research has demonstrated that, just as Mayer et al. [259] have argued, individuals differ in their abilities to perceive and identify emotions accurately. It has also revealed that individuals differ in another, closely related emotional skill: specifically, the ability to clearly express emotions. Overall, women are more skilled at both tasks, and happily married spouses are better both at expressing emotions and at identifying emotions than unhappily married spouses. What marital interaction studies have not revealed is the extent to which individuals vary in their abilities to perceive and accurately identify their own emotions. Even so, researchers have speculated about the extent to which some men may be unclear about their emotions, based on the fact that, overall, men are less likely than women to express (or admit to) feelings of fear, sadness, or vulnerability (e.g., see [242]). Researchers have suggested that many men feel threatened both by situations they cannot control and by the emotions of anxiety or sadness that such situations may evoke. When feeling vulnerable and powerless, such men tend to express anger, an emotion that gives them some sense of control. In the marital context, this may mean that a husband reacts to his wife's demands for more independence with anger at her effrontery, rather than with the anxiety he may actually be feeling over the possibility of losing her. This anger may then lead to confrontational and destructive behaviors, including physical intimidation and violence (e.g., see [247]).

It is difficult to gauge the extent to which men's anger in potentially anxiety or sadness-provoking situations comes from actual confusion over the meaning of their physiological symptoms. Gottman and others, for example, have proposed that in high-conflict marital interactions, even the most apparently stoic husband may be feeling overwhelmed and confused by the intensity of his negative feelings, including a churning stomach, rapidly beating heart, sweating palms, and pounding in the head. In such circumstances, men may automatically react with anger, which tends to be regarded as a natural and socially acceptable emotion for men (in Western cultures, at least). However, expressing anger in such situations also may be a deliberate and strategic response to feelings of vulnerability. In particular, some men may learn as they grow up that anger can provide an illusion of control and may even, in the short-term, help them achieve their goals.

Clearly, there is a need for more research to untangle these complex issues. Overall, however, the findings from marital interaction research suggest that for married partners to be able to make sense of their own and their partners' emotions and to be able to express them clearly to one another they need a good working knowledge of the causes, features, and consequences of emotions in the marital context. In the next section of the chapter, I will discuss some research that specifically has examined this aspect of EI in relation to forgiven and unforgiven marital offenses.

☐ Understanding and Reasoning about Emotions in Marriage

As I discussed in the first part of this chapter, people acquire knowledge as they grow up about how emotions are caused, what they feel like, and their likely outcomes. Emotion knowledge is both general (such as knowing what makes human beings angry) and context specific (such as knowing what makes spouses, in particular, angry with one another). Evidence suggests that most people have a minimum amount of context-specific emotion knowledge. For example, researchers have found that people's imaginary accounts of what would make spouses angry, loving, hateful, or jealous, and the consequences of these emotions, are remarkably consistent with recalled accounts of actual emotion instances in marriage [253], [252]. However, people differ in the complexity and accuracy of their emotion knowledge, differences that may well influence spouses' abilities to understand and deal effectively with the emotional ups and downs of marriage.

The results of a recent study on marital forgiveness provide some support for the important role of emotion knowledge and understanding in marriage (see [250]). This study explored people's experiences of guilt, shame, and forgiveness in relation to either self- or partner-caused marital offenses (e.g., involving betrayal, neglect, or abusive behavior) and examined the role of EI in people's responses to such offenses. In particular, it was hypothesized that higher EI might enable people to more effectively manage the delicate emotional negotiations involved in seeking and granting forgiveness: knowing, for example, how and when to say you are sorry and, conversely, knowing how sorry is sorry enough, and when to stop "rubbing it in."

Ninety long-term married and 70 divorced men and women were asked to recall and write about either a forgiven or an unforgiven marital offense. They provided details of who had offended, what had happened, and how they and their partners had felt and behaved in relation to the offense. They also completed questionnaires about various aspects of their marriages and personalities, including one of the earliest published measures of EI, the Trait Meta-Mood Scale (TMMS) [266]. This 30-item scale consists of three subscales that measure what were, in the early 1990s, considered to be the major dimensions of EI: attention to feelings (e.g., I pay a lot of attention to how I feel); clarity of feelings (e.g., I am rarely confused about how I feel); and mood repair (e.g., when I become upset I remind myself of all the pleasures in life). Although these dimensions are not exactly equivalent to current conceptions of EI, they are fairly close approximations, especially the emotion clarity (understanding) and mood repair (emotion regulation) dimensions.

The first point to note about the results of this study is that only two facets of the TMMS, emotion clarity and mood repair, were positively associated with one another. Being attentive to feelings was associated with neither of these facets. These results confirm, in line with theoretical predictions, that the ability to regulate and manage emotions is linked to the ability to understand emotions. However, the results also confirm that being highly attentive to feelings is not, on its own, necessarily adaptive. Rather, feelings may be both confusing and overwhelming if one is unable to clearly identify, understand, and effectively manage them.

With respect to the role of EI in marital forgiveness, only emotion clarity, or the ability to understand and reason about emotions, was important. First, and perhaps most critically, individuals who reported higher emotion clarity also tended to report greater marital happiness, irrespective of age or sex. Second, individuals with higher emotion clarity reported significantly less difficulty in forgiving a partner-caused offense than lower emotion-clarity participants, regardless of how serious the offense had been, how much hurt and pain it had caused, or how happily or unhappily married the individual was. Together, these findings suggest that the ability to understand the causes, features, and outcomes of emotions facilitates the constructive resolution of even the most hurtful marital transgressions and contributes significantly to perceptions of marital satisfaction.

Finally, low emotion-clarity offenders reported experiencing significantly more shame (but not guilt) in relation to their offenses and were more likely to believe their partners hated them because of those offenses than high emotion-clarity individuals. These findings are particularly interesting in light of theorists' arguments that shame is an intensely painful emotion that typically triggers defensive anger; guilt, in contrast, is held to be a more constructive emotion that typically involves attempts to make restitution for an offense (e.g., see [267]). Perhaps it is the case, then, that highly shameful, low emotion-clarity offenders are more prone to attack their injured partners than to apologize and show remorse for an offense. Similarly, it may be the case that low emotion-clarity offenders wrongly interpret their injured partners' hurt and distress as signaling hate and rejection; thus, rather than expressing guilt and remorse, they may act hatefully in return. Either of these reactions is likely to exacerbate marital conflict and diminish marital happiness over time.

These are issues that require more fine-grained research to resolve. Overall, however, the findings of this study suggest that the ability to understand and reason about emotions has a potentially important role to play in weathering marital ups and downs. Furthermore, the results of a second study on aspects of marital forgiveness with newlywed participants also found a positive association between emotion clarity and marital happiness, so this appears to be a reliable finding [251]. However, these studies do have some limitations with respect to measurement issues. For example, the TMMS asks people to rate how well they believe they understand their emotions, rather than assessing their actual abilities to understand them. In addition, neither study tracked spouses' emotion clarity or marital happiness over time. Thus, we cannot tell whether having more fine-grained emotion knowledge actually leads to greater marital happiness (mediated, perhaps, by greater empathy and fewer misunderstandings) or whether marital happiness provides a supportive context within which spouses can acquire accurate knowledge of both their own and their partners' emotions over time. In fact, the relationship most likely works both ways.

Clearly, although the results of the current studies are inconclusive, they are at least consistent with the hypothesis that the more complex and finely tuned our knowledge and understanding of emotions, the more adaptively we may behave in intimate relational contexts like marriage. This is turn brings us to consider the third aspect of EI: managing and regulating emotions.

☐ Managing and Regulating Emotions in Marriage

As noted in previous sections of this chapter, whether you are happily married appears to depend most importantly on your own and your partner's abilities to cope constructively with conflict and to understand and manage negative emotions like anger and hate. The results of several studies confirm the importance of self-control and emotion regulation in marital happiness and stability. For example, researchers have found that in comparison with unhappy spouses, happy spouses are more likely to accommodate than to retaliate during conflict interactions. This means that happy spouses tend to inhibit their impulses to react destructively when their spouses express anger or behave unreasonably and try to respond instead in a conciliatory or constructive manner (e.g., see [265]).

Other evidence that points to the important role of emotion management and regulation in marriage comes from the personality and clinical psychology literature. Researchers have theorized that accommodation and emotion regulation in marriage may actually be easier for some spouses to achieve than others because they naturally have more even temperaments. In fact, several negative emotional traits, including impulsivity, emotional instability, fearfulness, and depression, have been found to reliably predict poorer marital adjustment (see [263]). Similarly, negative marital outcomes have been associated with a cluster of emotional traits, collectively referred to as "negative affectivity," or the predisposition to experience relatively frequent episodes of anxiety, tension, anger, feelings of rejection, and sadness. Individuals with high negative affectivity tend to overreact to even mildly unpleasant or anxiety-inducing situations; they are also highly self-critical and tend to ruminate over perceived injustices wrought by others. As might be imagined, such negative emotional traits can spell disaster for marital happiness in the long-term [241].

The inability to control the expression of anger also has been shown to negatively impact on marital happiness and stability. For example, one longitudinal study by Caspi, Elder, and Bem [243] found that nearly 50% of men with a long-standing history of temper tantrums from childhood had divorced by the age of 40, compared with only 22% of men without such a history. Similarly, nearly 25% of women with a history of bad temper had divorced by midlife, compared with only 12% of women with a more good-tempered history. Furthermore, the husbands of bad-tempered women who had not divorced reported less satisfying and more problematic marital relationships than the husbands of more even-tempered women.

Overall, these findings suggest that the ability to manage one's negative emotions and control their expression is a prerequisite for marital happiness and stability. However, this does not mean that emotionally inexpressive spouses have the happiest marriages. Indeed, as noted in a previous section of this chapter, there may be nothing so infuriating as an excessively "rational," stonewalling spouse. In fact, researchers have found that spouses generally regard emotional openness and expressiveness as both positive and desirable in marriage and that more emotionally expressive spouses tend to have happier partners [257]. There is, however, an important caveat to this finding. Specifically, marital happiness critically depends on the overall number of expressed positive emotions outweighing the number of expressed negative emotions (optimally, by about five to one, according to Gottman [256]).

Studies of long-term marriages confirm the importance of predominantly positive emotional expression to marital happiness and stability. For example, in a large-scale study of middle-aged and older (in their sixties) couples, Carstensen, Gottman, and Levenson [244] found that although happy spouses still expressed negative emotions like anger and sadness in their interactions with one another, they more frequently expressed love, affection, and good humor in those interactions. In addition, happy spouses were skilled at interrupting and deescalating the kinds of destructive negative interaction sequences characteristic of unhappy couples. For example, they tended to react to a spouse's expression of anger with neutral or caring, empathic responses, rather than with retaliatory anger.

In short, the literature suggests that the intelligent regulation and management of emotions is an important factor in maintaining marital harmony. However, it also suggests that such intelligent regulation goes beyond "biting your tongue" when upset, or controlling the expression of negative emotions like anger, anxiety, and depression. In the marital context, emotion management involves the frequent expression of positive emotions like love, and a willingness to empathize and engage with one's partner in a climate of trust and affection. In this respect, it may not be unreasonable to conceptualize EI within the context of long-term marriages as an emergent property of happily married couples' interactions, rather than as a set of abilities residing within one spouse or the other. Again, this points to the need for more research to help identify the nature and features of the emotionally intelligent marriage and to explore the ways in which marital happiness itself may lead to more emotionally intelligent behavior over time.

☐ Is Emotional Intelligence the Key to a Successful Marriage?

The research reviewed in this chapter suggests that various emotion-related abilities are important for a happy, long-term marriage. These abilities include the accurate perception and identification of emotions, the clear expression of emotions (especially positive ones), emotion knowledge and understanding, and effective emotion regulation. It could be argued that all these abilities are potentially involved in EI, though the status of emotional expressiveness is unclear (see Chapter 2).

It should be noted, however, that the link between the various facets of EI and marital happiness may not be entirely straightforward. For example, although accuracy in perceiving and identifying emotions is one factor in marital happiness, evidence suggests that a certain amount of perceptual *inaccuracy* also may be important for a happy marriage. Researchers have found, for example, that happy spouses tend to perceive their partners through rose-colored spectacles, glossing over or simply not noticing their faults and attributing charitable intentions to each other in the face of less than exemplary behavior (e.g., see [260]). No doubt this ability to "turn a blind eye" is adaptive at times with respect to handling potentially difficult marital situations.

It is also important to consider that the proposed facets of EI may not always be used adaptively in marriage. Researchers frequently have assumed that the emotionally intelligent individual's empathic skills necessarily make him or her a good-hearted and popular person. However, as Epstein [248] pointed out, someone who is skilled at reading other people's emotions could just as well use this ability for destructive as for constructive purposes. Other researchers also have noted that empathy, in the sense of accurately reading and even vicariously feeling another's emotions, may or may not lead to sensitive and compassionate responding; other potential reactions include escape and avoidance [255]. In the context of marriage, spouses could conceivably use their EI to accurately identify their partners' vulnerabilities and insecurities, and exploit these for their own purposes.

One chilling example was obtained from the marital forgiveness study cited earlier, whereby a woman with high emotion clarity described how she manipulated her former spouse into a jealous rage. She then used his violent behavior as an excuse to "play the victim" and desert her loveless marriage. This woman clearly had sufficient emotion knowledge to achieve her goals; she also knew what would most upset her husband, how he would be likely to respond, and how best to win the sympathy and support of her friends. In contrast, a more touching account was written by a man with high emotion clarity who described how his wife had spotted him having a clandestine lunch with a former lover. He recounted in detail his wife's hurt and anger and his own distress at her pain; he also explained the steps he took to convince her of his remorse and express gratitude at her forgiveness.

In short, it seems that EI, or at least certain aspects of it, has the capacity to enrich marriage; however, EI alone is not sufficient to guarantee marital happiness. Spouses must also want to be married and be committed to the idea of being married. In addition, spouses must be committed to each other, look out for each other, care for and show compassion toward each other, and be willing to assume responsibility for each other's needs (e.g., see [246]). Such motivations, goals, and behaviors may have very little to do with EI per se.

☐ Conclusions

The literature reviewed in this chapter reveals a relatively long-standing and rich tradition of psychological research on emotions in the context of marital relationships. In particular, marital researchers have demonstrated that the better spouses are at perceiving, accurately identifying, regulating, and expressing emotions, the happier their relationships are. These findings are consistent with the hypothesis, derived from the EI literature, that people differ in their abilities to accurately perceive, identify, and express emotions; understand and reason about emotions; and effectively regulate and manage emotions. Thus it may be argued that the marital literature supports the suggestion that some individuals are indeed more "emotionally intelligent" than others. Moreover, these differences in emotion-related abilities are reliably associated with what may be considered an adaptive and desirable life outcome: marital happiness and stability.

Whether the construct of EI has anything new or useful to offer marital researchers will likely depend on what progress is made in more precisely defining and measuring it. Specifically, scholars must come to some agreement on the constituents of EI, and decide whether it would make more theoretical sense to conceptualize people's emotion-related abilities as interrelated but separable competencies, rather than as a unitary form of intelligence. In a related vein, scholars also need to devise more reliable ways of measuring EI, or emotion-related abilities. In particular, they must find ways of measuring people's abilities to clearly express their own emotions and accurately interpret others' emotions, abilities that marital researchers have shown to be especially important in adaptive interpersonal functioning (see also Chapter 2).

One final important point is that EI currently is conceived as an exclusively intrapersonal mental ability; however, as the research in this chapter has demonstrated, emotions like anger, guilt, jealousy, and love are profoundly interpersonal phenomena that are played out over time between individuals. Indeed, it could even be argued that people's emotion accuracy, expressiveness, understanding, and regulation only come to life within interpersonal and relational settings. Emotional intelligence theorists, then, might well look to the marital literature for data and theoretical insights about adaptive emotion functioning, particularly in the context of real-time behavioral interactions. However, EI scholars also have a potentially important contribution to make toward enhancing our understanding of adaptive emotion functioning in marriage. For example, research using the TMMS suggests that the accurate perception and understanding of how emotions like anger, shame, guilt, and love unfold over time may play an important role in the maintenance of satisfying long-term relationships, although we are a long way from understanding how the two are linked.

Clearly, emotion and close relationship scholars have much to offer one another with respect to theoretical insights and methodological expertise. I hope that in the future these researchers will work together to build more dynamic models of the features, predictors, and outcomes of EI in emotion-rich contexts like marriage.

☐ Acknowledgment

The author would like to acknowledge the very helpful comments of Trevor Case, Jill Duffield, and Doris McIlwain on a draft of this chapter.

CHAPTER

7

Judith Flury
William Ickes

Emotional Intelligence
and Empathic Accuracy

According to Salovey, Hsee, and Mayer [308], there are three primary domains of EI: the accurate appraisal and expression of emotion; the adaptive regulation of emotions; and the use of emotions to plan, create, and motivate action. This chapter focuses on the first domain as it relates to friends and dating partners, and we expand this focus to include the accurate appraisal of other people's thoughts as well as their feelings. For more than a decade now, the topic of inferring others' thoughts and feelings has been addressed by a field of study known as *empathic accuracy*. Empathic accuracy involves "reading" people's thoughts and feelings on a moment-to-moment basis; it is, by definition, a measure of the ability to accurately infer the specific content of these successive thoughts and feelings [290]. In the sections to follow, we draw on available theory and research to discuss the role of empathic accuracy and EI in the relationships of friends and dating partners.

☐ Ability to Infer Other People's Thoughts and Feelings

The ability to infer the attentional and intentional states of others is clearly evident in most normally developing children by the age of 3 or 4 [269], [275]. The ability to identify others' emotional states takes longer to emerge and is often not well developed until early or late adolescence [275], [308].

The ability to accurately infer the specific content of other people's thoughts and feelings represents the fullest expression of a perceiver's empathic skills. This level of insight is beyond the capability of most autistic individuals [269], [306], but is clearly evident—though in varying degrees—in most normally developing adolescents and adults [285].

From a personality standpoint, what are empathically accurate people like? Historically, researchers searched for the attributes of the good judge of others' personality traits and they did not pay much attention to the more methodologically daunting problem of what might determine perceivers' accuracy in inferring other people's thoughts and feelings. Taft's [320] qualitative review of the early trait accuracy research suggested that the best potential correlates of this ability for adult participants were intelligence, good psychological adjustment, and aesthetic interest.

Forty-two years later, when Davis and Kraus [274] published their quantitative metanalysis of the data from 36 "post-Cronbach investigations" (251 effects involving 32 individual-difference variables and 30 interpersonal accuracy measures), their list of the best potential correlates was only slightly longer than Taft's. Expanding on Taft's finding that "good judges" tend to be intelligent, Davis and Kraus found that they also tend be cognitively complex, field independent, and nondogmatic. And qualifying Taft's finding that "good judges" tend to be psychologically well adjusted, Davis and Kraus found that "good judges" tend to be more mature, trusting, and well socialized, but not less neurotic or anxious.

A recent attempt to extend this profile of the "good judge" of personality traits to the empathic accuracy domain produced findings that can only be regarded as tentative and equivocal [285]. Ickes and colleagues found that only two—verbal intelligence and interpersonal trust—of the four predictor variables that Davis and Kraus [274] used—were related to perceivers' empathic accuracy scores. However, verbal intelligence was positively correlated with men's, but not women's, empathic accuracy. And, contrary to the findings of Davis and Kraus's [274] metanalysis, interpersonal trust was negatively correlated with empathic accuracy. Although these relationships clearly warrant further study, the psychological portrait that they draw of the empathically accurate perceiver must be regarded as sketchy rather than detailed, and as tentative rather than definitive.

☐ Empathic Accuracy in Friendships and Dating Relationships

Knowing Each Other "From the Inside"

Gesn [278] predicted that the more background information we have about a friend or acquaintance (e.g., his or her work schedule, hobbies, career goals, current dating partners), the better we will be at inferring the specific content of that person's thoughts and feelings. However, Gesn's [278] findings offered a surprise: empathic accuracy was predicted not by the amount of background knowledge the perceiver had acquired about a target, but by the degree to which the perceiver characterized the relationship with the target as being psychologically close. It appears that simply knowing a lot of objective facts about a friend's life is not enough to ensure success in "reading" his or her thoughts and feelings; we must also acquire extensive information about the target's subjective—and intersubjective—experience. In other words, the perceiver must get to know the target "from the inside" instead of merely "from the outside."

Stinson and Ickes [319] point to the same conclusion from their study. They found that male friends could infer the specific content of each other's thoughts and feelings better than that of male strangers. Through a series of ancillary analyses, Stinson and Ickes analyzed the data and found that this difference in empathic accuracy could not be attributed to the fact that the friends exchanged more information than the strangers (although they did), or to the fact that the friends had more similar personalities than the strangers (although, on the single dimension of sociability, the friends were indeed more similar). Instead, there was evidence that the friends' advantage derived primarily from the large store of intersubjective knowledge that they had acquired in their previous interactions with each other—the type of knowledge that the strangers had not yet been able to acquire.

How do individuals get to know each other "from the inside"? As Colvin, Vogt, and Ickes [273] have noted, different authors have proposed complementary, but conceptually distinct, answers to this question. For example, Smither [317] has emphasized "empathy via role taking," which occurs when a person actively attempts to understand another's thoughts or feelings. Accurate knowledge of this target person's inner world is increased to the extent that the target discusses with the perceiver the "concerns, commitments, beliefs, and ideals" surrounding his or her current emotional state. The more a perceiver has observed a target's behavioral and emotional reactions to different situations, and the more that the two of them have discussed the psychological meaning of these situations, the better the perceiver will become at "reading" that target person's thoughts and feelings.

Karniol [292] offers a somewhat different perspective. She suggests that strangers initially rely on social stereotypes to infer each others' thoughts and feelings and then modify their inferences to rely on more individuating information the longer they have been together. For Stinson and Ickes [319], the most important type of individuating information is that which the partners have come to "share" through their intersubjective experience. By doing things together and discussing their present and past experiences, partners tend to develop overlapping (i.e., "shared") knowledge structures that facilitate their inferences about each other's thoughts and feelings. Similarly, Kenny [293] has noted that observations of a partner's behavior often lead to opportunities to discuss with the partner the thoughts and feelings associated with those events.

All of the activities noted by these authors—discussing with one's partner the beliefs, ideals, and concerns surrounding one's current feeling states, dealing with the partner in an individualized rather than a stereotyped way, sharing with the partner many life experiences and the subjective and intersubjective reactions to these experiences, and discussing with the partner the thoughts and feelings that led to certain behaviors, reactions, and emotional expressions—should lead to a greater knowledge of the partner's inner world. Collectively, these activities make up the process of getting to know the other person "from the inside."

Friends and dating partners should have an advantage, then, when it comes to reading each other's thoughts and feelings. The interactions typical of friendships and love relationships are usually of the type that result in shared experiences and corresponding discussions of these experiences. Acquiring and making effective use of this "inside" knowledge is not guaranteed, however. It depends upon many factors, including characteristics of the perceiver, characteristics of the target, characteristics of their relationship, and characteristics of the situation in which their immediate interaction is occurring. Some relevant factors in each of these categories are reviewed below.

Characteristics of the Perceiver

Empathic Ability

Perceivers not only differ in their overall levels of empathic ability but also tend to maintain similar rank orders when they infer the thoughts and feelings of different target persons [299], [279]. Although ability differences account for an important source of the variance in empathic accuracy scores, self-report measures of empathically relevant traits and dispositions have typically proved to be rather poor and unreliable predictors of these differences in empathic performance [274], [285]. One interpretation of these null results is that perceivers do not have the necessary metaknowledge of their own empathic ability [289], [285], [288].

Attentiveness

According to both theory and research, how much the perceiver attends to the target is an important determinant of empathic accuracy. Attending to the target person's behavior is the first stage in Funder's [276] realistic accuracy model—the stage upon which the success of all subsequent stages of the perceiver's inference-making ultimately depends. Consistent with this reasoning, Ickes, Stinson, Bissonnette, and Garcia [291] found that empathic accuracy in mixed-sex dyads is significantly correlated with the degree to which perceivers look at their partners (behavioral attentiveness) and the percentage of partner-relevant thoughts and feelings they report (cognitive attentiveness). Similarly, Gesn and Ickes [279] found that perceivers' ratings of their attention to and interest in an empathic accuracy task significantly correlated with their performance on the task. Finally, Trommsdorf and John [323] found that a manipulation that encouraged the members of heterosexual couples to focus on their partner's, rather than their own, feelings during a videotaped discussion caused the couples in the former condition to more accurately decode each others' emotional states from the videotape.

Motivation

There is increasing evidence that perceivers' motivation to be accurate also affects their performance on empathic accuracy tasks. In the first study hinting at the importance of motivation, Ickes and colleagues [291] found that opposite-sex strangers better inferred their target partners' thoughts and feelings to the extent that these partners were physically attractive. In a recent metanalytic study, Ickes, Gesn, and Graham [286] reviewed evidence suggesting that significant gender differences favoring female over male perceivers should be attributed more to differential motivation than to differential ability. Klein and Hodges [296] reached essentially the same conclusion and also noted that men and women achieve similar levels of empathic accuracy when they are motivated by the same financial reward.

Attachment Orientations

Simpson, Ickes, and Grich [315] found that perceivers' attachment orientations can affect their level of empathic accuracy in relationship-threatening situations. When anxious–ambivalent perceivers see a threat to the relationship, they become hypervigilant (exceptionally accurate) with regard to their partner's potentially threatening thoughts and feelings. In contrast, avoidant perceivers tend to avoid inferring partner's thoughts and feelings in relationship-threatening situations, resulting in generally lower levels of empathic accuracy.

Communal Orientation

According to Rothbaum, Weisz, and Snyder [307], people differ in their relationship to the environment. Those with a "primary" control orientation tend to work on changing the environment to fit their own needs and goals, whereas those with a "secondary" control orientation tend to work toward accommodation—restructuring their own needs and goals according to the perceived realities of the social and physical environment. Trommsdorf and John [323] examined the control orientation of the relationship partners in their study of emotion decoding in intimate relationships. They found that people who were more accommodating (had secondary control orientation) could read their partner's emotions more accurately. They also found, however, that the correlation between accurate emotional decoding and secondary control orientation fell from .25 (p <.05), to .09 when they separated out those who rated themselves as feminine. Thus, the effect of secondary control orientation appeared to be due primarily to having a feminine gender-role orientation.

In a more recent study, Vogt and Colvin [324] reported evidence that those who said they were communal tended to be more accurate in trait judgment. Unfortunately, however, neither self-rated communality nor self-rated femininity have reliably predicted individuals' performance in the empathic accuracy studies conducted to date [287], [296], [285].

Characteristics of the Target

How "readable" a target is has a lot to do with the variance in empathic accuracy scores, accounting on average for about 25% of the variance in the studies reviewed by Ickes and colleagues [285]. At this point, we don't know much about the personal characteristics that distinguish more "readable" targets from less "readable" ones. However, characteristics such as self-directedness, consistency, and coherence appear to be the best-candidate predictor variables identified so far.

Self-Directedness

Hancock and Ickes [281] reported that interaction partners who were more self-directed in terms of the relevant items on Snyder's [318] 18-item self-monitoring scale had thoughts and feelings that were generally easier to "read" than those of their more other-directed partners. Hancock and Ickes [281] speculated that other-directed targets are more difficult to "read" because (1) they allow their interaction partners to take the initiative in conversations and therefore do not disclose much themselves, and/or (2) they mask or suppress the expression of their actual thoughts and feelings in an attempt to behave in what they perceive to be a socially desirable manner.

Consistency and Coherence

The idea that people who are self- rather than other-directed are easier for their partners to "read" may be analogous to Colvin's [272] argument that people who have a coherent personality structure and who manifest consistent and non-erratic behavior are more "judgable" in terms of their personality traits [273]. The importance of consistency and coherence on target "readability" is also evident in the study reported by Marangoni et al. [299], in which 80 perceivers inferred the thoughts and feelings of three female clients who were videotaped during individual sessions with the same male, client-centered therapist. Marangoni and her colleagues found that the thoughts and feelings of one client were considerably more difficult to infer than the thoughts and feelings of the other two clients. A review of the respective videotapes revealed why: the difficult-to-"read" client was inconsistent in the presentation of her problem, her mood was labile, her affect changed periodically, and she gave conflicting accounts of her feelings toward the same situation at different times.

Characteristics of the Perceiver–Target Relationship

Acquaintanceship and Intimacy

Many studies have shown that well-acquainted partners can read each other's thoughts and feelings better than strangers can [278], [280], [319]. When the data from these studies were combined to create a cross-sectional picture of how empathic accuracy varies with the degree of acquaintanceship, the results suggested that most of the gain in partners' ability to "read" each other occurs within the first few weeks of their relationship, with only minor gains occurring after the second month [282]. As Gesn's [278] findings indicate, however, empathic accuracy may be more closely related to the degree of intimacy and closeness in the relationship than to the length of acquaintanceship per se.

Relationship Discord

Researchers have shown that relationship discord can reduce empathic accuracy, and that reduced accuracy can in turn lead to even more discord. For example, Kirchler [294], [295] had spouses rate their own affect and their partner's affect at randomly selected times throughout each day, for several weeks. He found that participants could more accurately identify their partner's current mood during times of agreement than during times of conflict. In a similar vein, Noller and Ruzzene [304] reported that distressed couples had a particular problem in identifying the specific emotions experienced by their partner during times of conflict.

A possible reason for this effect is suggested by the results of a study by Gaelick, Bodenhausen, and Wyer [277]. They found that spouses were not as accurate at decoding their partner's expressions of love as they were at decoding their expressions of hostility. This means that the decoding of a partner's positive, rather than negative, emotions may suffer the most in conflict situations. In addition, the Gaelick and colleagues' study showed that spouses tend to reciprocate whatever emotion they *thought* their partner was expressing.

What implications do these findings have for friendships and dating relationships? It depends, of course, on their generality. If such findings prove to be the rule, rather than the exception, we can expect that, during times of conflict, friends and dating partners—particularly those with an anxious attachment style—will more accurately read each other's negative or hostile thoughts or feelings than their positive feelings or expressions of love. If this is indeed the case, then the affect that they are, by inference, "receiving" from their partner during conflict should be experienced as being mainly negative or hostile. Furthermore, because couples tend to reciprocate whatever emotion they *think* their partner is conveying, and because they are mainly perceiving hostility or negativity, they are likely to convey hostility back to the partner. It is therefore easy to see how, despite their initial expressions of both love and hostility, the partners might increasingly respond to each other's hostility and therefore escalate the levels of hostility that they reciprocate.

Relationship Vulnerability

On the other hand, couples who feel that their relationship is especially vulnerable may display a contrasting effect—a tendency to avoid accurately "reading" each other's relationship-threatening thoughts and feelings. Simpson, Ickes, and Blackstone [316] documented this tendency in a study of more than 80 dating couples. They predicted that couples in vulnerable relationships would be especially likely to display empathic *in*accuracy in situations in which the partners were experiencing relationship-threatening thoughts and feelings. For the purposes of their study, vulnerable couples were defined as those who were highly dependent on each other but were also highly insecure about the future of their relationship.

When the vulnerable couples were asked to infer each other's thoughts and feelings in a relationship-threatening situation, they displayed unusually low levels of empathic accuracy. In fact, their average empathic accuracy scores were not significantly different from a chance baseline, and were significantly lower than the average empathic accuracy scores obtained by opposite-sex strangers in an earlier study. Simpson et al. [316] argued that the "motivated inaccuracy" displayed by these couples could actually help to preserve their vulnerable relationships in the face of a strong situational threat. Their argument was supported by the fact that the vulnerable couples, who were unusually inaccurate, were all still dating at a 5-month follow-up, whereas nearly 30% of the other couples in the study had broken up by that point.

☐   How Can Empathic Accuracy Be Improved in Casual and Close Relationships?

Theory and research have already begun to address this question [278], [319], [280], [299], [273]. Ironically, the preliminary answer appears to be that strangers should in some ways act more like intimates, whereas intimates should in some respects act more like strangers.

Improving the Empathic Accuracy of Strangers

For strangers, the evidence clearly suggests that empathic accuracy can be improved in at least two ways—by increasing their acquaintanceship with the target and by obtaining immediate feedback about the target's actual thoughts and feelings.

The Effect of Exposure and Acquaintanceship

Stinson and Ickes [319] found that the male friends were, on average, about 50% more accurate than the male strangers in inferring each other's thoughts and feelings. This effect (both the friends' advantage and its magnitude) was later replicated in a follow-up study by Graham [280], who found that it extended to the comparison of female friends with female strangers as well. Evidence for a more passive "acquaintanceship" effect was reported in a study by Marangoni and colleagues [299]. The perceiver-observers in this study were asked to infer from standardized videotapes the thoughts and feelings of three female clients who discussed their personal problems with a male, client-centered therapist. The results indicated that the observers' empathic accuracy improved substantially from the beginning to the end of the tapes. However, this effect was limited to the two clients whose accounts were relatively coherent and straightforward, and whose thoughts and feelings were therefore easier to read.

Limitations of the Acquaintanceship Effect

Although increased exposure to and acquaintanceship with a target does generally lead to an increase in the perceiver's empathic accuracy, there are limits to this effect. First, some people are particularly bad judges—even when they try to infer the thoughts and feelings of a friend [281]. Second, some targets are extremely difficult to read—even by perceivers who have known them for a very long time (see, for example, [272] research on target "judgability" and Hancock and Ickes's [281] research on target "readability"). Third, there may be circumstances when an individual is motivated to make *in*accurate inferences to preserve a close relationship. We talk more about the topic of motivated inaccuracy later in this chapter.

Obtaining Feedback about the Target's Thoughts and Feelings

Marangoni and colleagues [299] further demonstrated that when a target provides a perceiver with immediate, veridical feedback about his or her actual thoughts and feelings, it helps the perceiver to read the target better in the future. Specifically, they reported that perceivers who received such feedback during the middle portion of each therapy tape were generally more accurate during the final portion of the tape than were control subjects who had received no feedback. This feedback effect was not significant, however, for the highly ambivalent client whose thoughts and feelings were particularly difficult to read.

Summary

These findings suggest that strangers can improve their empathic accuracy by acting more like friends—by becoming better acquainted with each other, and by seeking a lot of feedback about each other's actual thoughts and feelings. The success of these strategies will be limited, however, by the overall empathic ability of the perceiver and by the overall "readability" of the target person.

Improving the Empathic Accuracy of Intimates

Surprisingly, there is evidence that the empathic accuracy of spouses actually declines following the first few years of their marriage [322]. This finding not only suggests a curvilinear relationship between length of acquaintanceship and empathic accuracy, but it also raises the important question of why such a decline occurs and how it can be reversed. Thomas and colleagues found that this decline was because couples who had been married for longer periods of time tended to have fewer shared thoughts and feelings (and, by implication, more idiosyncratic ones) during their interactions than did more recently married couples; and it was this difference in the level of "shared cognitive focus" that accounted for the lower levels of empathic accuracy attained by couples married for longer periods of time.

Thomas and colleagues interpreted this finding as evidence that "partners in long-standing relationships become complacent and overly familiar with each other" [322, p. 840]. They therefore lack the motivation to actively monitor each other's words and actions and to attain the kind of common, intersubjective focus in their thoughts and feelings that facilitates empathic accuracy. If this explanation is correct, it suggests that intimates become more empathically accurate by in some respects acting more like strangers. Specifically, they pay more attention to each other's words and actions and work harder to maintain a "shared cognitive focus" in their daily interactions.

☐ What Factors Can Impair Empathic Accuracy in Close Relationships?

What factors can *impair* empathic accuracy in friendships and love relationships? On the basis of existing theory and research, Ickes and Simpson [283] have proposed a number of likely factors.

1. Most obvious, perhaps, is that if the target person is unable or unwilling to *express* what he or she is thinking and feeling through verbal and nonverbal channels, the perceiver's empathic accuracy will be impaired.
2. Almost as obvious, empathic accuracy should also be hurt if the perceiver is unable or unwilling to correctly *interpret* the target's behavioral cues. The perceiver's impairment in some cases may be because he or she just does not have empathic ability. In other cases, however, it may be attributable to either a chronic or temporary lack of empathic motivation or to a phenomenon called "motivated inaccuracy." We will discuss this in more detail below.
3. Stress—both acute and chronic—should also impair the perceiver's empathic accuracy. Worries and concerns that arise in the context of both short- and long-term life stressors (e.g., problems related to health, work, and finances) should draw a perceiver's attention and cognitive effort away from deciphering those behavioral cues in everyday inter-

action that help to convey the true content of a partner's thoughts and feelings [309].

4. Despite the fact that increased acquaintanceship generally leads to increased empathic accuracy, the advantages conferred by greater knowledge of one's partner may at times be offset by perceptual biases that originate from knowing the partner *too* well. Sillars [312] has proposed that three features of close relationships can short-circuit accurate empathic understanding: excessive familiarity with the partner, high levels of behavioral interdependence, and strong emotional involvement.

   Familiarity frequently breeds overconfidence in inferential tasks [310] and if overconfidence extends into areas where partners know little about one another, greater familiarity can result in less understanding. As partners become more *interdependent*, they must interpret each other's actions under more complicated interpersonal contexts. By creating greater attributional ambiguity (i.e., "*Which* of these many contextual factors is/are relevant now?"), these numerous "background" variables should lower the perceived correspondence between the partner's overt behavior and his or her underlying dispositions, and thus impair empathic accuracy. Finally, *strong emotional involvement* should—in some circumstances—also attenuate empathic accuracy in close relationships, either by activating self-serving biases [326] or by restricting the acquisition of new information and the retrieval of old information.

5. Certain situational factors should also impair the perceiver's empathic accuracy. As likely candidates, Ickes and Simpson [283] have targeted situational factors that either (1) draw the perceiver's attention away from their partner's behavioral cues that are relevant to the inferential task (such as being absorbed in one's own thoughts about what to say next), or (2) require difficult, novel, or unfamiliar inferences to be made.

☐ Empathic Accuracy: Is It Good or Bad for Relationships?

Is empathic accuracy good or bad for relationships? At first glance, the answer to this question seems obvious. To the casual observer who relies on conventional wisdom, the apparent answer is, "Of course empathic accuracy is good for relationships; if everyone just understood each other better, the world would be a wonderful place."

When we think about it, though, there may be times when an accurate understanding of the thoughts and feelings of one's partner could actually harm or destabilize the relationship. Thus, while accurate understanding should be good for relationships as a general rule, too much understanding in certain contexts may have a negative outcome. In the following sections, we briefly review some theory and research that will help to disentangle the general rule from its important exceptions.

The Rule: Empathic Accuracy Is Good for Relationships

Many studies in the *marital adjustment literature* have documented a positive association between marital adjustment and understanding of the attitudes, role expectations, and self-perceptions of one's spouse (see [313] for a review).

Similarly, the *empathic accuracy literature* also provides some evidence that partners' accuracy in inferring each other's thoughts and feelings is associated with positive relationship outcomes. Bissonnette, Rusbult, and Kilpatrick [270] reported that high empathic accuracy was significantly correlated (r's in the range of .4 to .6) with such variables as commitment to the relationship, willingness to accommodate the partner's bad behavior, and adjustment to the partnership (dyad). These effects, which were found when the couples were in the first 12 to 18 months of their marriages, generally lessened over time, so that only the couple-level correlation between empathic accuracy and dyadic adjustment was still significant (.35) two years later. Bissonnette and colleagues speculated that the positive effects of empathic accuracy on relational outcomes may decrease over time for couples who, having learned each other's idiosyncratic cognitive, emotional, and behavioral quirks, have developed habits that automatically accommodate them.

If the link between empathic accuracy and positive relationship outcomes is likely to be most evident in the earlier stages of a relationship, it makes sense that empathic accuracy was significantly related to marital adjustment in Bissonnette and colleagues [270] newlywed sample but was not significantly related to marital satisfaction in Thomas, Fletcher, and Lange's [322] sample of longer-married couples. From this standpoint, it also makes sense that Ickes, Stinson, Bissonnette, and Garcia [291] found that opposite-sex strangers were more accurate in inferring each other's thoughts and feelings to the extent they found each other physically attractive, because—like the recently married couples in the Bissonnette et al. [270] study—they were presumably highly motivated to monitor each other closely and try to achieve a "shared cognitive focus." In general, then, the available empathic accuracy studies offer more evidence that empathic accuracy contributes to positive relationship outcomes, particularly during the formative stages of close relationships.

Collectively, these studies support the view that, as a rule, more understanding (i.e., greater empathic accuracy) is good for relationships. Noller [301–303] and Sillars (e.g., [312]), however, have questioned the generality of this rule. They argue that the association between understanding and marital adjustment is more complicated than earlier theorists and researchers supposed. In addition, recent empirical and theoretical work indicates that circumstances may exist in which greater empathic understanding might actually *reduce* partners' satisfaction with their relationships.

The Exceptions: When Empathic Accuracy Is Bad for Relationships

To date, Sillars and his colleagues (e.g., [311], [314]) have done the most integrative theoretical work on the question of when empathic accuracy might be bad for relationships. In a recent review, Sillars [312] suggested three such conditions:

1. *Irreconcilable differences.* When the partners' thoughts and feelings involve irreconcilable differences that cannot be resolved through greater clarifications of each others' respective views about an issue, greater empathic accuracy should increase the level of conflict and dissatisfaction in the relationship [268], [297].
2. *Benevolent misconceptions.* When benevolent misconceptions facilitate the stability and satisfaction that partners experience in their relationship, enhanced understanding that alters or destroys these misconceptions should destabilize the relationship through the decreased satisfaction of one or both partners [298].
3. *Blunt, unpleasant truths.* When the partner's words and actions cause the perceiver to experience pain and distress because they appear to express blunt, unpleasant "truths" rather than tactful and benign interpretations of the perceiver's character, motives, or behavior, increased understanding of the partner's thoughts and feelings should impair relationship stability and satisfaction [268], [305], [325].

What do these three conditions have in common? They all represent cases in which greater empathic accuracy leads to insights that are not only painful and distressing to one or both partners, but also raise doubts about the strength and permanence of their relationship.

☐ A Theoretical Model of How Empathic Accuracy Is "Managed" in Close Relationships

To further specify the conditions in which empathic accuracy will either benefit or harm close relationships, Ickes and Simpson [283], [284] have proposed a theoretical model of how empathic accuracy is "managed" by relationship members. The following is adapted by Ickes and Simpson [283], [284].

This model starts by assuming that the range of empathic accuracy (the upper and lower boundaries) that can be attained by a couple in a given interaction is set by respective levels of their (a) "readability," and (b) the partners' respective levels of empathic ability (the degree to which each partner can accurately decipher the other's valid behavioral cues). Within these broad constraints, however, the model presumes that empathic accuracy should be "managed" very differently depending on several factors. The most fundamental elements are shown in Figure 7.1.

Figure 7.1 characterizes behavior at the individual, rather than the dyadic, level of analysis. According to the model, each partner makes a preliminary assessment of whether or not the current situation is likely to evoke a *danger zone* topic or issue in the relationship. The term "danger zone" means having to confront a topic or issue that could threaten the relationship by revealing thoughts or feelings harbored by one's partner that might distress or upset the perceiver.

Of course, everyone is different in what he or she finds upsetting in their partners' thoughts and feelings. Male partners, for example, might find their female partner's thoughts about her actual or potential sexual infidelity more threatening than her thoughts about her actual or potential emotional infidelity, whereas the reverse might be true for female partners [271]. Thus, the model begins by acknowledging that relationship partners can follow different "paths" or trajectories if one partner anticipates a danger zone emerging in the current situation whereas the other partner does not. Although developing the theoretical implications of this more complex "dyadic" model is beyond the scope of this chapter, we consider a few of these implications below.

At the first branching point in the model, each partner infers whether the current situation is or is not likely to evoke a danger-zone issue. Let us first consider the part of the model that applies when one perceives that a situation is nonthreatening in the sense that no danger-zone issue is likely to emerge that might force the partners to confront each other's deepest relationship-threatening thoughts and feelings.

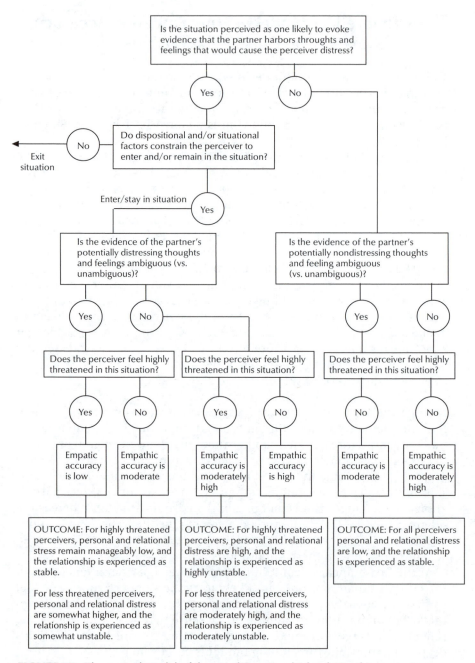

FIGURE 7.1. Theoretical model of the conditions in which relationship partners are motivated to accurately infer or *in*accurately infer each other's thoughts and feelings. Reprinted from Ickes and Simpson [284].

Empathic Accuracy in Nonthreatening Contexts

When perceivers expect to discuss issues that should not have threatening implications for their relationship (see the right-hand portion of Figure 7.1), the model predicts that they should be at least somewhat motivated to accurately infer their partners' thoughts and feelings. Because experience should have taught the partners that mutual understanding usually facilitates their ability to coordinate their actions in the pursuit of individual and dyadic goals, and because the behaviors needed to achieve such understanding typically become habitual through repeated reinforcement [270], perceivers should be motivated to attain at least minimal levels of accuracy when inferring their partners' thoughts and feelings in nonthreatening contexts.

Accordingly, in nonthreatening situations in which no danger zones are perceived (e.g., everyday conversations about trivial or mundane issues), perceivers should display a habit-based "accuracy orientation." This orientation should help them to clear up misunderstandings about nonthreatening issues, keep minor conflicts from escalating into major ones, and gain a deeper understanding of their partners, all of which should enhance feelings of satisfaction and closeness in the relationship. Thus, as long as situations do not lead perceivers to anticipate the emergence of issues that could evoke and reveal their partners' relationship-threatening thoughts and feelings, perceivers should be motivated to attain at least a moderate level of empathic accuracy.

On the other hand, the motivation of perceivers to be accurate should be attenuated to some degree by the routine, taken-for-granted nature of most mundane, nonthreatening interactions (cf. [321], [322]). The level of empathic accuracy displayed by perceivers in nonthreatening interactions should, therefore, be moderate to moderately high rather than high (see the lower right portion of Figure 7.1). Finally, levels of relationship satisfaction and stability should correlate positively with empathic accuracy in nonthreatening situations, consistent with the premise that higher levels of empathic accuracy are generally good for relationships. These effects may be small, however, because they are likely to be attenuated by the restricted ranges of both the empathic accuracy and the relationship-outcome variables in most nonthreatening interactions.

Empathic Accuracy in Relationship-Threatening Contexts

Inevitably, perceivers will encounter situations in which "danger zones" are anticipated—encounters that have the potential to destabilize their relationships (see the left-hand portion of Figure 7.1). When these situations arise, the model predicts that the first impulse of most perceivers should be to avoid or escape from them, if possible. In other words, the tactic of avoiding or escaping from danger-zone situations should be the first "line of defense" that perceivers can use to keep themselves from having to confront their partners' relationship-threatening thoughts and feelings.

The use of this tactic presumes, of course, that perceivers can recognize—and even anticipate—potential "danger zone" areas in their relationships (e.g., positive feelings about old flames or lustful thoughts about other attractive people). Over time, perceivers in most (but not all) relationships should learn to identify and avoid such danger-zone areas to protect their own self-esteem, their partners' self-esteem, and their cherished views of the relationship (cf. [300]). In doing so, perceivers can avoid dealing with danger-zone topics directly, based on the presumption that it is better (and easier) to avoid confronting one's worst fears than it is to have one's worst fears confirmed and then be forced to deal with them.

But we cannot always avoid danger-zone issues (see the left and middle portions of Figure 7.1). When perceivers feel that they have to stay in a relationship-threatening situation, the model predicts that they should use motivated inaccuracy—consciously or unconsciously fail to accurately infer the specific content of their partner's potentially hurtful thoughts and feelings—as their second "line of defense." How successful this will be will depend on whether the partner's distressing thoughts/feelings are perceived as ambiguous or unambiguous.

If the perceivers cannot identify what their partners are thinking and feeling (see the left-hand portion of Figure 7.1), they should be able to use motivated inaccuracy as a defense. Or if they deny, repress, or rationalize, to avoid having to deal with the most threatening implications of their partners' potentially destructive thoughts and feelings, perceivers should *mis*infer such thoughts and feelings and therefore display low levels of empathic accuracy. Their defensiveness should provide them with an important payoff, however, by decreasing their distress and by helping to keep their relationship more stable.

Simpson, Ickes, and Blackstone [316] reported some intriguing evidence that romantic partners may indeed use motivated inaccuracy to ward off impending threats to their relationships. Eighty-two dating couples took turns rating and then discussing with each other the desirability of several opposite-sex persons as "potential dating partners." Immediately afterward, the members of each couple independently viewed a videotape of the rating-and-discussion task. On the first pass through the tape, each partner listed all of the thoughts and feelings that he or she had had during the task. Then, on the second pass through the tape, each partner was asked to infer each of his or her *partner's* thoughts and feelings at the exact points on the tape at which they had been reported.

As predicted by Ickes and Simpson's [283], [284] model, partners who reported the greatest perceived threat to their relationships displayed the least empathic accuracy. Even more interesting is that all of the highly threatened/low-accuracy couples were still dating at four-month follow-up, whereas 28% of the remaining couples in the study had broken up. That is, couples who displayed the least accuracy in this relationship-threatening situation were the most stable at follow-up, suggesting that motivated inaccuracy might indeed function as a preemptive relationship maintenance strategy.

Just as the empathic accuracy model predicts, then, there appear to be circumstances in which motivated inaccuracy can actually help to stabilize and sustain relationships in the face of serious perceived threats. There are other circumstances, however, in which motivated inaccuracy is simply not an option. What happens, for example, when perceivers feel obliged to remain in a relationship-threatening situation but cannot use motivated inaccuracy as a secondary strategy for dealing with the threat? The middle portion of Figure 7.1 depicts one case of this type, in which the relationship-threatening content of the partner's thoughts and feelings is perceived to be clear and unambiguous (e.g., the partner openly admits that he or she loves someone else). Because the message is so blatant, the perceiver will be forced to have at least moderately high levels of empathic accuracy, along with, obviously, little relationship satisfaction or stability.

Clearly, this case is one in which increased empathic accuracy can actually harm relationships. However, because the perceiver is forced to be accurate by virtue of the sheer truth, this is not an illustration of a case in which *motivated* accuracy hurts relationships. Such a case should occur, however, if the perceiver has a strong personal need to confront the truth about the partner's relationship-relevant thoughts and feelings. Recently, Simpson, Ickes, and Grich [315] demonstrated that more anxiously attached (preoccupied) dating partners tend to display motivated accuracy (rather than motivated inaccuracy) in response to at least one type of relationship threat—the possibility of breaking up. This finding suggests that a strong, dispositionally-based accuracy motive can override such tendencies as avoiding danger-zone situations or using motivated inaccuracy to stave off relationship-threatening information.

☐ Conclusions

In this chapter, we have examined several aspects of EI and empathic accuracy as they relate to friendships and dating relationships. Knowing one's partner "from the inside," as friends and dating partners typically come to do, can facilitate empathic accuracy for the partner's thoughts and feelings. But just because we have the information does not mean we will use it well. This depends on many factors that include characteristics of the perceiver (empathic ability, attentiveness, motivation, attachment orientation), characteristics of the target (self-directedness, consistency, coherence), and characteristics of their relationship (e.g., intimacy and relationship discord).

A perceiver can become more empathically accurate by getting to know the target better (although there are limits to the acquaintanceship effect), and by obtaining feedback about the target's thoughts and feelings. On the other hand, if couples want to reduce their tendency to lose empathic accuracy for each other's thoughts and feelings over time, they would do well to act a little more like strangers in some respects—paying close attention to each other's behavior during interactions and attempting to maintain a shared cognitive focus.

Research and theory have also suggested factors that may impair empathic accuracy in close relationships. These factors include the target's inability or unwillingness to express thoughts and feelings, the perceiver's inability or unwillingness to interpret the target's behavioral cues, and the perceiver's current level of stress. And, paradoxically, there are at least three reasons (overconfidence, interdependence, strong emotional involvement) why knowing one's partner *too* well can also contribute to a lack of empathic accuracy.

Perhaps the most interesting aspect of empathic accuracy is its capacity to generally help, but sometimes hurt, close relationships. Ickes and Simpson [283], [284] present a theoretical model that not only specifies the conditions in which empathic accuracy will either benefit or harm close relationships but also examines the processes by which empathic accuracy is "managed" by relationship partners.

Maurice J. Elias
Lisa Hunter
Jeffrey S. Kress

CHAPTER 8

Emotional Intelligence and Education

What does it mean to be educated? The current view is that to be educated involves being knowledgeable, responsible, and caring, and many would add, nonviolent [343]. It means that the traditional focus on intellectual skills—IQ—must be supplemented by a strong concern with social and emotional skills—"EQ," the skills of emotional intelligence (EI). The reasons for this are many, but none are more compelling than what we have learned about brain function, human memory, and the difference between learning for test performance and learning for the purpose of living one's everyday life. For the latter, social and emotional factors are paramount.

A primary principle of EI is that caring relationships form the foundation of all genuine and enduring learning [358]. A moment's reflections on one's own educational experiences will reveal the fundamental truth of this point of view. We all have learned under adverse conditions, but it is not the best way to produce regular and lasting learning, and we need to bring our educational systems into alignment with this reality.

Although EI recently has received a lot of attention, the concept is not new. In the 1920s and 1930s, the psychologist E. L. Thorndike proposed that social intelligence, the ability to understand others and act appropriately in interpersonal relations, was one aspect of a person's IQ [347]. Thorndike's view of social intelligence as an important component of IQ, however, was not particularly popular at the time or the subject of much research.

John Dewey thought deeply about the nature of classrooms and concluded that they were places where students had to learn about democracy: the skills needed to preserve it, the reflective state of mind needed to advance it, and the social and emotional climate needed to convey it. To Dewey, there was a seamless relationship between the material to be learned, the context in which it was learned, and the arenas to which that learning needed to be applied [336]. In his book, *How We Think*, Dewey [335] outlined many of the skills that we view as necessary for citizens in a democracy—not only analytic skills, but also skills for perspective taking, social debate and exchange, and interpersonal commerce.

In the 1980s, the work of Robert Sternberg and Howard Gardner rekindled interest in social/emotional intelligence. Sternberg found that when asked to describe an "intelligent" person, social skills were among the characteristics listed by subjects [363]. He emphasized the value of social intelligence and distinguished it from academic abilities.

Howard Gardner, famous for his concept of multiple intelligences, added a cross-cultural perspective. By examining a range of social contexts and ethnic groups across many countries, Gardner was able to identify seven intelligences that are essential to effective human functioning. In addition to the two areas held as essential in American education, logical–mathematical and verbal–linguistic intelligences, Gardner also identified interpersonal and intrapersonal intelligences. Gardner [345] defined interpersonal intelligence as "the ability to understand people: what motivates them, how they work, how to work cooperatively with them" (p. 9). He defined intrapersonal intelligence as "the capacity to form an accurate, veridical model of oneself and to be able to use that model to operate effectively in life" (p. 9). Clearly, these are precursors to what we now have come to understand as EI.

In the early 1990s, Educators for Social Responsibility took the work of Dewey and others to the next level when it called for schools to make all children socially engaged and responsible [330]. An array of skills was identified that allowed children to move in the world as students and as citizens, including skills for group participation, decision making, and social awareness. This work began to integrate theoretical and research knowledge with a strong advocacy perspective designed to help bring the new ideas into the mainstream of education.

Despite this compelling historical background, however, it was the recent research of Mayer and Salovey [357], combined with the publication of Dan Goleman's 5-million copy best-selling book, *Emotional Intelligence* [347], that has put EI and its applications on the public, professional, and scientific agendas. According to Mayer and Salovey [357], emotional intelligence involves:

the ability to perceive accurately, appraise, and express emotion; the ability to access and/or generate feelings when they facilitate thought; the ability to understand emotion and emotional knowledge; and the ability to regulate emotions to promote emotional and intellectual growth. (p. 10)

This model proposes four branches of EI (perception, appraisal, and expression of emotion; emotional facilitation of thinking; understanding and analyzing emotion; and reflective regulation of emotions) that are arranged in order from the most basic psychological processes to the more psychologically integrated processes. (See Chapter 1 for a complete description of this model.) Within each branch, there are representative abilities, which develop along a continuum. The model emphasizes the diversity and intricacy of the concept. Emotional intelligence is not a single ability. Rather it is a set of abilities that ranges from the relatively simple, such as distinguishing emotional facial expressions, to the more complex and integrated, such as understanding the causes and consequences of emotions in everyday interpersonal situations and how they interplay with motivation.

In his book, *Emotional Intelligence*, Daniel Goleman also emphasizes the multiple aspects of EI. Drawing from the work of Mayer and Salovey, Goleman [347] identifies five domains of EI: knowing one's emotions, managing emotions, motivating oneself, recognizing emotions in others, and handling relationships.

The definitions of EI offered by Mayer and Salovey and Goleman highlight the central role it plays in human interactions. Emotional intelligence is likely to be involved in the home, school, work, and other settings. Given the broad scope of EI, considerable attention has been paid to how it can be enhanced.

Emotional intelligence is made up of a set of skills, and most skills can be improved through education [357]. Thus, it is not surprising that we should look to schools as the prime location for the promotion of EI. Goleman [347] considers schools as "the one place communities can turn to for correctives to children's deficiencies in emotional and social competence" (p. 279). The learning of emotional skills, however, begins at home, and children enter school at different "emotional starting places" [357]. As such, schools face the challenge of teaching as well as remediating the emotional skills of children. This challenge can be met by infusing emotional literacy into the standard curriculum as well as creating school climates that foster the development and application of emotional skills.

The Collaborative to Advance Social and Emotional Learning (CASEL) was founded in 1994 by Daniel Goleman and Eileen Rockefeller Growald to establish social and emotional learning (SEL) as an essential part of education from preschool through high school. CASEL accomplishes its work by advancing the science of SEL, translating our best knowledge into effective school practices, helping to prepare and train educators to carry out SEL, and creating networks of scientists, educators, advocates, policymakers, and interested citizens, all linked through its website, www.CASEL.org. CASEL has emerged not only as the national voice of SEL in the schools, but also as an international center. It has given rise to systematic, collaborative efforts to promote SEL in the schools in Denmark, Sweden, Israel, and Great Britain. CASEL also serves as the hub of a network of numerous other SEL initiatives.

At this point, we would like to take a step backward and fill in some of the details about how and why EI fits into education. After we provide some examples, we conclude by addressing the areas in which we expect exciting future progress to take place.

☐ How Does Emotional Intelligence Fit into Education?

The State of Mental Health/Prevention in the Schools

Because most children go to school, focusing efforts on promotion of social competence and prevention of problem behaviors in the schools makes sense. Schools are also an ideal place for prevention, because research indicates low school achievement is a major risk factor for a host of problem behaviors such as drug abuse and delinquency [365]. Thus, school-based prevention efforts can protect against the development of problem behaviors as well as promote mental health.

Although we know how important school is in preventing problem behaviors and promoting mental health, the scope of such efforts varies widely. Six types of school-based programs for elementary-age children and adolescents have been identified: (a) school-level organizational strategies, (b) classroom climate and structure, (c) social-competence-enhancing programs, (d) targeted prevention programs, (e) comprehensive health education programs, and (f) multicomponent strategies [365].

School-level organizational strategies aim to help collaborative and productive relationships among the key stakeholders in a school community (i.e., administrators, teachers, parents, and students). These relationships can help a school coordinate its prevention efforts and create a climate conducive to learning and the promotion of mental health. This is especially important when addressing such areas as smoking and other substance use. James Comer's School Development Program [334] and the Positive Action through Holistic Education (PATHE) project [348] are examples of promising coordinated school-level organizational development and planning strategies.

Prevention programs that focus on *classroom climate and structure* seek to enhance students' school performance and social behavior. These programs try to achieve this goal by increasing classroom opportunities for active participation in learning and the development of supportive relationships with adults and peers. Success for All (SFA) [362], an example of such a program, focuses on offering high-quality curriculum instruction, frequent assessment of children to assure adequate progress, and cooperative work with parents. The Child Development Project [329], the Seattle Social Development Project [352], [353], and the School Transitional Environment Project [353] are other examples of successful prevention programs at the school-organizational level.

Among the most effective *social-competence enhancement programs* identified by CASEL [332], [343] are the New Jersey–based Social Decision Making and Social Problem Solving Project; the Promoting Alternative Thinking Strategies (PATHS) curriculum, based at Penn State University; the Massachusetts-based Responsive Classroom and Open Circle programs; the Lions Club-Quest International program based in Ohio; the spiritually focused Passages program of Rachael Kessler in Colorado; and, on the West Coast, the Raising Healthy Children and Second Step programs. All these programs share a common focus on developing and improving children's self-control, stress management, problem-solving, and decision-making skills, as well as building their affective awareness and reflective capacities.

Targeted prevention programs have a more specific focus than the programs discussed so far and aim to prevent identified problem behaviors such as substance abuse, high-risk sexual behavior, or violence. These types of programs will be discussed in more detail in the section on guidelines for establishing EI programs in schools.

Comprehensive health-education programs are designed to promote the mental and physical health of students and prevent an array of health-compromising behaviors (e.g., high-risk sexual behavior, smoking, substance use). Some of the more successful health-education programs, as identified by Weissberg and Greenberg [365], include the School Health Curriculum Project, the Teenage Health Teaching Modules, and the Minnesota Heart Health Program [355].

Multicomponent prevention strategies target several domains of functioning (i.e., academic, social, and health behaviors) and are typically implemented on a school-district or community level or both. Examples from Weissberg and Greenberg [365] include the New Haven School Development Project and Communities that Care.

The various school-based prevention programs described by Weissberg and Greenberg [365] and CASEL share a common focus on enhancing the lives of children and preventing problem behaviors. The programs differ, however, in the extent to which they involve the entire school community in these efforts. Overall, it appears that more inclusive programs are more likely to have a lasting impact on social–emotional and learning outcomes in children.

EQ Makes a Difference in Education:
Four Exemplary Programs

There is much evidence that shows programs to promote social and emotional learning/EI are effective. Elias, Zins, Weissberg, and Associates [343] and Weissberg and Greenberg [365] give summaries, and they can be found on the CASEL website, www.CASEL.org. Here, we provide information from four exemplary programs so that readers can better understand what they try to accomplish and what kinds of outcomes they have achieved.

The Child Development Project (CDP) focuses on creating schools in which children feel part of a caring community of learners. In the classroom, children learn the skills of EI, how to cooperate on academic tasks, and how to develop self-control. This is complemented by schoolwide community-building activities to promote a sense of bonding and parent involvement activities to build family–school partnerships. Results from experimental studies over many years included program-related improvements in substance use, social skills, and the degree to which students felt their school was a community [328]. A program with similar emphases, the Seattle Social Development Project, not only found positive results in more than a decade of research in such factors as discipline and substance abuse, but also found that how involved teachers were in implementing the program could predict students' actual classroom involvement, reinforcement for involvement, and higher student bonding to their school [327].

Many programs have integrated into school curricula and focus on providing students with intensive, ongoing opportunities to build their EI skills over multiple years. Promoting Alternative Thinking Strategies (PATHS) emphasizes teaching students to identify, understand, and self-regulate their emotions. In a randomized controlled trial with 200 second- and third-grade regular education students, children showed improvements on social problem solving, emotional understanding, self-report of conduct problems, teacher ratings of adaptive behavior, and cognitive abilities related to social planning and impulsivity. Improvements were maintained at one-year follow-up, and additional significant reductions in teacher and student reports of conduct problems appeared at two-year follow-up. Similar results also were obtained for children with special needs [349], [350]. The Social Decision-Making and Social Problem Solving Program focuses on skill building to promote social competence, decision making, group participation, and social awareness. In a two-year program given to students before they transitioned to middle school, Elias and colleagues found improvements in youth self-report of coping with stressors related to middle school transition and teacher reports of behavior. Children receiving the program were followed up after six years and continued to appear better adjusted that children in comparison schools. Boys who did not receive the program had higher rates of drinking alcohol, behaving violently toward others, and having self-destructive/identity problems compared with those in the program. Girls who did not receive the program reported higher rates of cigarette smoking, chewing tobacco, and vandalism relative to girls who were in the program [331], [339].

EI and Academics

Discussing the schools' role in promoting EI may lead us to ask: "If schools focus on social and emotional issues and promote EI, are they neglecting their role in teaching academics?" In fact, forms of this question often are raised by educators new to the idea of promoting social and emotional skills. One aspect of this involves practical concerns: Where will the time come from, in already packed curricula, to teach social and emotional skills? Another aspect is more theoretical and involves the mission of schools in general. Some view schools as places to learn academics—math, social studies, literature—whereas social and emotional skills should be learned elsewhere (i.e., the home, faith communities).

Although we do not dispute that the promotion of EI skills involves coordinated effort with parents and communities, we do take issue with the idea that EI and "academics" are in some way incongruent or at odds with one another. We see a convergence in efforts to build academics and EI. We have already outlined how social and emotional skills are intertwined with abilities needed for classroom success. But the connections go further.

EI and Academic "Standards"

When we look closer at "academics," we can see further similarities of curriculum content areas and EI and see that EI skills rest clearly within the central mission of the schools. Recently, much discussion over schools' academic mission has focused on the area of curriculum standards. Standards outlining expectations for student attainment for all content areas have been developed by each state for each level of education. Each state has codified, for example, the social studies skills students should have when they complete eighth grade. An analysis of curriculum standards reveals that expectations for curriculum attainment contain many essential EI skills. For example, in analyzing literature, students are expected to be able to understand the feelings and motivations of characters. In social studies, students should understand the consequences of historical events. A literature lesson that does not touch on the goals of characters or the emotions that a poem stir in a student misses an EI "teachable moment" *and* overlooks an important aspect of the academic content area. Similarly, if we study just the dry facts of historical events, we may well repeat our past mistakes. It is clear that the role of schools in promoting academic competence and EI cannot be separated [360].

Taking this even further, the state of New Jersey has added a section of Cross Content Workplace Readiness Standards, which makes it clear that children are expected to learn skills such as decision making, self-awareness, getting along with others, effective communication, self-presentation, and motivation. An instructive case study can be drawn from the New Jersey State Core Curriculum Cross Content Workplace Readiness Standards. The first of these focuses on career planning and workplace readiness skills and contains indicators, which include skills in decision making, self-awareness, getting along with others, self-presentation, effective communication, and motivation. Think of the standards as the blueprint for tomorrow's workforce and the qualities of people we would like to see in our workplaces. Emotional Intelligence skills are indeed "cross content" because they are important throughout the school day and in productive life outside the school, not just in one particular subject area [360].

At the time we were writing this chapter, an important line of research was beginning to focus on the link of EI to students performance on standard academic tests. Preliminary research in Israel by Reuven Bar-On and in the United States by the four exemplary programs mentioned earlier, as well as by the Northeast Foundation for Children, provides encouraging data that suggest the important role that social–emotional learning and EI play in all aspects of children's functioning in school, including academic achievement. (See www.CASEL.org to monitor the continued progress of this research.)

☐ Guidelines for Implementing Emotional Intelligence/Social and Emotional Learning in Schools

For reasons not hard to figure out, schools have been slow to incorporate EI/SEL into their structure. Schools continue to be test driven and focused on a narrow range of academic outcomes, in part because they lack clear guidance as to how to proceed differently. Fortunately, work has been done to help schools incorporate new ideas about what it means for our children to be "educated."

What is needed is not "either–or" thinking, but rather a "both–and" point of view. As noted earlier, children need to be knowledgeable, responsible, *and* able to deal effectively with their emotions. Our education system must work for the integration of all these. Our schools have long and frequently suffered from a program-of-the-month approach, as a revolving door of disconnected, narrow, problem-specific programs have been invoked in schools, typically in response to crisis. The response to tragic shootings such as occurred in Columbine High School, or when there is a suicide in a school, are clear examples. The result, even when the specific programs that are put in place have been individually acclaimed, is educational chaos. This is represented by the jumble of puzzle pieces in the schoolhouse figure (Figure 8.1).

What is needed is represented by the bottom schoolhouse. Here, SEL provides synergy. Under this conceptual umbrella, an array of life skill promotion and problem behavior prevention efforts can be organized and unified in a proactive way. There is continuity and coordination. Because we know children bring their problems to school with them, we can help them, we can help them by having an SEL firmly in place as a facet of schooling. As children see schools as places where their social and emotional needs are addressed in a focused and concerned way, they are likely to open themselves up to academic learning to a greater degree.

CASEL has established a set of guidelines for schools to use to bring their jumbled programs into synergistic organization [343], [358]. The first of these, presented below, provides clear guidance to schools as to how to organize their SEL efforts.

Educators at elementary, middle, and high school levels need explicit plans to help students become knowledgeable, responsible, and caring. We need to build and reinforce skills in four major SEL domains:

1. *Life skills/positive social competencies* involve generic life, health, citizenship, and workplace skills such as problem solving, assertiveness, self-confidence, decision making, and problem solving; social skills; family

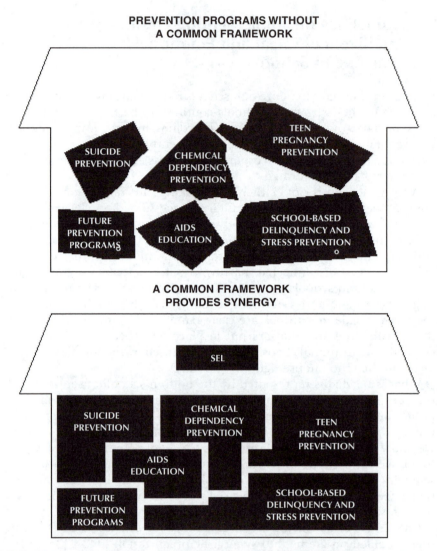

FIGURE 8.1. An integrated and coordinated framework provides synergy.

life/sex education; stress management; communication skills; and spiritual development.
2. *Health promotion, problem prevention/risk reduction skills* include strategies and behaviors related to specific problems such alcohol, tobacco, drugs, violence, AIDS, sexually transmitted diseases, premature sexual behavior, delinquency, suicide, as well as positive health behaviors and lifestyles.

3. *Conflict resolution and coping and social support for transitions and crises* involve systematic structures for conflict resolution, corrective discipline, positive adult modeling and caring, career and future (postgraduation) planning, and event-triggered coping and support. (The latter refers to prevention-oriented services that are available and initiated when critical life events occur, such as divorce or serious parental illness, rather than after a child has experienced severe behavioral or learning disruption as a consequence of one of these life events.)

4. *Positive, contributory service* includes within-class and cross-age tutoring and mentoring; classroom, school, or community service; buddying; and serving as peer mediator, orienter for new students, and assistant for special needs/special education students.

☐ School-Based Applications of SEL: Emotional Intelligence across Domains

Domain 1: Primary Prevention via Curriculum-Based Programs

The Social Decision Making and Social Problem Solving (SDM/SPS) Program [338], [340] is a broad-based preventive intervention, focusing on the promotion of social competence in the schools. Effective implementation targets an entire classroom, grade level, or school and addresses a range of social and emotional skills. In addition to its roots in social skills and problem-solving therapies, SDM/SPS is based on the premises of "primary prevention" (or intervention to a general population before problems occur) and ecological systems theory (focusing on how the program is implemented in a way that is matched to the context of a particular setting).

SDM/SPS was created in 1979 by a multidisciplinary collaborative that brought together the perspectives of clinicians, researchers, and educators on the issue of promoting social competence. These initial efforts grew into curricula for elementary and middle school classes. Although research, curriculum development, and training are based at the University of Medicine and Dentistry of New Jersey and at Rutgers University, it is the classroom teachers who are the primary program implementers and who introduce lessons to the students as part of regular classroom activities.

The skill areas addressed by SDM fall into the broad categories of self-control, social awareness, and problem solving. In the SDM curricular structure, the first two of these areas are included in the Readiness Phase of the curriculum, whereas the latter makes up the Instructional Phase. Conceptually, the readiness skills are seen as tools or building blocks that mediate problem solving and provide the social and emotional contexts to make solutions work. A third curricular phase, the Application Phase, focuses on bringing the self-control, social awareness, and problem-solving skills into academic and social situations.

The Readiness Phase consists of lessons emphasizing particular skill areas. The teacher who works with the students to develop a rationale and motivation for the use of this skill, introduces these lessons. He or she spells out clear and consistent expectations for the students' behavior. The teacher models the behavior and gives behavioral feedback in the classroom. The teacher also establishes a prompt for use of each skill that serves as common language that staff throughout the building can use to call for desired behaviors. Once students can successfully use the skill in classroom situations, teachers can then generalize and transfer the skill (to the playground, for example).

A key readiness self-control skill is a self-calming procedure called Keep Calm. A teacher may introduce this skill by leading a discussion of times when the students had difficulty staying under control, and what happened as a result. They may give examples of people with stressful occupations (for example, an athlete during an important point in a game) and discuss how this individual may handle the stress. The Keep Calm skill consists of four behavioral steps: (1) Tell yourself to "Stop." (2) Tell yourself to "Keep Calm." (3) Breathe in through your nose while you count to five, hold for the count of two, and exhale through your mouth to the count of five; keep doing this until you feel calm. (4) Praise yourself for a job well done. Teachers help students practice this skill in the classroom and prompt them, with the term "keep calm" to use it in increasingly stressful situations (e.g., before a quiz or test, or before dismissal). Teachers can give feedback and students can share times when they successfully used the skill in real-life situations.

In the Instructional Phase of SDM, students learn an eight-step strategy for decision making. The skills involved include recognizing feelings, identifying problems, setting goals, generating options, thinking about consequences, choosing a solution, planning, and observing outcomes. Students can use these skills in their academic subjects, such as when they consider decisions made by characters in a story or historical figures, as well as in interpersonal situations, such as during arguments at recess.

SDM aims to build self-control, social awareness, and problem solving in elementary and middle school students. The approach to EI promotion is characterized by addressing a broad range of skills to an entire "population" (be it a classroom, grade level, school, or district) of students rather than a specified risk group.

Domain 2: Problem Behavior Prevention: Violence

We must target prevention programs specifically at problem behaviors, such as smoking, taking drugs, and acting violently, and at appropriate developmental periods. Ideally, these will be carried out in a way coordinated with the particular primary prevention curricula in their schools. We use the example of violence prevention, because, as Noguera says, "concerns about violence have even surpassed academic achievement . . . as the highest priority for reform and intervention" in the schools [359].

There are two violence prevention approaches that we want to highlight. Many schools have implemented conflict resolution programs, but our focus here is on a curriculum-based approach presented to all students, whether or not they have been involved in conflicts. The Resolving Conflict Creatively Program (RCCP), founded by Linda Lantieri, is based on teaching all students how to settle school arguments that may escalate into violence. Students learn how to recognize and name feelings, how to empathize with the feelings of others, and how to stand up for themselves without resorting to violence. The program also trains some students to be mediators who are available to help resolve conflicts where they are most likely to occur: the cafeteria and playground. Data suggest that RCCP has a positive impact on children's hostile attributions and aggressive problem-solving strategies [354].

A more general skills-training approach to preventing violence comes from the significant body of literature demonstrating that "aggressive children and teenagers display a variety of interpersonal, planning, aggression management, and other psychological skill deficiencies" [346, p. 34]. Positive Adolescents Choices Training (PACT) helps children make non-violent choices in anger-provoking situations and has identified six key areas for skill development: (1) giving positive feedback, (2) giving negative feedback, (3) accepting negative feedback, (4) resisting peer pressure, (5) solving problems, and (6) negotiating. Participants in the program, as compared with nonparticipants, had less involvement in violence-related school behavior and violence-related suspensions from school as shown in a preliminary report [351].

Conclusions about well-designed, targeted preventive efforts seem consistent across content areas. When they teach specific skills with sufficient frequency and intensity, they appear to have a positive impact. However, the evidence suggests that they are most effective when implemented systematically and in conjunction with multilevel, school-wide efforts to create a social–emotional skilled and caring school community [343], [364].

Domain 3: Programs for Transitions and Social Support: Divorce

When a child's parents separate and/or divorce, the child is faced with a wide array of stressors. These include the emotions of loss, guilt, blame, and anger, the cognitions of worrying about the future and about possible reconciliation, and the behaviors linked to having one's daily routines disrupted. Is there any doubt that difficult life events such as this impair the student's ability to learn in school? Yet it has been standard practice—until SEL theory came along—to wait until a child showed significant behavioral or emotional problems before providing any needed services.

A more humane and educationally sound approach is to provide event-triggered services: supportive services that are initiated once the school learns of a difficult life situation. Joann Pedro-Carroll has developed the Children of Divorce Project, operating out of the Primary Mental Health Project at the University of Rochester, so that children can receive peer support and skill building as early as possible. Meeting in groups, children learn to recognize the common feelings they are experiencing, find out about misconceptions, and learn stress management and problem-solving skills. One of the most important skills they learn is what problems they can try to solve and which ones are really beyond their control. They learn how to adjust to new routines and painful feelings, often by calling upon their peers for support.

Data consistently confirm the benefits of the program in terms of positive mental health and reduced problem behaviors, and the schools report fewer disruptions of the learning process. The divorce program, or similar programs concerning bereavement, parental illness, incarceration, death, unemployment, relocation, changes in family structure, and the like, are most effective when the skills and concepts used are consistent with the curricular flow of programs in the first two domains described earlier [361].

Domain 4: Positive, Contributory Service

When CASEL went in search of the most effective empathy-building procedures in the schools, it concluded that there was nothing more powerful than an orientation toward positive, contributory service. It is better to begin as early as preschool, in Head Start programs, and not to wait until high school, which is where introduction to contributing service usually begins. In the early grades, all children need to learn that they are valued contributors to their classrooms and their schools. Getting to know and appreciate the diversity of students in their classroom and school communities helps build both empathy and perspective. Beginning in middle school, there are programs that help prepare children for service outside the classroom and broaden their perspectives.

The Giraffe Heroes Program teaches kids to "stick their necks out" and make a difference in their communities. It does so in part through understanding historical and local examples of heroes and what they did that made them special. Then they follow this with planning ways to address issues in their local communities (www.giraffe.org). Lions-Quest International's Skills for Action Program (www.Quest.edu) is based on an empirically supported process of organizing service learning experiences: preparation (find out who you are helping), action (provide meaningful service with real consequences, based on appropriate social–emotional and academic skills), reflection (keep records of your experience, discuss your thoughts and feelings, look at broader perspectives), and demonstration (show others what you have done, learned, accomplished through service, perhaps including carrying out projects in the community).

If programs are carried out in a coordinated and continuous way across all domains, there is greater likelihood that the synergy of the SEL-oriented schoolhouse will occur. But, there are certain conditions that need to be in place in schools to optimize both social–emotional and academic learning.

☐ What Needs to Happen in Schools for SEL Initiatives to Work?

Schools as Learning Communities

Even though there have been advances in research, many schools continue to address EI by implementing short-term, add-on programs. Although students may get short-term social–emotional benefits, the impact they have usually does not last. To truly improve the social–emotional lives of children and maximize learning, schools must become learning communities where social–emotional learning is integrated with academic learning. According to Comer [333] "acquisition of a reasonably high level of cognitive skills in knowledge is most often made possible through whole child development—physical, cognitive, psychological, language, social, and ethical" (p. 11). This means that students probably will not learn a subject well until all aspects of their development, including the social emotional, are addressed. Transforming schools into learning communities is one way to accomplish this goal.

Comer's School Development Program focuses on school as a learning community. Consensus, collaboration, and no-fault are the guiding principles of this program. These principles nurture a positive school climate that allows teachers, parents, and students to work together to promote learning [334]. By focusing on relationships and social processes, schools can become communities characterized by the kind of learning that becomes a true part of children's lives, rather than by learning for tests. As Comer puts it, "Strong relationships build community whether that community is in the classroom or among the teacher, parents, and students in the community of learners we call the school" [334, p. 46].

Preparation of Teachers and Administrators to Build Social–Emotional Learning

School personnel are confronted with issues of EI on several levels. Teachers must be concerned not only with the social and emotional skills of their students, but also must be aware of their own EI level and apply their EI skills. Administrators are concerned with the EI of students, teachers, and, of course, themselves. School personnel also are in contact with parents, who have different levels of EI and different ways of using their EI skills with their children. Further, because of various state mandates and programs, schools often are already running EI-promotion programs. For these reasons, it is important to assess teachers' and administrators' EI strengths, needs, and resources in the particular setting [343].

Trainers must introduce the importance of EI skills to teachers and administrators, discuss how school staff can be models of EI behavior, and train them in how to address these skills directly through curriculum-based instruction. To make the teacher training and program development appropriate to the particular context of the school, school-based personnel should take an active role in program planning and curriculum development. Trainers must be sensitive to legitimate reservations that staff might have regarding programming, such as how to fit EI instruction into an already busy school day [337]. Finally, staff should receive ongoing support and encouragement for efforts in the area of EI [356]. Teachers must be given opportunities to meet together to share successes and brainstorm solutions to obstacles to not only move programming ahead, but also to set a positive social and emotional climate for school personnel.

Parents Must Be Brought Along

Just as it is important for parents to support academic learning to improve progress, the same can be said for EI. Two resources have been developed for parents, based on the work of Daniel Goleman and CASEL and are consistent with their principles:

Emotionally Intelligent Parenting: How to Raise a Self-Disciplined, Responsible, Socially Skilled Child [341] focuses on applying EI to all areas of parenting, particularly issues related to schooling (homework, competition from media, after-school activities, and peers), time demands on all families, and the various interpersonal stresses and strains of the daily routine. This book has been published in eight international editions as of the time of this writing, showing the strong cross-cultural relevance of the issues addressed. *Raising Emotionally Intelligent Teenagers: Parenting with Love, Laughter, and Limits* [342] focuses especially on the stressors of school, relationships, career decisions, and family. There also is an EI quiz and a clinical corner chapter to help parents recognize the difference between normal teenage quirks and serious deficiencies in EI skills. These tools can help parents work in parallel with school-based efforts to build children's EI skills.

☐ Conclusion

Emotional intelligence now has an indelible place in education. Although educators recognize this, integrating it into the curriculum is slow. Guidelines provided by CASEL were presented to help schools systematically infuse SEL into their overall structure. Examples were provided for each of the four domains at which EI must be brought into the schools. In addition, EI theory suggests that schools must be set up as inclusive learning communities, with teachers and administrators being skilled in SEL and its implementation and parents using EI with their children. As CASEL and other organizations continue their collaboration, EI should move into an increasingly prominent role in education, which in turn will deepen students' academic learning and actually enhance progress toward meeting national and state education goals. The evidence thus far suggests that EI and social–emotional skills are necessary if our children are to grow up into adults who are going to be effective in their families, workplaces, and communities and are more likely to experience positive physical and mental health. It is an exciting area for future research and practice.

9
CHAPTER

David R. Caruso
Charles J. Wolfe

Emotional Intelligence in the Workplace

Consider, for a moment, the cases of an unhappy research analyst, a group of unproductive new associates, and a leader in charge of a floundering project team. Paul, a research analyst at a major securities firm, hated his job. Yet he felt that he had no choice except to tough it out and cope with the stress and job dissatisfaction. The job was a prestigious one, an important factor for Paul. More importantly, his father was a founding partner of another financial services firm and Paul knew his father would be devastated if he left the industry.

The client in the second case was John, the head of human resources (HR), who complained to us that productivity and morale were problematic among new associates. The associates had difficulty working with each other, experienced conflicts with senior staff, and had problems handling the stress of their roles. John told us, "I want to provide training for the associates that will help them better manage themselves in this competitive environment."

An e-commerce team was floundering. There was little enthusiasm for the project, with a lot of energy being expended in blaming others for the lack of progress. The team leader was not the cause of the problems, but, clearly, it was going to be up to Janet to turn the situation around.

What do an unhappy research analyst, a team with poor morale, and a floundering project have in common? On the surface, not much. But in each of these three cases, we applied the Mayer–Salovey four-branch ability model of emotional intelligence [376] (EI; see Chapter 1) to help diagnose and resolve the core problems. As readers of this book know, there are many approaches to EI. We utilize the Mayer–Salovey model in our consulting practice but integrate this model with other approaches to understand and optimize workplace performance. In this chapter, we discuss how we apply EI to career development, selection, training, and management development, and we offer a blueprint for EI workplace programs.

☐ Emotional Intelligence and Career Development

When clients approach us complaining about their jobs and saying that they want to leave, the first thing we try to find out is whether the dissatisfaction is due to the job itself (job activities), the environment (situational factors such as a dictatorial boss), or the person (personality traits such as depression and stress tolerance). In many instances, people are running from one situation only to re-create the same bad situation in a new place.

Our career development process relies heavily upon assessment, or testing. Typically, we use tests to evaluate a client's interests, work-related values, job skills, personality traits, interpersonal style, and EI. We use an ability measure of EI, initially, the Multifactor Emotional Intelligence Scale (MEIS), and then its successor, the Mayer–Salovey–Caruso Emotional Intelligence Test (MSCEIT). Both of these tests are based upon Mayer and Salovey's four-branch model of EI and yield scores for each branch, as well as a total EI score.

The first branch of the Mayer–Salovey model is identifying emotion in others and oneself. Often, self-reported skills in this area do not match the actual ability of a person to read others' emotions accurately. As a result, employees may miss critical information in their interactions with colleagues and customers, even though they may believe themselves to be emotionally perceptive.

The second branch is using emotions. This is the ability to use emotions to help achieve outcomes, solve problems, and capitalize on opportunities. The use of emotions to motivate and excite people has been a focal point of our professional practice.

The next branch is understanding emotions—the ability to understand complex emotions, what causes them, and how emotions change from one stage to another. With this knowledge, we can understand what might motivate or unmotivate individuals or groups and better plan how to work with them.

The fourth branch is managing emotions—the ability to manage emotions in yourself and in others. There are many possible responses to a workplace situation: deny the feelings, avoid the problem, acknowledge the situation but not process it, or utilize emotions to solve the problem and to integrate emotion and thought. How a person manages his or her own and others' emotions in the workplace can have a profound impact on job performance and satisfaction.

The MEIS and MSCEIT measure people's actual performance, rather than their self-reported skills, on emotional problem-solving tasks (see Chapter 2 by Ciarrochi et al. for a discussion of these tests). Performance on these ability tests is only slightly related to personality traits, as measured by self-report personality tests. But that is not the case with other purported tests of EI. In our view, other EI models and tests (sometimes called emotional or socioemotional competency models) are just repackaged models and tests of traditional personality traits such as optimism, motivation, and stress tolerance. Most workplace practitioners, us included, cover this ground by using a personality inventory such as the NEO [371] as part of the assessment process. The NEO measures five broad personality factors, each of which is broken down into six facets. The five factors are neuroticism, extraversion, openness, agreeableness, and conscientiousness. Neuroticism includes anxiety, anger, depression, impulsiveness, and vulnerability to stress. Extraversion's facets are warmth, gregariousness, assertiveness, activity level, stimulation seeking, and optimism. Openness is a measure of fantasy, openness to emotions, openness to new actions and intellectual curiosity, and openness to values. Agreeableness includes trust, straightforwardness, compliance, altruism, and tender-mindedness. Finally, the facets of conscientiousness are self-confidence, orderliness, duty, achievement motivation, self-discipline, and deliberation.

We address the interpersonal, or social components that some subsume under the EI banner by measuring the extent to which people are outgoing and warm, and how much they need or enjoy being included in groups and/or close to others. We typically use a simple test of interpersonal needs, the Fundamental Interpersonal Relations Orientations test (FIRO-B), to measure a client's expressed and desired social needs.

Let us look at Paul's career assessment results. He had very high interest and confidence in sales, marketing, design, analyzing, producing, and risk taking. He was somewhat anxious and a bit moody at times, but, importantly, he could handle stressful situations without falling apart. He was optimistic and open to new experiences. Paul also had a strong work ethic. Paul had excellent social skills—he was inclusive and warm—and he enjoyed working in a team environment. His MEIS results showed that he was okay at reading people, good at understanding others and managing emotions, but that he was brilliant at using emotions to think creatively. Here was a hidden asset, or ability, that was not being used in his job as an analyst.

After reviewing these results with Paul, we began to explore alternative career paths. Although he could adequately perform the analyst job, it was too narrow for him. In this case, it was the job, and not the person, that was at the root of the problem. Paul's skills—technical and emotional—could best be put to use in a broader, more creative role such as marketing. Initially, Paul resisted making any changes and unilaterally ended his career counseling program. He was struggling with crucial identity and acceptance issues. However, Paul eventually took action: His openness and flexibility won the day. Five months after our last meeting, Paul called to say that he had taken a job as the director of marketing for a new company a month earlier. The firm was in the same industry that he had tracked as an analyst. Thrilled with the new job, he said that for the first time in his career he was being challenged and was having fun. As for his father, he had resisted the change for a few weeks, but once he saw how happy Paul was, he came around and thought that the move was a great idea.

What Do We Know about Emotional Intelligence and Careers?

The story of Paul illustrates how EI—defined in different ways—plays a role in career development and selection. One of the difficulties with an emotional assessment approach to careers is that in the absence of hard data, the matching of personality traits or emotional competencies to different careers often is based upon the personal experience or bias of career development professionals. Unfortunately, such experience and bias may yield inaccurate perceptions of certain careers and a list of personality prerequisites that have little to do with successful performance in a particular job.

However, although this is true for EI, it is not true for personality models, which have decades of research behind them. For instance, Barrick and Mount [366] reviewed a number of research studies that examined the role of personality traits in three job areas: job proficiency, training proficiency, and personnel data such as salary, turnover, and tenure, for several types of careers. Using a popular personality framework known as the "Big Five" model, they found that people who worked hard (who were high on the trait called conscientiousness) were also higher on all three job criteria for all career areas. Extraverts performed better than introverts, but only for management and sales positions. People who were more creative and flexible (high on openness) tended to get more out of training, as did extraverts. Last, trusting and agreeable people (they scored high on a trait called agreeableness) did not differ from those who were cynical, skeptical, and aggressive. Those who were less anxious and depressed (high on emotional stability) did not perform better than people who were high on these traits. In fact, more anxious professionals performed better than their more emotionally stable peers!

Whereas another review by Tett and colleagues [380] found that job performance could be predicted from some of these traits, it is important to note here that the traits accounted for about 10% of the variation in measured job performance.

An extensive database of jobs and EI comes from work using the Bar-On Emotional Quotient Inventory (EQ-i; see Chapter 5), a self-report measure of 15 personality traits or emotional competencies (assertiveness, emotional self-awareness, empathy, flexibility, happiness, impulse control, independence, interpersonal relationships, optimism, problem-solving ability, reality testing, self-actualization, self-regard, social responsibility, and stress tolerance). Stein and Book [378] examined relationships between EQ-i scores and self-reported workplace success for thousands of people. The five most important EQ-i factors in terms of workplace success were self-actualization, happiness, optimism, self-regard, and assertiveness. Interestingly, Stein lists the top five factors for a number of different careers. For example, a group of 104 HR professionals rated the top five factors as happiness, self-actualization, optimism, assertiveness, and stress tolerance. Management consultants' top five were: assertiveness, emotional self-awareness, reality testing, self-actualization, and happiness. Engineers' five factors were self-actualization, happiness, optimism, empathy, and interpersonal relationships.

Not surprisingly, strong social and emotional skills seem to be part of getting the job offer that you want. Recent research by Kingsbury and Daus [375] suggests that mood management has an impact on interview success, and Caldwell and Burger [369] found that extraversion and agreeableness are related to getting more job offers.

Last, we cannot forget that some psychologists believe the best predictor of workplace performance is academic intelligence. At the same time, researchers such as Sternberg [379] have forcefully argued for the importance of other factors in workplace success such as successful or practical intelligence.

How to Use Emotional Intelligence in Career Development and Selection

As Paul's story illustrates, EI can play a role in career development if it is part of a comprehensive approach. We recommend a three-step process that incorporates EI into career development and selection.

Step 1—Specify the Job Description

The job's requirements need to be explicitly stated in behavioral terms or objectives. It is not good enough to state that a job requires *people skills*. Instead, we need to state that the job requires one-on-one customer interaction skills. In essence, the job description needs to be translated into a trait list. As part of this step, consultants would do well to review the literature on personality and job performance.

Step 2—Select Assessment Tools

Armed with a specific trait-based job description, the appropriate assessment tools can be selected. Assessment should focus on those areas that are not adequately addressed by existing selection methods (e.g., interviews and background checks).

Step 3—Evaluate and Recommend

Most evaluators rank order the job finalists or prepare individual summary reports. The test data should be part of the decision-making process, not a replacement for it. Issues of person–job fit must be addressed and strategies for developing the person and enhancing the fit offered.

☐ Emotional Intelligence and Training

John, the HR person with productivity and morale problems among new associates, asked for a one-day seminar to teach the group about EI and to enhance their skills. We explained that we could conduct a one-day seminar, or even a one-hour seminar, but that an effective program would take longer and consist of multiple sessions. We indicated that although knowledge can be imparted using techniques such as lectures, teaching EI skills needs a knowledge-based component and an *experiential* component.

We were able to conduct three sessions with the team, over a six-week period. Before the first session, we held several interviews with John to find out more about the organization, the team members, and the issues they faced. From these discussions, we drew up a plan of attack that combined knowledge-based and experiential components.

The first session started with cases from our own practice, and then brought in the participants' stories. We used lectures to present the structure of EI and its role in the workplace. Assessment featured prominently in our work: We had each participant take the MEIS and we used the results in two ways. First, the results provided a useful diagnostic for each individual. Second, we used the results to fine tune the workshop, focusing on areas of weakness while also providing ways for the participants to leverage their strengths.

We relied heavily upon case studies and role plays. The case studies were customized for this group, based upon our discussions with the HR person and the participants' experiences. We used the office as a living laboratory, setting up observation posts in different areas. Later, we returned to the training room to discuss our observations, develop optimal strategies, and then role play these strategies to cement the learning.

We structured the cases around the Mayer–Salovey model. A case would start with identifying how each person was feeling. We identified the mood of the group and why they felt the way they did. We discussed what would happen next. Then we generated and analyzed alternative management strategies. Training also was structured around the model. We had a unit on improving the accuracy of emotional identification, and another on strengthening the ability to see different emotional points of view. Practicing emotional strategies was another key, as was teaching more effective social behaviors, such as engaging others and listening carefully.

Assignments were given after each session so that the team members would use the skills they had learned during the workshop. The assignments included different exercises, observations in the office, keeping an emotions diary, and trying to be more aware of the emotional undercurrents in meetings.

Between-session communication and postworkshop follow-ups are important aspects of successful training. We required participants to send us e-mail with observations or cases between sessions to further their learning, encouraged them to utilize their training, and addressed their individual concerns and needs. Postworkshop follow-up is also critical to ensure that the material is retained and applied. Although many companies often balk at such extensive training, a small, but growing, number understand that the real payback from training comes from such intensive follow-up. In this case the company did not have the budget for formal follow-up work, but we strongly encouraged each participant to stay in touch with us by phone and e-mail to address ongoing issues and concerns.

Did it work? It did, at least in the short term. We know that we provided many people with new insights into themselves and their work style. We made a difference in their behavior and expectations. Postworkshop evaluations were extremely positive. Certainly, long-term impact could be enhanced if we had more formal access to the associates, but even our remote continued assistance seemed to be enough for the associates to maintain their newly acquired skills.

The Right Way to Conduct Emotional Intelligence Training

This multi-day workshop illustrates several principles for conducting EI training:

1. Determine the organization's goals.
2. Tie training to these goals.
3. Assess participants to understand their baseline skills and individual needs.
4. Revise the plan to reflect the skills and weaknesses of the individuals.
5. Provide structure for the sessions. We use the Mayer–Salovey four-branch model.
6. Stress the use of experiential exercises, case studies, and role plays.
7. Cases and examples should tie to the participant's real-world experience.
8. Provide opportunities for practice.
9. Provide multiple opportunities for feedback.
10. Use the group setting to demonstrate, teach, and role play social behaviors.
11. Address the unique needs of each individual privately.
12. Provide a means for follow-up support and reinforcement.

☐ Emotional Intelligence and Management Development

Group-based EI training programs can be cost effective. The cost per participant is relatively low, and resulting increases in productivity provide a high return on investment. In addition, because much of what is being trained happens in a group context, group workshops provide a real-world training ground. However, in-depth development often requires one-on-one training or *executive coaching*. Such coaching can be applied to individual managers as well as to teams.

Emotional Intelligence Coaching

As part of the coaching we were doing with a technology team, Janet, one of the high-potential managers, asked if we could continue coaching her while working with an e-commerce project team that she would be leading. Our role was to act as a team-building facilitator to help people work effectively across organizational boundaries. We accepted the challenge and attempted to minimize possible role conflict by making clear to the team that the team leader was our key client.

The difficulties surrounding the project were many. The team members represented different functional groups, each of whom have e-commerce projects that were planned for the year. The goal of the project team was to bring the groups together to develop an overall technical plan to promote efficiency and cost effectiveness. Although failure of the project would be costly, the team spent a lot of time blaming each other, refused to cooperate, and spent most of their energy defending their own turf. The organizational culture was hierarchical, and people were used to doing what they wanted without outside interference.

In our role, we anticipated difficulties that happen to cross-functional teams and used the Mayer–Salovey EI model as a guide for avoiding common pitfalls. We observed the team in action over a several-week period and debriefed key participants. It became clear that there was more to the problem than organizational politics. There was a great deal of negativity among the team members, finger pointing and lack of accountability. Janet was not the cause of these problems, but it appeared that it was up to her to turn things around. We formally evaluated Janet using the MEIS, with the following results:

Total MEIS score:	Average
Identifying emotions:	High
Using emotions:	Low
Understanding emotions:	Average
Managing emotions:	Average

Janet is very good at reading people. She attends to people's emotions and her perceptions are generally quite accurate. She can switch points of view and see an emotional situation from both points of view, although, at times, she may take emotional sides. Janet can effectively manage others' emotions, but at times she may not choose the optimal strategy.

Because moods can influence the way we think, remember, and make decisions, Janet's low score on using emotions suggested she may have a tough time generating a certain emotional state, getting the team to feel "up" or motivated to perform. In conversations with senior management, team members, and Janet herself, we also discovered that she had been known to drive others very hard and that some team members were nervous about having her as the lead. We generated a set of coaching objectives based upon the MEIS data, our observations, and discussions with Janet and the team:

1. To have Janet accept the results and objectives:
   - Focus on how her one low score may impact her performance.
   - Leverage her strengths to improve how she uses emotions.
2. Tie results to meaningful life events:
   - Improve her influence skills in situations where she does not have control.
   - Plan for emotions to have a positive impact on the e-commerce project team.
   - Tie team-building activities to the EI model. Help Janet learn how to use EI to positively impact the team's performance.

The key in working with Janet was to have her accept these results. We did so through conversations with her about critical team incidents and by leveraging her ability to understand emotions. Next, we had to tie the results into real working situations. When we can show the possibility of a payoff that impacts the manager's ability to perform more effectively by bringing a new product on line ahead of schedule, or improving a relationship with a difficult customer, we have much greater success with our coaching assignments.

So individual coaching sessions for Janet focused on team interactions, beliefs, and behaviors using the four-branch EI model. We discussed how people who are on the project feel and how we want them to feel (identifying emotions). Together, we planned strategies and tactics to overcome negative feelings and build on positive emotions (using emotions). For example, when we had to decide on how we would prioritize which projects got funding, we reached out to each participant separately and asked them to comment on, suggest modifications, or simply accept our model for decision making *before* we had to make a tough decision. We knew people would not review this on their own until it was time to make a critical choice, so we went over the process with each individual and insisted that he share it with his managers so there would be no surprises. The decision-making process was a success. We also identified ahead of time those participants who had potentially overlapping responsibilities for technical systems architecture. We worked with each of them individually and together with them and their bosses to make sure that the experience is both collaborative and successful (understanding emotions).

Regarding team members in general, we dedicated part of our time to calling each key project participant after the monthly meeting to determine how he was feeling about what took place at the meeting. When people have been concerned about issues, we discussed them with Janet and addressed them to the best of our combined ability (managing emotions).

Although we were guided by the model, we supplemented our approach by examining key personality traits (such as optimism and stress tolerance) and social behaviors (such as warmth and control) that we know are critical to leadership success.

As we write this chapter, the story of this team is not yet complete. However, senior management all recently spoke glowingly about the participants' efforts to date. One sure sign of growing success is that we now have to turn people away from attending the monthly meetings! In the beginning, it was hard to get people to show up. Perhaps the most gratifying sign of success is that a separate effort modeled on this group's work is being started in another part of the company. To Janet's credit, she is doing an amazing job managing many disparate elements and bringing them together to collaborate and achieve meaningful outcomes for her organization.

The Right Way to do Emotional Intelligence Coaching

Although there is no single way to conduct effective coaching, we offer a set of guidelines to help practitioners conduct successful EI coaching.

Get Their Attention

A major, public problem is often enough to motivate a leader to seek or accept the services of a coach. However, managers who lack self-awareness may require a more direct approach to get their attention. Sometimes, a 360-degree assessment can be used as a wake-up call for such managers. A "360" is often a formal assessment wherein a manager rates himself on many traits, as does the manager's boss, peers, and subordinates.

But almost every manager we coach comes along willingly. We meet with him and explain that the process is developmental in nature. We tell him that "If they wanted to fire you, they wouldn't spend all of this time, money, and effort on you."

Determine Required Competencies

The consultant must next determine what competencies are required by leaders in the organization. Input for this stage should start with the organization's own competency model, if one exists. Next, other models can be used to round out the analysis. Goleman [372] lists five clusters of emotional competencies: self-awareness (emotional awareness, accurate self-assessment, self-confidence); self-regulation (self-control, trustworthiness, conscientiousness, adaptability, innovation); motivation (achievement, commitment, initiative, optimism); empathy (understanding others, developing others, service orientation, diversity, political awareness); and social skills (influence, communication, conflict management, leadership, change catalyst, building bonds, collaboration/cooperation, team capabilities).

We find that most of these traits have been described, studied, and measured for years. For instance, in 1981, Yukl's leadership competency model [381] included a number of traits and skills. Traits include being adaptable, alert to social environment, achievement-oriented, assertive, cooperative, decisive, dependable, dominant, energetic, persistent, self-confident, tolerant of stress, and willing to assume responsibility. Skills include being intelligent, conceptually skilled, creative, diplomatic and tactful, fluent in speaking, knowledgeable about group task, organized, persuasive, and socially skilled. Also in 1981, Bass developed a leadership model [368] with these competencies: uses good judgment, knowledgeable, decisive, adaptable, alert, creative, has personal integrity, self-confident, emotionally controlled, independent, cooperative, popular, sociable, participates socially, and tactful.

In our work, we borrow heavily from these leadership theorists but ground our approach on the Mayer–Salovey four-branch model of EI. We find that these four skills have not been measured previously and only have been included tangentially in existing competency models. Inclusion of these four new competencies provides us with a structure for the coaching process and our clients with a competitive edge.

p. 33

?

Emotional Intelligence Assessment

The assessment phase is critical in successful coaching as it helps to identify the manager's skills and competencies. Many consultants run into problems by being wedded to a single assessment tool. For instance, if you employ a 360, then your entire focus is on observable behaviors— what a manager does. Bias, politics, and fear of retaliation can plague 360's, and for these reasons and others, we use this approach sparingly. But if you use a personality trait–based instrument, you only obtain information on what a manager thinks of himself. Utilizing the MEIS or MSCEIT tells you what underlying abilities, problems, and potential the person actually has.

In our work, we use multiple methods to measure key competencies. We often look at emotional stability, optimism, motivation, and other critical personality traits using a standard personality instrument such as the NEO [371] or California Psychological Inventory [373]. We examine a manager's social behavior, his social needs, and how these impact others' perceptions of the manager. We measure EI abilities via the MEIS or MSCEIT. The advantage of this assessment process is that it is comprehensive, does not focus solely on EI and is a confidential one, as only the coach and the manager are privy to the data.

Set Objectives

We meet one on one with the client to share the results of the assessments. In spite of e-mail and voice mail, we still find a personal meeting to be the best means of providing emotional intelligence feedback. In a face-to-face meeting, one can observe the client's body language, his acceptance of the results, his interest, and reaction to the feedback. Even more important, in terms of an EI feedback session, the skills can be demonstrated. For example, when a manager balks at his or her results for emotional identification, we can demonstrate the skill right then and there. I can ask how she is feeling, ask her how I am feeling, and discuss how these feelings are impacting our conversation about her scores. The whole model of identifying, using, understanding, and managing emotions can all be on display and applied to the client's perspective regarding his or her scores.

The specific goals of the feedback session are to (1) gain client acceptance of the results, (2) gain client agreement to discuss the applicability of the results, and (3) jointly develop a meaningful plan to address key deficiencies if they exist and/or determine how to leverage identified strengths.

Coaching Sessions

Next, we set a schedule that includes a combination of in-person and telephone coaching sessions. There are typically 10 biweekly sessions. It is a critical cornerstone of our work that we make sure the theoretical models we use are tightly connected to the person's real-world experience. Throughout the process, we ask individuals to use a reflective journal to capture their thoughts, feelings, and actions at different points during the coaching process.

Coaching sessions have an agenda. We get right to work, because we have been in communication with the manager via voice mail or e-mail. We discuss critical incidents, the manager's situation analysis, behaviors, and reactions, and then we analyze the response. If we can improve upon the process, we discuss how the manager can take this new approach and use it in the next situation. This always involves role playing and often provides a script for the manager to use to practice his lines. We employ the four-branch model as much as possible by (1) identifying the key player's emotions; (2) determining whether the mood facilitated the situation; (3) understanding why people felt the way that they did; and (4) discussing how they could best handle the situation.

For some clients, we become a shadow coach, or identify a person on staff who can serve in this role. A shadow coach follows the client to a meeting to observe the meeting and the client's behavior. Postmeeting discussion focuses on the client's read of the situation, his internal problem solving, and his behavioral approach to the situation. The shadow coach provides insight into each of these areas, providing the client with a corrective solution to a real-life, recent event.

Follow-Up

The progress that managers make in EI coaching can be remarkable. However, the gains can be lost if they fail to practice what they have learned. If coaching is tied directly to his everyday work activities, it is more likely that the manager will use these newly learned skills. Even then, practice and follow-up is critical. We recommend monthly follow-ups for several months, followed by a quarterly review. These reviews can be conducted over the phone or even via e-mail, because the coach–client relationship already has been formed.

Part of the follow-up involves checking in with the referral source or the manager's boss or peers. Although the coach can observe some of the manager's progress, much of it is hidden from view because it occurs in countless meetings and phone calls. There is an ulterior motive to this follow-up: It serves as an opportunity for the manager to reinforce to others the progress made during coaching. Many managers go through coaching and improve, yet they are not perceived as being different by others in the organization—especially those several layers removed from them. The manager must engage in self-marketing so that others' perceptions of them can be updated.

What Do We Know about Emotional Intelligence and Team Leadership?

As the case above demonstrates, the ability to use emotions, or generate emotions to facilitate problem solving, may play a role in team effectiveness. In fact, Sigal Barsade [367] of the Yale School of Management has conducted work on *emotional contagion*. She finds that the spread of positive emotions within teams facilitates cooperation, decreases conflict, and increases a team's rated effectiveness.

Rice [377], an American HR professional, administered the MEIS to

164 employees of an insurance company, as well as to 11 of their team leaders. The MEIS scores of the 11 team leaders correlated $r = .51$ with the department manager's ranking of those leaders' effectiveness. The correlation between average *team* MEIS scores and the department manager's ratings of the team performance for customer service was .46. The relationship between EI and performance was complex. For example, higher team leader EI, as measured by the MEIS, was negatively related to the manager's rating of the team's accuracy ($r = -.35$) in handling customer complaints, whereas performance ratings by team members correlated highly, and positively, with EI ($r = .58$).

An Australian research team led by Jordan [374] examined the performance of 44 teams over a nine-week period. Emotional intelligence was measured using a self-report workplace measure based on the Mayer–Salovey model. The researchers analyzed the performance of teams who were high or low on EI. At the start of the study, the high EI teams performed significantly better than did the low EI teams. By the end of the nine-week study, the performance of the low EI teams matched the performance of the more emotionally intelligent teams. It appears that EI can serve as a catalyst to team performance, allowing the team to quickly and efficiently form a cohesive group. Less emotionally intelligent teams seem to require more time to learn how to work effectively as a group.

☐ Conclusions

How Emotional Intelligence May Be Used at Work

What role might emotional abilities play in the workplace? Elsewhere, we have talked about how EI may contribute to leadership [370] but it likely plays a role in other aspects of work. Identifying emotions provides awareness of emotions and the ability to read accurately other people's emotions. Using emotions provides a means to generate ideas, a feeling, or a team spirit. Understanding emotions offers insights into what motivates people and others' points of view. Finally, managing emotions allows you to stay open to your emotions, which have valuable information, and use them constructively.

What of the other approaches to EI? Is there room for more than one point of view in this field? As we hope this chapter demonstrates, we urge workplace consultants to broaden their thinking about what skills, traits, or competencies they should study, train, and select upon. For instance, conscientiousness is an excellent predictor of job performance. Optimism is an important ingredient for some sales positions and certain leadership styles. Screening for high-stress positions may want to include stress tolerance. A person's expressed warmth and her desire for social interactions are critical aspects of many jobs. These traits and behaviors can be relabeled emotional competencies, but they are personality traits and behaviors that have been researched, measured, and trained upon for decades.

Developing Emotional Intelligence

The "new" news in EI views EI as a set of skills or as a form of intelligence. What happens, though, if you or a client does not possess these emotional skills? Can you actually increase your level of EI? As we hope we have demonstrated through our case studies, and some early research findings, it may be possible for a person to enhance their knowledge about emotions and to bolster their emotional skills. We next provide techniques that will help you or your clients learn more about emotions and provide for more effective emotion management strategies.

Reading peoples' emotions is a skill that can be improved. First, one must attend to emotional cues, especially in meetings and key one-on-one interactions. Second, one can learn to read between the lines when dealing with others. First, note whether the person's facial expression agrees with her words and her tone of voice. An example would be an employee who, when asked by her boss to work over the weekend, says, "no problem" while tightening her lips and frowning ever so slightly. When making sense of such discrepancies, the key is not to get caught up in the words, but also to be aware of the feeling conveyed visually.

Positive moods are believed to facilitate creative idea generation, whereas negative moods focus attention and facilitate analytic processing (such as reviewing a financial spreadsheet). Generating an emotion to help solve a problem, energize a group, or calm yourself prior to a big meeting or interview is also a skill that can be acquired. Relaxation techniques include breathing and progressive muscle relaxation. Visualization, imagery, and self-statements can assist you in becoming more upbeat and exciting, and perhaps more importantly, transmitting this excitement to others.

Sometimes people are able to understand emotions but they fail to pay attention to them. For other people, their thinking about emotions is faulty. It helps to ask why someone reacted the way he did. What was the other person feeling? You can also learn about emotions, what causes them, and what their functions are. For instance, anger usually arises out of a sense of wrong or injustice; we feel that someone is being unfair to us or to others. Disappointment or loss results in sadness, and mourning allows us to grapple with the idea that we will not have the thing we wanted.

If you have read the emotional situation accurately and understand the underlying emotional dynamics, then you will need to effectively manage the emotional situation. Mayer and Salovey identified four major ways in which most of us handle our emotional situations: defensive reaction, acknowledge and delay, social convention, and emotional management.

Defensive reactions keep emotions at arm's length, such as distracting oneself by watching a funny movie. This strategy can be fine in the short term. In a crisis situation, for instance, a minor problem does not have sufficient priority to be acknowledged and dealt with. Long term, a defensive coping strategy may not be effective because the underlying problem itself is never acknowledged or addressed.

The acknowledge and delay strategy initially recognizes the emotion but does not process it. For instance, a person might simply indicate the existence of a problem but does not expend energy thinking about it. This strategy can be effective in some situations where you need to simply acknowledge a problem or a feeling.

Social convention pays lip service to emotions by expressing awareness of the emotional component of a situation. Expressing your condolences to a grieving colleague, or indicating that you are angry with the way the negotiation was handled, are examples of this strategy if you merely express awareness but then drop any further reference to the emotion.

Emotional management, often the most effective way to manage emotions, begins with recognition of the emotions and then using them to solve the problem. For instance, a colleague makes a recommendation at a meeting that the team should use a certain vendor. This makes you uncomfortable, and you feel a little anxious. Anxiety signals that something bad may happen. Rather than ignoring this feeling, you use it to recall that the vendor had a quality problem a few years ago. You decide to speak to your colleague about this after the meeting.

Emotional management starts with awareness. An uncomfortable feeling signals that there is a problem. Analyze the situation by asking why are you feeling this way. Ask "what if" questions to help determine how different reactions to the problem will work out. Come up with alternative plans, and select the plan that has the best chance of succeeding. Include in your planning how others are likely to respond emotionally and how to use emotions to help you sell your plan.

Emotional Intelligence Has a Job to Do

Emotional intelligence's role in the workplace seems to be an important one. Yet the field is faced with some major issues. First, the approaches to the topic vary from traditional personality research to standard leadership research to a newer focus on emotional skills. Second, by defining any skill or trait that is not intelligence or expertise as "emotional intelligence," we are at risk of losing a rich history of science and practice. Third, although applied research on the Mayer–Salovey ability model is just beginning, it is likely that the relationship between EI and workplace outcomes is a complex one.

Of the several approaches to workplace EI, we believe that only the Mayer–Salovey ability model offers new and unique insights into career development, selection, team effectiveness, and leadership development. We urge researchers and practitioners alike to critically examine alternative approaches and hope that they see the power and broad applicability of the Mayer–Salovey approach to their work.

☐ Acknowledgment

Names and particulars of the cases presented in this chapter were altered to protect the confidentiality of our clients. Dr. Sigal Barsade designed and implemented much of the group training program described in this chapter. Given our preference for the ability model of Mayer and Salovey, we wish to disclose that Caruso is a codeveloper of both the MEIS and MSCEIT, that Charles J. Wolfe Associates distributes the MEIS commercially, and that MHS is the distributor of the MSCEIT.

CHAPTER

Peter Salovey

Applied Emotional Intelligence: Regulating Emotions to Become Healthy, Wealthy, and Wise

This chapter is going to be a little different from many others in this book. Rather than talk about emotional intelligence (EI) per se, I am going to discuss two particular applications of what we have learned about EI. The focus will be on staying physically well and on making good financial decisions: health and wealth. I will argue that the appropriate regulation of emotions is an important predictor of good health and a key to investing money wisely.

The view of EI that forms the backdrop for this chapter is that of Mayer and Salovey [409], [416] and their collaborators [417], [418]. This theory describes EI as a set of interrelated abilities organized along four dimensions: (a) identifying and expressing emotions, (b) using emotions, (c) understanding emotions, and (d) managing or regulating emotions. Although all four of these sets of skills may be important in staying healthy and accumulating wealth, in this chapter I focus only on the last of these four, managing one's feelings.

☐ Salubrious Consequences of Emotional Regulation

You are driving on the interstate and a car cuts in front of you at 70 miles per hour. Then the driver jams on the brakes. You do the same and feel yourself becoming enraged: "Where did this guy get his driver's license,

Sears?" Emotional challenges like this one present themselves every day: Should I express my anger—perhaps rolling down the window, yelling, or gesturing obscenely? Or should I "sit on" my emotions, suppressing them until, it would seem, they go away? The challenge of expressing versus suppressing is a fundamental dimension of emotional self-management. And I am going to argue in this section of the chapter that emotional expression and emotional suppression represent a double-edged sword: Both strategies can lead to health problems.

Emotional Expression and Health Outcomes

How would you answer the following questions, true or false? "Some of my family members have habits that bother and annoy me very much." True or false? "I tend to be on my guard with people who are somewhat more friendly than I had expected." True or false? "It makes me feel like a failure when I hear of the success of someone I know well." People who answer "true" to questions like these tend to be prone to hostile, angry outbursts [387] and it seems that the tendency to respond to social situations with hostility is associated with coronary heart disease [423].

What is interesting in this line of research is that it is not just any kind of hostility and anger that bodes poorly for the health of one's heart, but rather a particular kind: cynical hostility. Cynical hostility is a special example of the failure of emotional self-management. It is characterized by suspiciousness, resentment, florid displays of anger, antagonism, and distrust. These folks are not hard to find in a crowd. More often than not, they are men [408]. They tend to be verbally aggressive and behaviorally antagonistic. Not surprisingly, they have difficulty making friends or maintaining relationships [384], [404].

All of this cynical hostility takes it toll on the heart. First, it creates excessive cardiovascular reactivity. The heart and vascular system tend to overreact to minor stressors [421], and this is especially true in situations involving other people [426]. The blood vessels feeding the heart muscle tend to constrict, while the heart itself beats faster. This puts a real strain on the coronary system. The emotional arousal often experienced by cynically hostile people is associated with lipids being shunted to the bloodstream (perhaps to provide "fuel" for the ensuing fight that the body is expecting). This increase in blood cholesterol and triglycerides creates a risk for the buildup of plaques, which can block arteries feeding heart muscle and result in a heart attack [391]. Worse in some ways, when people are experiencing a lot of anger and hostility they may cope with it by smoking cigarettes, drinking alcohol, or eating fatty foods, which also can lead to longer-term health damage.

Emotional Suppression and Health Outcomes

So, is the answer simply to "stuff it"—to suppress hostile feelings, maintain a calm exterior, and minimize the expression of negative emotions? That strategy does not appear to be very healthy either. For one, suppressed anger seems to raise one's blood pressure just as much as expressed anger [385]. It is also possible—although the evidence is quite weak at this point—that suppressing negative emotions may increase susceptibility to and progression of cancer [383], [395], [427]. In fact, the course of the illness among cancer patients who are openly angry and combative may actually be better than for those who suppress their anger [390], [405]. Denial and repression, on the other hand, may be related to cancer progression [410].

In one set of studies, recent stressors and coping abilities were measured in more than 1,500 women sent to a specialist because of a lump or tenderness in a breast. Those women who were experiencing the most stress, but at the same time denied its existence, were especially likely to be diagnosed with breast cancer. However, women who indicated that they were comfortable expressing anger were less likely to receive this diagnosis [388], [389], [392]. So, acting as if the stressors in one's life are not bothersome may be dangerous to one's health. And, at least in the breast cancer context, expressing anger might protect a person from cancer. Again, it looks as if anger is a double-edged sword. Too much results in one kind of health problem, and too little another.

Luckily, we can learn to express the right amount of anger. David Spiegel and his colleagues at Stanford University enrolled women with metastatic breast cancer into a support group that met weekly and, in part, helped women to learn to express their feelings about having cancer, extract meaning from the experience, and develop a social support system [425]. A control group received only standard medical care. Those women who participated in the support group lived an average of 37 months from the start of the study; those women who received only standard medical care died, on average, after only 19 months. A large multisite study is currently underway to replicate these remarkable findings.

Confiding: Might This be the Answer?

If expression of cynical hostility is related to heart disease but suppressing emotions may be associated with cancer progression, what is a person to do with such feelings? Perhaps there is a "golden mean," as the Greeks suggested. We may need to express negative feelings, but in a way that is neither mean spirited nor stifled. It is likely that this is what he had in mind when Jamie Pennebaker at the University of Texas proposed that confiding our traumas may have beneficial effects on physical and mental health. Pennebaker has studied the effects of emotional disclosure extensively and found that the simple act of disclosing emotional experiences in writing, even anonymously, improves individuals' subsequent physical and mental health (see [412] for a review). For instance, students assigned to write about a traumatic emotional experience subsequently made fewer health center visits and received higher grades than students assigned to write about a trivial topic (e.g., [386], [413]). The benefits of emotional disclosure also include broadly enhanced immunological functioning (e.g., [414]), and decreases in self-reported physical symptoms, distress, and depression (e.g., [394], [415]). These impressive findings have proved robust across dozens of studies conducted by several investigators and among such disparate populations as college students, maximum security prisoners, and recently unemployed professionals (see [424] for a meta-analysis).

Learning to Regulate Our Emotions for Better Health

Perhaps the expression of emotions has only a positive impact on physical health when we are confident about our abilities to regulate them. In one study, we investigated the hypothesis that adapting successfully to a stressful experience depends, in part, on beliefs that one has the capacity to regulate feelings. Goldman, Kraemer, and Salovey [393] conducted a prospective study examining whether beliefs about one's moods, in particular the belief that one can repair negative moods, are related to physical health complaints. The reasoning behind this study was that individuals who cannot repair or regulate their feelings may look to others for help in doing so. As a result, they may be more likely to seek the attention of a physician when they are feeling stressed because they do not know how to regulate these feelings themselves. Such individuals simply may be using the health care system as a mood regulation strategy. Of course, it is also possible that these individuals are actually more likely to become physically ill when stressed.

Goldman et al. [393] assessed 134 student volunteers at three different times during the semester: at the start of the year, during midterm examinations, and during final examinations. At these times, Goldman et al. administered the Trait Meta-Mood Scale (TMMS), which includes an index of one's beliefs about being able to regulate feelings, as well as measures of stress, physical symptoms, and health center visits. When the researchers divided the sample into three groups of people (those with a high degree of skill in repairing negative moods, those with average skills in this area, and those with low skills), they found some intriguing results. When stress was low, the three groups differed very little. But, as stress increased, those individuals who said that they cannot easily regulate their feelings were more likely to visit the health center, and those individuals who were good at repairing negative moods actually visited the health center less often.

Summing Up

Affective self-regulation appears to be the aspect of EI most relevant to physical health. As we have seen, individuals unable to control their anger and hostility are prone to heart disease. The data connecting hostility to cardiovascular problems are quite strong. At the same time, individuals who suppress their anger and hostility—and negative feelings more generally—may be engaging in an emotional style that exacerbates certain kinds of cancer. However, the data linking suppressed negative emotions, like hostility, to cancer are, currently, not nearly as convincing as that linking hostility and heart disease. In general, the inability to regulate negative emotions, indeed even the belief that one does not have strong skills in this domain, seems to make one vulnerable to stress. When the going gets tough, the tough get going; but when the going gets tough for individuals who lack confidence in their emotional regulatory skills, they are more likely to end up going to the doctor's office.

☐ The Emotionally Intelligent Investor: Avoiding the Pathologies of Loss Aversion

It's January. You've paid off your holiday bills. For the first time in years, you have some extra cash—$4,000 to be exact. Usually you would just add this to your savings account, but you've noticed of late the paltry 2% interest rate the bank is paying. Maybe there is a better place to invest your money. What about the stock market? You read a book last year suggesting that even nonexperts like yourself can make money in stocks, just invest in what you know. Well, you know about General Motors; you have a 1993 Chevrolet parked in the garage and a 1997 Pontiac in the driveway. And your daughter works as a hostess in that new restaurant in town, the celebrity-endorsed Planet Hollywood. It always seems pretty crowded there when you drop by to see how she is doing.

So you set up an account with one of those electronic brokerages on your home computer and buy $2,000 worth of General Motors (50 shares at $40 each) and $2,000 in Planet Hollywood (100 shares at $20 each).

For a while, nothing much happens one way or the other. You check your stocks every day: They go up, they go down. But over a few months time, you notice a trend. General Motors seems to be creeping up just a bit, but the overall inclination of Planet Hollywood seems downward. After six months, General Motors is now worth $50 a share and Planet Hollywood $16.

"Time to make some decisions?" you wonder. You think about the situation with General Motors. In just a few months, you've made $500 on a $2,000 investment. "Pretty good," you think to yourself. "Let's lock in that gain and sell it." You log on to your electronic broker, type in a sell order, and find that you have $2,500 in cold hard cash, minus a few dollars commission. "This is pretty easy," you think to yourself. "But what to do about Planet Hollywood?" Your $2,000 investment there is now worth only $1,600. You mull over your options and decide, "why turn a $400 loss on paper into a real loss by selling? Might as well just hold on. Planet Hollywood will turn around. If it doesn't make a big run, I'll hang on at least until it drifts back to $20 a share. When I'm even, I'll sell it. Besides, I think Planet Hollywood is a pretty good restaurant. I am sure others will see how wonderful it is before too long. Maybe I should think about buying some more shares using some of the money in our household emergency account. Probably best just to sit tight."

Do these investment ruminations ring a bell with you? Most experts in behavioral finance and investor psychology would suggest that they have led to precisely the wrong choices: Selling winners quickly and hanging onto losers for a long time waiting for them to turn around are defeatist strategies. Taking risks in order to get out of a hole no matter how compelling is not an emotionally intelligent decision, and overvaluing what we already own is commonplace but irrational. And that making no decision at all—maintaining the status quo—often feels like the easiest decision, the path of least resistance. This section of the chapter explores some of the reasons why investors make these kinds of decisions and argues that by intelligently managing our emotions—our pride and, in particular, by not being quite so afraid of feeling regret, we may be able to make more profitable choices.

Prospect Theory

Obviously people feel better when their investments rise in value than when they fall. But why is it that, say, a 20% gain only makes us feel pretty good while a 20% loss leads to wretched misery? Winning some amount certainly brings pleasure. But take that same amount and lose it: Now we feel truly horrible. Before we can understand the investor pathologies described in this chapter, we need to appreciate this emotional imbalance.

How are we to comprehend this asymmetry between how winning and losing makes investors feel? We need to consider one of the most influential theories in both behavioral economics and psychology. It is called *prospect theory*, and it was articulated by Stanford University's Amos Tversky and Princeton's Daniel Kahneman. Although this theory has profound and complex implications, its essence can be captured in a single graph that looks like an "S." This graph, depicted in Figure 10.1, relates outcomes in the world—such as gaining or losing money—to how they make us feel, their subjective value [400], [401].

There are a few things to notice about this graph. First, if humans were completely rational creatures—mechanical androids like Commander Data on *Star Trek*—the figure would not be an S-shaped curve at all but rather a straight line. Every dollar gained makes us one unit happier; every dollar lost makes us one unit sadder. In terms of its influence on our emo-

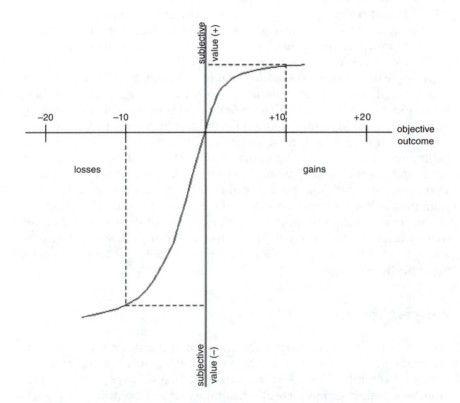

FIGURE 10.1. The value function of prospect theory.

tions, each dollar is like every other dollar. But this is not the case. As we "win" dollars, each new dollar adds less to our enjoyment than the previously won dollar. The first few dollars gained make us feel the best. No reason to take any risks to gain more dollars, once we have won a few; we already feel pretty good, right?

Now take a look at the left side of the graph. Here, with each dollar lost we feel worse and worse, but the losses that pack the strongest negative punch are those first few dollars lost. We already feel pretty badly when we lose, so if we lose more, we only feel a bit worse. If we are losing, perhaps we might as well take some risks; we are already feeling pretty badly, so who cares if we lose more?

There is something else that is interesting about this graph. Notice how the "S" curve is not as steep for winning as it is for losing. Start at the middle of the graph—called the "reference point"—and notice what happens to one's feelings as you move the same distance right (gain) or left (loss). The negative emotional reaction to losing is always bigger than the positive emotional reaction is to gaining the same amount. A $5 win is okay, but a $5 loss is sad. A $10 win is nice, but a $10 loss is miserable. A $1,000 win is terrific, but a $1,000 loss is total tragedy. As psychologists like to say, losses loom larger than comparable gains.

So why am I taking so much time telling you about this graph? Well, this simple S-shaped curve helps us to understand several classic and interrelated investor mistakes and the emotions that drive them: (a) refusing to sell losing investments but selling winners prematurely, (b) taking bigger and bigger risks when losing to "get even," (c) overvaluing an investment simply because we own it, and (d) staying with the investments we already have, that is, preserving a bias toward the status quo. In the remainder of this chapter, we discuss each of these emotionally rooted investor pathologies.

Refusing to Sell at a Loss

Some years ago, a manufacturer of sports apparel moved to New Haven, Connecticut, the city where I live. This company provides uniforms for many professional sports teams and also sells T-shirts and sweat clothes to the general public. With great fanfare, this company "went public," selling stock in an initial public offering for about $24 a share. Wanting to support a local employer and get in on this action, I began to follow the stock price of this company. When it dropped to about $12 a share a year later, I bought 500 shares. At half the initial offering price, it seemed like a bargain. The price of this stock, however, never saw $12 again. Over the next several years, in the face of labor problems in professional sports leading to strikes and shortened hockey and basketball seasons, it dropped to $6 then to $3 then to $2 and finally bottomed out near $1. A $6,000 initial investment was now worth a bit over $500.

As this situation unfolded, it would have been adaptive to have asked, "Is there a better place for my money?" If yes—and these were years when the market as a whole was rising dramatically, so nearly any investment alternative may have been better than this one—the rational thing to do was sell the stock, despite the loss, and put the money to work somewhere else. In fact, some money managers have a "stop-loss rule" that says if their initial investment drops in value more than some predetermined amount, often 10%, sometimes a bit more, they sell it. Period. No questions asked. But I would not be telling you about this particular investment if that is what I did. Instead, refusing to admit I was wrong about this company (even though I read their annual reports indicating negative earnings year after year), I hung on. "Why turn a paper loss into a real one?" I would tell my wife. "Someday, when all these strikes in professional sports end, I'll get even. Then I'll sell."

Well, this story has an interesting ending, which I will describe later when I talk about the pathology of risk taking in the face of losses. But for now, let me discuss the emotional turmoil that plagued and paralyzed me. Investment guru Leroy Gross [396, p. 150] in *The Art of Selling Intangibles: How to Make Your Million $ Investing Other People's Money* captures it very well:

> Many clients will not sell anything at a loss. They don't want to give up the hope of making money on a particular investment, or perhaps they want to get even before they get out. The "getevenitis" disease has probably wrought more destruction on investment portfolios than anything else. . . . Investors are reluctant to accept and realize losses because the very act of doing so proves that their first judgment was wrong.

This is called *loss aversion*, the reluctance to accept a loss [401], [402]. And it can manifest itself in two ways: the tendency to hold onto an investment that has declined in value for much too long, and the tendency to sell an investment that has appreciated prematurely. In other words, rather than stopping losses but letting profits run (as is usually advised), we are emotionally wired instead to refuse to cut our losses with a bad investment and fail to take full advantage of a good one. Behavioral economists Hersh Shefrin and Meir Statman note, we "sell winners too early and ride losers too long" [420, p. 778].

Refusing to sell losers and invest our money elsewhere is especially interesting, given that the IRS rewards us with a nice tax deduction if we could bring ourselves to admit we were wrong and sell that damn losing stock. But no, we hang on. Pride goeth before the fall: Why admit we made a mistake by turning a paper loss into a real one? And hope springs eternal: If we hold on just a little longer, we know that the investment will turn around.

The best way to understand this investor pathology is to consider, once again, the S-shaped curve earlier in this chapter. Notice how as one contemplates a gain—the right side of the figure—the curve from the reference point (the center) is concave, but that as one contemplates a loss—the left side of the figure—the curve from the reference point is convex. The way in which the curve flattens out for both gains and losses reflects the fact that once we feel good about a gain, it is hard to feel much better with additional gains, and once we feel pretty bad about a loss, it is unlikely we will feel even worse with additional losses. Hence, why not sell gainers and "lock-in" these good feelings now, without risking that they could go away. And why not hang onto losers; after all, how much worse could I feel? Sounds like a good emotional self-regulation strategy, no?

An emotionally intelligent investor might look at the tendency to hang onto losers but to sell winners in yet another way: as a battle between pride and regret [420], [428]. The potential pride in selling an investment at a profit ("I was right") is offset by the even stronger emotion of regret when one contemplates selling an investment at a loss ("Damn, I was wrong"). We are delighted to experience pride whenever we can, and hence sell our winners when, perhaps, we should hold onto them. But we will work very hard to avoid experiencing the more powerful emotion of regret. As a result, we postpone selling losers. Richard Thaler [428] suggests that "the regret at having erred may be exacerbated by having to admit the mistake to others, such as one's spouse or the IRS," admissions that never have to be made if one refuses to sell! Not surprisingly, then, an analysis of the accounts of 10,000 individual investors with a particular brokerage firm revealed that these investors were 50% more likely to sell a stock that had gone up as compared with one that had gone down [411]. In this analysis, if each investor had sold a loser rather than a winner, on average they would have made 4.4% more profit in the subsequent year. But "forgone gains are less painful than perceived losses" [398].

Emotionally intelligent investors can benefit from the advice of legendary Wall Street executive Alan C. (Ace) Greenberg, the chairman of the investment firm Bear Stearns. Considering his father's approach to selling clothing retail through a chain of stores in the Midwest, Greenberg says:

> If you've got something bad, sell it today because tomorrow it's going to be worse. . . . People don't hesitate for a minute to take a small profit, but they don't want to take losses. Which is, of course, just the opposite of what you should do. If you're wrong, you're wrong. Sell, and buy something else. (quoted in [422, p. 142])

An emotionally intelligent way to get over the concern about feeling regret when a losing stock position is sold is to reframe what one is trying to do. Rather than thinking in terms of selling a loser and buying something else with the proceeds, reframe this decision as the transferring of money from one investment to another. Do not even use the word "sell" in describing what you are doing. You are simply reallocating investments, not "buying" and "selling."

Risk Taking when Confronted by Losses

In one of their early papers on prospect theory, Kahneman and Tversky observed that "a person who has not made peace with his losses is likely to accept gambles that would be unacceptable to him otherwise" [400, p. 287]. Because losses are so painful, investors are motivated to take risks as a way to avoid them. Think about casino gambling for a moment. It is very hard to walk away from the table a loser, isn't it? But suppose that luck was not much of a lady for you last night, and today is the final day of your vacation in Atlantic City. What are you most likely to do? Frequently, people will head back to the casino and try one last time to get even. Now, because time is of the essence and they are already so far in the hole, they take much bigger risks—betting at the $20 blackjack table rather than the $5 table. Investors often engage in similar behavior—buying more and more of a loser as it drops in price hoping that if there is a price turnaround, they will break even. Perhaps, also, they are attempting to demonstrate to themselves (and anyone who is watching) that they did not make a mistake, that they have no regrets. Peter Lynch calls this, *watering weeds* [407].

Now, if you really believe in the fundamental value of your investment—it is an excellent company, in a leading industry, with quality management—but that it is just going through a temporary difficult period, by all means buy more of it. What was a good deal at $20 per share is an even better one at $10, right? Alas, often decisions to buy more do not represent taking advantage of temporary discounts—a New York Stock Exchange Fire Sale—but rather throwing good money after bad.

Recall my investment in the New Haven sports apparel company that I purchased at $12 and that sank like a stone for the next several years thereafter. How should I have handled that mistake? No doubt, when the stock dropped some predetermined amount—say to $9 or $10—and there was no reason to believe that the fundamental value of the company in terms of sales or profits was going to improve quickly—I should have cut my losses and sold. True, $6,000 would have turned into $5,000, or even less, but the loss could be used to offset gains at tax time. More importantly, the question to ask is, "If I had $5,000 to invest, would I buy shares of this company or put the money somewhere else?" No doubt, other options would have appeared to be better investment opportunities.

But is this what happened? Alas, no. Desperate and not being able to admit my folly by "booking" the loss, I bought more of the stock—at $6, then at $4, and then again at $2. With no hope on the horizon for this company, the value slipped to $1 per share, and now about a $15,000 investment was starting to look pretty worthless. With an overwhelming case of "getevenitis," I bought a final 2,000 shares at $1.25 each. Over the next several months, the stock price bounced around between $1.00 and $1.75. The likelihood that this company would ever make a profit was in great doubt. Maybe it would not even survive. What was bad only got worse.

This gamble paid off, but only because of a small miracle. Scanning the stock quotes on my office computer one afternoon (while I should have been working), I noticed unusual activity in the stock of this company: massive amounts of buying and selling. Volume was hundreds of times greater than normal. And the price was going up—$2, then $3, then, $4—all in a matter of 15 minutes. At just under $5, I sold everything I had, a small profit, actually. For five more minutes, the stock rose, to $6 7/8 or so, but then, just as quickly it sunk back to $4. One day later, it was trading at $2, and within a week it was back around $1.50. The company has since gone into bankruptcy and was "delisted" by the stock exchange.

What caused this unusual activity? It is not really clear—the company made no announcements during this period, and it was not covered in the financial media. Perhaps day traders were churning the stock and then lost interest. No one is quite sure. For me, the end of the story is a relatively happy one: I got out alive—after several years of stress—although my money during this time could have done much better invested elsewhere. But for every minor miracle of this kind are dozens of stocks that continue to sink and never rise to the level at which they were purchased. Should you sit around waiting for such lightening to strike and then sell them? I don't think so. Get out. Put your money somewhere else. Pretend you had the cash in hand that you would if you sold the investment; would you now invest that cash in this company? If the answer is "no," and it probably is, "book the loss."

The tendency to take big risks when losing, hoping against hope that one can get out from under the loss, results in investors throwing good money after bad. They are engaging in what is called a *sunk-cost strategy* [382, 428]. The more money we have thrown at some idea—consider how I continued to throw money at the losing sports apparel stock—the more we ignore associated risks and justify throwing even more money at it. As every owner of an old car knows, the reason for not selling your jalopy is that you just put $500 into a new exhaust system for it (despite knowing that the transmission is likely to go next, and that will be even more expensive to fix). The emotional power of sunk costs is illustrated at the theater when we do not leave at intermission even though we are not enjoying the play, at restaurants when we overeat simply because the meal was expensive, and at the department store when we value something more after paying full price than when we purchase the same item on sale.

Endowment Effect: If It's Mine It's Worth More

Losers are the hardest investments for us to get ourselves to sell. But, in fact, we have emotional difficulties selling anything. The subjective value of what we own (that is, its value to us) is always higher than its actual, objective value (its price in the marketplace). This is called *the endowment effect*: Investors overvalue what they own and devalue what others own. More formally, people demand much more to give up something than they would be willing to pay to buy it [428].

If humans were the rational automatons on which traditional economic theory is based, the value of something would not change depending on whether one owned it or not. I should be as willing to sell my laptop computer for $1,500 as I would be willing to buy the exact same one from my neighbor at the same price. But this is not what happens. I want $1,800 for mine, and I would not touch my neighbor's for more than $1,200. Similarly, people fall in love with their investments, especially stocks and mutual funds, and have great difficulty parting with them.

The endowment effect is another implication of that S-shaped function of prospect theory described earlier in the chapter. It is a kind of loss aversion. Because of the extra emotional impact associated with losing something as compared with winning it, we have strong motivations not to lose things—not to let go of anything we have. This behavior often is seen among homeowners who sell their houses without help from real estate brokers. These FSBO—for sale by owner—homes often are priced above the market because their owners so desperately want to avoid the regret associated with accepting too low a price, and there is no broker to encourage them to set a more realistic figure. How many of you know someone who refused to sell their house, despite a reasonable offer, hoping to get full price (even with a broker encouraging them to accept) only to find that a better offer never materialized?

The endowment effect is demonstrated easily in the laboratory. For example, suppose I recruit individuals to participate in one of my experiments and compensate half of them with $1 and the other half with a state lottery ticket. At the end of the experiment, I give the folks who received the dollar the option of exchanging it for a lottery ticket and the folks who received the lottery ticket the option of exchanging it for a dollar. It turns out that most individuals, regardless of whether they first received a dollar or a lottery ticket, are reluctant to give it up in exchange for the alternative option. Because they own it, it is now worth more to them (after [403]). Similar results have been obtained for individuals given coffee mugs or ballpoint pens: For mugs, the average "owner" was unwilling to sell for less than $5.25, but the average "buyer" was unwilling to pay more than about $2.75; the ratio of selling to buying prices for pens was also about 2 to 1 [397].

Perhaps in the most dramatic demonstration of *instant endowment,* George Loewenstein and Daniel Kahneman gave half of the students in a class a nice ballpoint pen and the other half a token redeemable for a mystery gift. Everyone was then asked to rate the attractiveness of various possible gifts and then to choose between a pen and two chocolate candy bars. Fifty-six percent of the individuals who already had a pen preferred it as the gift of choice, but only 24% of the others chose the pen. However, when everyone rated the attractiveness of the gift options, the people given a pen did not rate it as more attractive than those who did not get one. It appears that the endowment effect is driven more strongly by the emotion of regret at having to give something up than an enhanced pride of ownership [406].

The potential impact of regret is so strong that people often make very strange financial decisions merely to avoid regret. For instance, suppose you can choose Retirement Plan A or Retirement Plan B. Last year, Retirement Plan A featured two mutual funds, a very risky small-cap stock fund that returned a whopping 50% and a more conservative blue-chip stock fund with a 20% return. If you select Retirement Plan A, your employer will only let you invest in the conservative blue-chip fund option. Alternatively you can pick Retirement Plan B, which has only one fund, a different conservative blue-chip fund that last year returned 15%. Surprisingly, many people will choose Retirement Plan B, even though its blue-chip fund wasn't as successful as a comparable fund with Retirement Plan A. Why? Well, to choose Retirement Plan A means to experience the regret of not being allowed to invest in its very successful small-cap fund. With Plan B, this nonoption is not salient—you don't see its fantastic return in the quarterly fund report—and regret is less likely to be experienced. In an actual experiment, Richard Thaler found that people would rather win $100 than $150, if winning $150 also meant that someone else won $1,000. They would take less money to avoid feeling the regret at not having been the "big" winner [428]. In this study, regret avoidance was purchased for $50.

The endowment effect creates a bias that plagues investors, making it difficult to "pull the trigger" on a transaction. Is it any wonder that manufacturers risk very little when they offer money-back guarantees on their products? Once possessed, these products are worth more than their purchase price to the consumer. The same status quo bias holds, of course, for all kinds of financial products, and so we turn to this issue next.

Status Quo Bias: Paralyzed in the Present

It all starts to add up: If investors fear selling stocks that have gone down, value what they have more than what they don't have, and are willing to pay a premium not to experience regret, the overwhelming psychological bias must be to do nothing at all. After all, if all of one's ducks appear to be swans, why sell them? And if no one else has anything that is worth what they want me to pay for it, why buy? Besides, if we just hang on, it will all work out, we convince ourselves. Even in the end, Pandora's box contained one last item: hope. As the prospect theory S-shaped function suggests, the disadvantages of change always loom larger than the advantages of remaining in the status quo [398].

   The status quo bias may be the dominant emotion management strategy among investors. All things being equal, options that have the appearance of being the status quo—of requiring no change to maintain them—are favored. For example, in one experiment individuals were told that they would receive a substantial inheritance. Some of these individuals were told that they were to decide on an investment portfolio for these funds (high-risk stock, moderate-risk stock, treasury bills, or municipal bonds); others were given these options but told that the money was already invested predominantly in one of them. Anticipated returns for each of these options were provided. Both groups were told to allocate the inheritance in any way that they wanted and that they should ignore any tax consequences or possible commissions. The participants who were given a preexisting portfolio allocation showed a strong bias toward the status quo—they generally left things invested in the way that they already were. For example, 32% of the individuals chose the municipal bond option when no prior investments were mentioned. The number of individuals choosing municipal bonds rose to 47% when they were told that the money they were to receive was already invested that way—when it was the status quo option. The status quo option was especially attractive when the number of investment choices was increased. The more alternatives for investment people were given, the more they simply wanted to leave things alone [419].

   Once one decides on an investment strategy, it is important to stick with it. "Stay the course" is a mantra, for example, of the Vanguard family of mutual funds. However, often an investment strategy is selected precisely because it is the course that things were already on, without an active decision that this is the most appropriate one. So avoiding excessive buying and selling is certainly a good investment principle, but only once a strategy has been developed, a strategy that is decided upon actively, not merely inherited.

Summing Up

So let's return to our investor from the beginning of the chapter—the person who purchased $2,000 worth of General Motors (50 shares at $40 per share), only to sell it a few months later when it went to $50 and was worth $2,500. What if this investor, who also bought $2,000 worth of Planet Hollywood (100 shares at $20 per share) and decided to hold onto it, even after a 20% drop in its value, rode her winner, General Motors, but sold the loser, Planet Hollywood, instead?

In today's newspaper, as I write this chapter, is a story about General Motors opening a new luxury car plant in Lansing, Michigan, and revealing plans for a new Saturn small sport utility vehicle to be available in 2002. There is also a column about Planet Hollywood. Under the headline, "Planet Hollywood Spinning Out of Orbit," is a discussion of the restaurant chain's $238 million loss in 1998, reflecting an 18% drop in sales. Accounting firm PricewaterhouseCoopers is quoted as saying they are concerned about Planet Hollywood's ability to continue as a going concern. In May 1999, to pick a date at random, General Motors was selling for $95 per share and Planet Hollywood for 81 cents. We can only hope our hypothetical investor repurchased General Motors but sold Planet Hollywood while it still had some market value.

The trouble, though, is that our psychological instincts and consequent emotional reactions are more likely to lead us to make the same mistakes as this investor. Because realizing losses packs such an emotional punch and forces us to confront the fact, semipublicly, that we were wrong, it is easier to hang onto stocks like Planet Hollywood, hoping they will turnaround and we will get even. Not only that, we tend to fall in love with what we own, and so we are overly optimistic about the prospects of Planet Hollywood despite objective data to the contrary—we might even be tempted to take a risk and buy more in the face of mounting losses and sinking stock prices. Does Planet Hollywood really look like it will be selling around $20 a share in the near future? Finally, because we feel pretty good about having made some money on General Motors, we get out early, locking in those warm feelings along with a small profit. Regret is no longer risked. Alas, we miss out on even larger gains.

If there is one overarching lesson as we contemplate the pathology of loss aversion and its close cousins, instant endowment and status quo biases, it is that the past tends to be too much with us. We get emotionally hung up on the history of our investments, from whence they came. Ask yourself, "If all my investments were liquidated now, and I had the cash in hand and the freedom to put it anywhere, what would my investment portfolio look like? Where is the best place to put my money for the future?" To the extent that your current portfolio deviates from this ideal one, transferring investment dollars may be desirable—and you should think of it as just that, a transfer or shift of funds. Our emotions are likely to be more cooperative with our investment goals if we think in terms of reallocating our money rather than buying and selling.

☐ Conclusion

This chapter has discussed some of the pathologies and advantages of intelligent emotional self-management. In the health arena, appropriate levels of emotional expression may help us to avoid the negative consequences of, for example, anger expression or of emotional suppression. As for investing, learning to manage regret and anxiety seems like the key to avoiding the pathologies of loss aversion. Emotional intelligence, then, appears to be central to maintaining good health and making the most of the money we earn in life. It is a twist on the old saying, but being emotionally wise may help a person become healthy and wealthy.

☐ Acknowledgments

Preparation of this manuscript was facilitated by the following grants: American Cancer Society (RPG-93-028-05-PBP), National Cancer Institute (R01-CA68427), and National Institute of Mental Health (P01-MH/ DA56826). I also acknowledge funding from the Ethel F. Donaghue Foundation Women's Health Investigator Program at Yale University. I also thank the Rockefeller Foundation, as this chapter was written during a sabbatical residence at the Bellagio Study and Conference Center.

INTEGRATION
AND CONCLUSIONS

CHAPTER Robert J. Sternberg

Measuring the Intelligence of an Idea: How Intelligent is the Idea of Emotional Intelligence?

We have tests to measure the intelligence of people [442] and of various kinds of animals [461], including dogs [433]. Can we also measure the intelligence of an idea? One might argue that ideas differ from people and animals in that ideas are abstract, whereas people and animals are concrete; or that people and animals, unlike ideas, are alive. But ideas do seem to have a life of their own, and there is now an entire science devoted to the life and propagation of ideas, *memetics* [435].

I have proposed that the intelligence of people should be measured by examining their analytical, creative, and practical abilities (e.g., [450], [452]). In this chapter, I suggest that the same "triarchic" theory I have applied to people can be applied as well to ideas—that the "intelligence" of an idea inheres in analytical, creative, and practical aspects of the idea. Because the "intelligence" of an idea sounds strange, I will speak instead of the "intellectual value" of an idea.

An idea can be intellectually valuable in three ways. The analytical value of an idea refers to whether the idea is "correct" or is consistent with available evidence. The creative value of an idea refers to whether the idea is novel and appropriate in accomplishing what it is supposed to. The practical value of an idea refers to its usefulness. How does the idea of emotional intelligence (EI) hold up by these three criteria?

☐ The Analytical Value of Emotional Intelligence

For an idea to have analytical value, the idea needs to be plausible in some sense. Because we are dealing with the realm of science in discussing EI, we should use the standard of *scientific* plausibility in evaluating the idea.

The analytical value of the construct of EI probably depends largely on the conceptualization of EI. As Mayer points out in his exceptionally lucid chapter, "'A Field Guide to Emotional Intelligence," Chapter 1, there are actually several rather different conceptions of EI. Mayer discusses early conceptions—which date back to the early twentieth century—and later conceptions, which date back at least to Leuner ([445] see also Chapter 5). Perhaps the most well-validated conception is from Salovey and Mayer [449], who conceive of EI as "the ability to monitor one's own and others' feelings and emotions, to discriminate among them and to use this information to guide one's thinking and actions" (p. 189). More recently, Mayer and Salovey have expanded their definition to include the capacity to perceive emotions, assimilate emotion-related feelings, understand the information of those emotions, and manage them.

Goleman [438] proposed a somewhat different conception, including knowing one's emotions, managing emotions, motivating oneself, recognizing emotions in others, and handling relationships. This conception was then expanded further by Goleman [439] to include a vast array of skills, such as emotional awareness, accurate self-assessment, self-confidence, self-control, trustworthiness, conscientiousness, adaptability, innovation, achievement drive, commitment, and so forth. This kitchen-sink approach undermines the credibility of Goleman's approach, which at this point probably should be viewed as commercial rather than scientific. The overblown claims made in the book, such as that EI is twice as important as IQ, simply have no scientific backing, as Salovey points out in Chapter 10 (see also [454]).

Emotional intelligence has been operationalized as well as conceptualized. Ciarrochi, Chan, Caputi, and Roberts's Chapter 2, "Measuring Emotional Intelligence," provides a very useful review of some of the empirical evidence for the construct. They argue that when EI is measured objectively, we can obtain a reliable score that shows discriminant validity with respect to measures such as positive and negative affectivity and other personality traits. Such tests (in this case, the Multifactor Emotional Intelligence Scale [MEIS]; [446]) also show convergent validity with respect to measures of related constructs such as happiness, relationship success, parental warmth, and engaging in behavior that tends to maintain or increase positive mood. The MEIS further shows some but not high overlap with measures of verbal intelligence, as we would expect.

Researchers have also found that emotional perception is distinct from mental health and that, somewhat counterintuitively, emotionally perceptive people respond more strongly to stress, perhaps because they are more aware of the interpersonal and other contextual circumstances that precipitate stress [432]. Another measure, the Levels of Emotional Awareness Scale (LEAS), is also a maximum-performance test [444]. It too shows good convergent-discriminant validity.

Ciarrochi and his colleagues are less favorably disposed toward typical-performance tests (questionnaires) than they are toward maximum-performance tests, arguing that the former measure perceived rather than actual EI. If a participant does not have insight into his or her own emotional skills, or lies, then the results are likely to be suspect. Moreover, the investigators believe that such measures are closer to personality tests than are objective measures. We might therefore look for evidence of the validity of typical-performance tests.

The author of one such test, Bar-On, Chapter 5, "Emotional Intelligence and Self-Actualization," used his Bar-On Emotional Quotient Inventory (EQ-i; [429]) to assess the extent to which people who are more emotionally intelligent according to his inventory are higher self-actualizers. He found that higher emotional intelligence is associated with higher self-actualization. Higher EI was not associated with higher cognitive intelligence (IQ), however. These results must be interpreted cautiously. First, Bar-On used as a measure of self-actualization a subscale of his complete scale and so in the overall correlations presented (.75 in North America, .72 in Israel, .71 in Holland), there may be a part–whole correlation, which would be in part artifactual. Second, even in the multiple regression, which regresses self-actualization on the other subscales, the fact that the scales are all from the same test may create some overlap due to shared instrumentation. Thus these results need to be replicated with a conceptually and operationally independent measure of self-actualization.

EI does respectably well in terms of the internal and external validation criteria that are used in psychological research to substantiate the value of a new construct. What is especially impressive is the amount of research that has been done in such a short amount of time. The first serious article on EI appeared in 1990, and only 10 years later there is already a substantial body of work empirically testing the theory. This active empirical experimentation is in stark contrast to the lack of hard empirical work that has emerged to validate other related theories (e.g., that of [436]).

What is especially appealing about EI or any new intelligence is that it redefines the issues that dominate twentieth-century research on intelligence, such as whether there is a general factor of intelligence. Thousands of studies have been done investigating that question—arguably, ad nauseam (see [441] for a review)—and it is not clear that the issue will be resolved definitively any more than the issue of whether learning is continuous versus discrete was ever resolved. If one includes the somewhat narrow range of tests typically included in conventional intelligence-test batteries, we are likely to obtain some kind of g factor. The question is whether the range of tests adequately samples all the behavior needed for success in everyday life. New constructs of intelligence, such as that of EI, make a persuasive case that the conventional tests are too narrow: They sample important skills, but not all relevant skills.

Were it to turn out that EI was not a viable construct, the efforts put into validation still would have been well worth the time. First, they have provided a model for the validation of a new construct. Second, they have been, in many cases, scientifically rigorous. Third, they have moved intelligence research away from stagnancy. I have been somewhat skeptical of the construct of EI, but I have also found that the chapters in this book, as well as other empirical research, especially by Mayer and Salovey, have made a persuasive case for the plausibility of the construct.

☐ The Creative Intellectual Value of Emotional Intelligence

The creative intellectual value of a new construct is a function of how different it is from previous constructs and how well it does what it is supposed to do. As shown above, EI seems to be filling the bill, although there is some evidence to suggest that the definition of the construct that holds together psychometrically is narrower than the definitions used by the investigators in this book [434].

One question of course is whether EI differs from IQ, that is, intelligence as it has traditionally been defined (see [455] for various definitions). Unquestionably, EI differs from IQ, both conceptually and, as discussed above, statistically. Although there may be some operational overlap, it is at best modest, as pointed out in Chapters 2 and 5.

EI is much more similar to social intelligence (see [443], [457], [458], [459]) and may also bear some relation to the behavioral facet of Guilford's [440] structure-of-intellect model. Social intelligence is, to a large extent, the ability to understand and interact effectively with other people. Bar-On even largely combines the two constructs in his own conceptualization, as described in this volume. Nevertheless, when we compare two recent chapters reviewing the literatures on each construct [443], [447], we see somewhat different intellectual antecedents, conceptualizations, and measurement strategies. The relationship between the two constructs remains something of an open question, one that will be difficult to resolve until very refined measures of both constructs are forthcoming.

Finally, EI bears some relationship to practical intelligence [456], [460] as well as to interpersonal and intrapersonal intelligences [436]. These kinds of intelligence pertain to the ability to adjust effectively in the everyday world, in the case of practical intelligence, with respect to tasks as well as people. But none of these constructs focuses on emotional regulation, as does EI. Practical intelligence, in particular, is broader, including aspects of EI but also of adaptation that are more cognitive in nature.

A second question is whether EI differs from more personality-based constructs. Goleman's [439] current conception appears to differ little. Rather, his conception seems to be a general lumping together of characteristics of a "good person." Bar-On's [430] conception also seems quite closely linked to what in the past would have been described as aspects of personality. Nevertheless, his conception at least puts together those aspects of personality that focus on emotion, and so in this way the conception may provide a valuable function. The Salovey–Mayer [449] conception seems, now, to be the most distinctive with respect to past global constructs.

Two chapters in the book consider this question more specifically. Taylor's Chapter 4, "Low Emotional Intelligence and Mental Illness," focuses on alexithymia, which appears to be related to low EI. In general, it refers to difficulty in identifying feelings, difficulty distinguishing between feelings and the bodily sensations of emotional arousal, difficulty describing feelings to others, an impoverished fantasy life, and a cognitive style that is literal and focuses on the minute details of external events [448]. It may further reflect deficits in the ways in which emotions are mentally represented.

Alexithymia does seem close to being a description of the low end of some aspects of EI. But it would be unfair to characterize EI as merely the opposite of this syndrome. When conceptualized and measured as an ability, as in the Salovey–Mayer model, EI seems truly to be closer to an intelligence than to the opposite of a dysfunctional personality syndrome.

Forgas, in Chapter 3, "Affective Intelligence: The Role of Affect in Social Thinking and Behavior," introduces the concept of affective intelligence, which seems close or identical to EI. Almost certainly it is not some separate set of skills. Forgas observes many interesting aspects of affect regulation, such as that affect has a greater influence on judgments that require a great deal of reflection than on those that can be rendered automatically.

In sum, EI seems to have value added vis-à-vis past related constructs. Although the construct of EI goes back some way, probably credit for the first theory regarding it should go to Salovey and Mayer and credit regarding its popularization should go largely to Goleman. The field of psychology, which just a few years ago was overly focused upon general intelligence, may now find itself with an embarrassment of riches concerning new "intelligences." What the field now needs with all these creative ideas is a sorting out to determine how they all fit together. It will probably turn out that no existing theory quite captures their structure.

Carroll [431] has provided a compelling hierarchical model for cognitive intelligence. What will be the structure of intelligences, broadly defined? Only time (and empirical research!) will tell.

☐ The Practical Intellectual Value of Emotional Intelligence

The chapters in the book show very well the practical intellectual value of the construct of EI. Salovey's Chapter 10, "Applied Emotional Intelligence: Regulating Emotions to Become Healthy, Wealthy, and Wise," applies the construct of EI to two domains: health regulation and financial regulation. An interesting finding with regard to health is that too much expression of anger can lead to heart attacks, and too little, to cancer. Not a good choice for anyone to face! Salovey and his colleagues also have found that those who cannot regulate their own emotions may need to seek out other people, such as physicians, to do it for them [437]. Salovey also shows (a bit more loosely) how EI is related to financial success. He concludes from his analysis that trying to save oneself from the pain of regret can be a remarkably counterproductive strategy. Of course, he may regret saying this, but according to his own analysis, so what?

Two chapters consider the relevance of EI for close relationships. In Chapter 7, "Emotional Intelligence and Empathic Accuracy," Flury and Ickes examine the relationship of EI to empathic accuracy in friendships and dating relationships. They argue that what creates empathic accuracy is not necessarily knowing a person for a long time or even knowing a person well, but rather, knowing the person "from the inside"—understanding what makes the person tick. Partners can actually lose empathic accuracy with respect to each other if they start to live comfortably together but not in a way that encourages them constantly to challenge what each other is thinking and feeling. As time goes on, people may become reluctant to express thoughts and feelings for fear of hurting their partner; at the same time, the partner may self-protectively close his or her eyes to what the other person is feeling. Thus couples should not assume that intimate understanding of each other will increase with time. It may actually decrease [453].

Fitness investigated the relevance of EI for marital success in Chapter 6, "Emotional Intelligence and Intimate Relationships." She found in reviewing the literature that EI is associated with marital happiness and stability. Although this result is not terribly surprising, it does help validate the construct of EI. Had the results come out the opposite way, one would have been very skeptical of EI, indeed!

Fitness has found that emotional misperception may lead directly to marital conflict, as when a neutral look is mistaken for an angry look. Thus, emotion perception is particularly important given the complexity and ambiguity of emotion signals in marriage. More emotionally perceptive people have happier marriages than do people who are less emotionally perceptive. On average, men have different emotional perception than do women. But EI does not guarantee marital happiness. It can be used for evil as well as good, as when a spouse identifies the weaknesses of the partner and exploits him or her.

Two other chapters examine the relevance of EI for education and for the workplace. These chapters are somewhat different from the others because they are more oriented toward a lay audience and less toward providing new scholarship to persuade an academic audience of the value of EI.

Chapter 8, by Elias, Hunter, and Kress, "Emotional Intelligence and Education," traces back interest in EI to the work of E. L. Thorndike and John Dewey, and then through Gardner and me. The article then discusses how EI can be relevant to schools.

In Chapter 9, "Emotional Intelligence in the Workplace," Caruso and Wolfe show how to use existing instruments for measuring EI (such as the MEIS) to counsel clients who wish (or whose employers wish them) to be more adaptive in work environments. The prescriptions are quite specific and therefore useful, and there is a bit of (unpublished) data suggesting the usefulness of the approach. This approach has advantages over the more diffuse approach of many others who target business applications, because it is theory-based, specific, and measured: Unlike some other consultants, Caruso and Wolfe make no claims that stretch credibility.

In conclusion, EI already is showing practical intellectual value. The cottage industry it has spawned is probably unmatched in the history of psychology since the early days of intelligence testing. Much of what is being done under the banner of *emotional intelligence* appears to be conceptually weak and oriented more toward commercial exploitation than toward increasing psychological understanding. But the programs represented in this book show that the concept can lead to serious interventions with the power to change people's lives as well as the lives of institutions.

☐ Acknowledgments

Preparation of this chapter was supported by Grant REC-9979843 from the National Science Foundation and by a government grant under the Javits Act Program (Grant R206R0001) as administered by the Office of Educational Research and Improvement, U.S. Department of Education. Grantees undertaking such projects are encouraged to express freely their professional judgment. This chapter, therefore, does not necessarily represent the positions or the policies of the U.S. government, and no official endorsement should be inferred.

REFERENCES

Introduction

1. Pascal, B. (1643/1966). *Pensees*. Baltimore: Penguin.

Chapter 1

2. Bar-On, R. (1997). *The Emotional Quotient Inventory (EQ-i): Technical manual*. Toronto, Canada: Multi-Health Systems, Inc.
3. Bar-On, R., & Parker, J. D. A. (2000). Introduction. In R. Bar-On, & J. D. A. Parker (Eds.), *The Handbook of Emotional Intelligence*. San Francisco: Jossey-Bass.
4. Boyatzis, R. J. (1982). *The competent manager: A model for effective performance*. New York: John Wiley and Sons.
5. Britton, P. (1997). *The jigsaw man*. London: Corgi Books.
6. Buck, R. (1984). *The communication of emotion*. New York: Guilford.
7. Buss, A. H., & Finn, S. E. (1987). Classification of personality traits. *Journal of Personality and Social Psychology, 52*, 432–444.
8. Cobb, C. R., & Mayer, J. D. (in press). Emotional intelligence: What the research says. *Educational Leadership, 58*, 14–19.
9. Cooper, R. K., & Q-Metrics (1996/1997). *EQ map: Interpretation guide*. San Francisco: AIT and Essi Systems.
10. Costa, P. T., & McCrae, R. R. (1992). Normal personality assessment in clinical practice: The NEO Personality Inventory. *Psychological Assessment, 4*, 5–13.
11. Dabrowski, K., & Piechowski, M. M. (1977). *Theory of levels of emotional development* (vol.1). Oceanside, NY: Dabor Science Publications.
12. Damasio, A. R. (1994). *Descartes' error: Emotion, reason, and the human brain*. New York: Putnam.
13. Davies, M., Stankov, L., & Roberts, R. D. (1998). Emotional Intelligence: In search of an elusive construct. *Journal of Personality and Social Psychology, 75*, 989–1015.
14. Dyer, M G. (1983). The role of affect in narratives. *Cognitive Science, 7*, 211–242.
15. Ekman, P. (1973). *Darwin and facial expression: A century of research in review*. New York: Academic Press.
16. Epstein, S. (1998). *Constructive thinking: The key to emotional intelligence*. Westport, CT: Praeger.
17. Eysenck, H. J., & Eysenck, S. B. (1969). *Personality structure and measurement*. San Diego, CA: Knapp.
18. Fancher, R. E. (1985). *The intelligence men: Makers of the IQ controversy*. New York: W. W. Norton.

19. Gardner, H. A. (1983). *Frames of mind.* New York: Basic Books.
20. Gardner, H. (1993). *Frames of Mind* (10th Anniversary Edition). New York: Basic Books.
21. Gardner, H. (1999, February). Who owns intelligence? *Atlantic Monthly, 283,* 000-000.
22. Goleman, D. (1995). *Emotional intelligence.* New York: Bantam Books.
23. Goleman, D. (1998). *Working with emotional intelligence.* New York: Bantam.
24. Goleman, D. (1998). What makes a leader? *Harvard Business Review, 76,* 93–102.
25. Goleman, D., Boyatzis, R. E., & Hay/McBer (1999). Emotional competencies inventory. Boston: Hay/McBer.
26. Gough, H. G. (1994). *California Psychological Inventory.* Palo Alto, CA: Consulting Psychologists Press.
27. Marlowe, H. A. (1986). Social intelligence: Evidence for multidimensionality and construct independence. *Journal of Educational Psychology, 78,* 52–58.
28. Mayer, J. D. (1986). How mood influences cognition. In N. E. Sharkey (Ed.), *Advances in cognitive science* (pp. 290–314). Chichester, West Sussex: Ellis Horwood.
29. Mayer, J. D. (1995). A framework for the classification of personality components. *Journal of Personality, 63,* 819–877.
30. Mayer, J. D. (1998). A systems framework for the field of personality psychology. *Psychological Inquiry, 9,* 118–144.
31. Mayer, J. D. (2001). Rater analyses of traits in regard to Primary Parts Theory. Unpublished raw data.
32. Mayer, J. D. (2000). Emotion, intelligence, emotional intelligence. In J. P. Forgas (Ed.). *The handbook of affect and social cognition* (pp. 410–431). Mahwah, NJ: Lawrence Erlbaum.
33. Mayer, J. D., Caruso, D., Zigler, E., Dreyden, J. (1989). Intelligence and intelligence-related personality traits. *Intelligence, 13,* 119–133.
34. Mayer, J. D., Caruso, D., & Salovey, P. (1999). Emotional intelligence meets traditional standards for an intelligence. *Intelligence, 27,* 267–298.
35. Mayer, J. D., Caruso, D. R., & Salovey, P. (2000). Selecting a measure of emotional intelligence: The case for ability testing. In R. Bar-On & J. D. A. Parker (Eds.), *Handbook of emotional intelligence* (pp. 92–117). New York: Jossey-Bass.
36. Mayer, J. D., DiPaolo, M. T., & Salovey, P. (1990). Perceiving affective content in ambiguous visual stimuli: A component of emotional intelligence. *Journal of Personality Assessment, 54,* 772–781.
37. Mayer, J. D., & Gaschke, Y. N. (1988). The experience and meta-experience of mood. *Journal of Personality and Social Psychology, 55,* 102–111.
38. Mayer, J. D., & Salovey, P. (1993). The intelligence of emotional intelligence. *Intelligence, 17*(4), 433–442.
39. Mayer, J. D., & Stevens, A. (1994). An emerging understanding of the reflective (meta) experience of mood. *Journal of Research in Personality, 28,* 351–373.
40. Mayer, J. D., Salovey, P., & Caruso, D. R. (2000). Models of emotional intelligence. In R. J. Sternberg (Ed.). *Handbook of intelligence* (pp. 396–420). Cambridge, UK: Cambridge University Press.
41. Mayer, J. D., Salovey, P., & Caruso, D. R. (in press). Emotional intelligence as *Zeitgeist,* as personality, and as a standard intelligence. In R. Bar-On & J. D. A. Parker (Eds.), *Handbook of emotional intelligence.* New York: Jossey-Bass
42. McAdams, D. P. (1996). Personality, modernity, and the storied self: A contemporary framework for studying persons. *Psychological Inquiry, 7,* 295–321.
43. Newsome, S., Day, A. L., & Catano, V. M. (2000). Assessing the predictive validity of emotional intelligence. *Personality and Individual Differences, 29,* 1005–1016.
44. Payne, W. L. (1986). A study of emotion: Developing emotional intelligence; Self-integration; relating to fear, pain and desire. *Dissertation Abstracts International, 47,* (01), 203A. (University Microfilms No. AAC 8605928)

45. Salovey, P., & Mayer, J. D. (1990). Emotional intelligence. *Imagination, Cognition, and Personality, 9*, 185–211.
46. Salovey, P., Mayer, J. D., Goldman, S., Turvey, C., & Palfai, T. (1995). Emotional attention, clarity, and repair: Exploring emotional intelligence using the Trait Meta-Mood Scale. In J. W. Pennebaker (Ed.), *Emotion, disclosure, and health* (pp. 125–154). Washington, DC: American Psychological Association.
47. Schutte, N. S., Malouff, J. M., Hall, L. E., Haggerty, D. J., Cooper, J. T., Golden, C. J., & Dornheim, L. (1998). Development and validation of a measure of emotional intelligence. *Personality and Individual Differences, 25*, 167–177.
48. Stein, S. & Book, H. (2000). *The EQ edge.* North York, ON: Stoddart.
49. Sternberg, R. J. (1997). The concept of intelligence and its role in lifelong learning and success. *American Psychologist, 52*, 1030–1037
50. TenHouten, W. D., Hoppe, K. D., Bogen, J. E., & Walter, D. O. (1986). Alexithymia: An experimental study of cerebral commissurotomy patients and normal control subjects. *American Journal of Psychiatry, 143*, 312–316.
51. Terman, L. M., & Merrill, M. A. (1973). *Stanford-Binet Intelligence Scale: 1972 norms edition.* Boston: Houghton-Mifflin.
52. Van Ghent, D. (1953). *The English novel: Form and function.* New York: Harper and Row.
53. Wechsler, D. (1981). *WAIS-R Manual: Wechsler Adult Intelligence Scale—Revised.* San Antonio, TX: Psychological Corporation.

Chapter 2

54. Adams, E. M. (1998). Emotional intelligence and wisdom. *The Southern Journal of Philosophy, 36*.
55. Anastasi, A., & Urbina, S. (1997). *Psychological testing.* Upper Saddle River, NJ: Simon & Schuster.
56. Bagby, R. M., Parker, J. D., & Taylor, G. J. (1994). The twenty-item Toronto Alexithymia Scale-I. Item selection and cross-validation of the factor structure. *Journal of Psychosomatic Research, 38*, 23–32.
57. Bagby, R. M., Taylor, G. J., & Parker, J. D. A. (1994). The twenty-item Toronto Alexithymia Scale—II. Convergent, discriminant, and concurrent validity. *Journal of Psychosomatic Research, 38*, 23–32.
58. Bar-On, R. (1997). *The Emotional Intelligence Inventory (EQ-I): Technical manual.* Toronto, Canada: Multi-Health Systems, Inc.
59. Bar-On, R. (2000). Emotional and social intelligence: Insights from the Emotional Quotient Inventory (EQ-i). In R. Bar-On & J. D. A. Parker (Eds.), *Handbook of emotional intelligence.* San Francisco: Jossey-Bass.
60. Bar-On, R., Brown, J. M., Kirkcaldy, B. D., & Thome, E. P. (2000). Emotional expression and implications for occupational stress: An application of the Emotional Quotient Inventory (EQ-i). *Personality and Individual Differences, 28*, 1107–1118.
61. Barth, J., & Bastiani, A. (1997). A longitudinal study of emotion recognition and preschool children's social behaviour. *Merril-Palmer Quarterly, 43*, 107–128.
62. Carver, C. S., Scheier, M. F., & Weintraub, J. K. (1989). Assessing coping strategies: A theoretically based approach. *Journal of Personality and Social Psychology, 56*, 267–283.
63. Cassidy, J., Parke, R., Butkobsky, L., & Braungart, J. (1992). Family-peer connections: The roles of emotional expressiveness within the family and children's understanding of emotions. *Child Development, 63*, 603–618.
64. Ciarrochi, J., Chan, A., & Bajgar, J. (2000). Measuring emotional intelligence in adolescents. Manuscript submitted for publication.

65. Ciarrochi, J., Chan, A., & Caputi, P. (2000). A critical evaluation of the emotional intelligence construct. *Personality and Individual Differences, 28,* 539–561.

66. Ciarrochi, J., Chan, A., & Caputi, P. (2000). [Measuring emotional intelligence]. Unpublished data.

67. Ciarrochi, J., & Deane, F. (2000). *The relationship between emotional intelligence and the willingness to seek help from nonprofessional and professional sources.* Manuscript submitted for publication.

68. Ciarrochi, J., Deane, F., & Anderson, S. (2000). *Emotional intelligence moderates the relationship between stress and psychological adaptation, as measured by depression, hopelessness, and suicidal ideation.* Manuscript submitted for publication.

69. Cooper, R. K., & Sawaf, A. (1997). Executive EQ: Emotional intelligence in leadership and organizations. New York: Grosset/Putnam.

70. Costa, P. T., Jr., & McCrae, R. R. (1992). Revised NEO personality inventory (NEO PI-R) and NEO five-factor inventory (NEO-FFI). Odessa, FL: Psychological Assessment Resources.

71. Costa, P. T., & McCrae, R. R. (1992). Normal personality assessment in clinical practice: The NEO Personality Inventory. *Psychological Assessment, 4,* 5–13.

72. Davies, M., Stankov, L., & Roberts, R. D. (1998). Emotional intelligence: In search of an elusive construct. *Journal of Personality and Social Psychology, 75,* 989–1015.

73. Dawda, D., & Hart, S. D. (2000). Assessing emotional intelligence: Reliability and validity of the Bar-On Emotional Quotient Inventory (EQ-i) in university students. *Personality & Individual Differences, 28,* 797–812.

74. Field, T. M., & Walden, T. A. (1982). Production and discrimination of facial expressions by preschool children. *Child Development, 53,* 1299–1311.

75. Friedman, H. S., & Miller-Herringer, T. (1991). Nonverbal display of emotion in public and in private: self-monitoring, personality, and expressive cues. *Journal of Personality and Social Psychology, 61,* 766–775.

76. Friedman, H. S., & Riggio, R. (1999). Individual differences in the ability to encode complex affects. *Personality and Individual Differences, 27,* 181–194.

77. Friedman, H. S., Riggio, R. E., & Casella, D. (1988). Nonverbal skill, personal charisma, and initial attraction. *Personality and Social Psychology Bulletin, 14,* 203–211.

78. Goleman, D. (1995). *Emotional intelligence.* New York: Bantam Books.

79. Gregory, R. J. (1996). *Psychological testing: History, principles, and applications* (2nd ed.). Boston, MA: Allyn & Bacon.

80. Lane, R. D., Quinlan, D., Schwartz, G., Walker, P., & Zeitlin, S. (1990). The levels of emotional awareness scale: A cognitive-developmental measure of emotion. *Journal of Personality Assessment, 55,* 124–134.

81. Lane, R. D., Reiman, E. M., Axelrod, B., Yun, Lang-Sheng, Holmes, A., & Schwarz, G. E. (1998). Neural correlates of levels of emotional awareness: Evidence of an interaction between emotion and attention in the anterior cingulate cortex. *Journal of Cognitive Neuroscience, 10(4),* 525–540.

82. Lane, R. D., Sechrest, L., Riedel, R., Shapiro, D., & Kaszniak, A. (in press). Pervasive emotion recognition deficit common to alexithymia and the repressive coping style. *Psychosomatic Medicine.*

83. Mayer, J. D., Salovey, P., & Caruso, D. R. (in press). Technical manual for the MSCEIT V. 2.0. Toronto, Canada: MHS.

84. Mayer, J. D., Caruso, D., & Salovey, P. (2000). Emotional intelligence meets traditional standards for an intelligence. *Intelligence, 27,* 267–298.

85. Mayer, J. D., & Cobb, C. D. (2000). Educational policy on emotional intelligence: Does it make sense? *Educational Psychology Review, 12,* 163–183.

86. Miller, S. M., Brody, D. S., & Summerton, J. (1988). Styles of coping with threat: Implications for health. *Journal of Personality and Social Psychology, 34(1),* 142–148.

87. Nolen-Hoeksema, S., & Morrow, J. (1991). A prospective study of depression and distress following a natural disaster: The 1989 Loma Prieta earthquake. *Journal of Personality and Social Psychology, 61,* 105–121.

88. Paulhus, D. L., Lysy, D. C., & Yik, M. S. (1998). Self-report measures of intelligence: Are they useful as proxy IQ tests? *Journal of Personality, 66,* 525–554.

89. Petrides, K. V., & Furnham, A. (2000). On the dimensional structure of emotional intelligence. *Personality and Individual Differences, 29,* 313–320.

90. Roger, D., & Najarian, B. (1989). The construction and validation of a new scale for measuring emotion control. *Personality and Individual Differences, 10,* 845–853.

91. Roberts, R. D., Zeidner, M., & Matthews, G. (2001). *On being emotionally intelligent: An emotion-less, intelligence perspective.* Research report A2000-1, Center for Interdisciplinary Research on Emotions. Haifa, Israel: University of Haifa.

92. Ryback, D. (1998). *Putting emotional intelligence to work: Successful leadership is more than IQ.* Boston: Butterworth-Heinemann.

93. Saarni, C. (1999). *The development of emotional competence.* New York: Guilford.

94. Salovey, P., & Mayer, J. D. (1990). Emotional intelligence. *Imagination, Cognition and Personality, 9,* 185–211.

95. Salovey, P., Mayer, J. D., Goldman, S., Turvey, C., & Palfai, T. (1995). Emotional attention, clarity, and repair: Exploring emotional intelligence using the Trait Meta-Mood Scale. In J. W. Pennebaker (Ed.), *Emotion, disclosure, and health* (pp. 125–154). Washington, DC: American Psychological Association.

96. Schmidt, F. L., & Hunter, J. E. (1998). The validity and utility of selection methods in personnel psychology: Practical and theoretical implications of 85 years of research findings. *Psychological Bulletin, 124,* 262–274.

97. Schutte, N., Malouff, J., Hall, L., Haggerty, D., Cooper, J., Golden, C., & Dornheim, L. (1998). Development and validation of a measure of emotional intelligence. *Personality and Individual Differences, 25,* 167–177.

98. Schwarz, N., & Clore, G. L. (1983). Mood, misattribution and judgments of well-being: Informative and directive functions of affective states. *Journal of Personality and Social Psychology, 45,* 513–523.

99. Smith, S. M., & Petty, R. E. (1995). Personality moderators of mood congruence effects on cognition: The role of self-esteem and negative mood regulation. *Journal of Personality and Social Psychology, 68,* 1092–1107.

100. Taylor, G. J. (2000). Recent developments in alexithymia theory and research. *Canadian Journal of Psychiatry, 45,* 134–142.

101. Taylor, G. J., & Taylor, H. L. (1997). Alexithymia. In M. McCallum & W. E. Piper (Eds.), *Psychological mindedness: A contemporary understanding* (pp. 77–104). Mahwah, NJ: Lawrence Erlbaum Associates.

102. Watson, D., & Clark, L. A. (1992). On traits and temperament. General and specific factors of emotional experience and their relation to the five-factor model. *Journal of Personality, 60,* 441–476.

103. Watson, D., & Clark, L. A. (1997). Measurement and mismeasurement of mood: Recurrent and emergent issues. *Journal of Personality Assessment, 68,* 267–296.

104. Watson, D., & Tellegen, A. (1985). Toward a consensual structure of mood. *Psychological Bulletin, 98,* 219–235.

105. Weinberger, D. A., Schwarz, G. E., & Davidson, R. J. (1979). Low-anxious, high-anxious, and repressive coping styles: Psychometric patterns and behavioural and physiological responses to stress. *Journal of Abnormal Psychology, 88,* 369–380.

106. Weisinger, H. (1998). *Emotional intelligence at work: The untapped edge for success.* San Francisco: Jossey-Bass.

107. Zins, J. E., Elias, M. J., Greenberg, M. T., & Weissberg, R. P. (in press). *Promoting social and emotional competence in children.*

Chapter 3

108. Adolphs, R., & Damasio, A. (2001). The interaction of affect and cognition: A neuro-biological perspective. In Forgas, J. P. (Ed.), *The Handbook of Affect and Social Cognition.* Mahwah, NJ: Erlbaum.

109. Berkowitz, L., Jaffee, S., Jo, E,. & Troccoli, B. T. (2000). On the correction of feeling-induced judgmental biases. In J. P. Forgas (Ed.), *Feeling and thinking: The role of affect in social cognition* (pp. 131–152). New York: Cambridge University Press.

110. Bless, H. (2000). The interplay of affect and cognition: The mediating role of general knowledge structures. In J. P. Forgas (Ed.), *Feeling and thinking: The role of affect in social cognition* (pp. 201–222). New York: Cambridge University Press.

111. Bower, G. H. (1981). Mood and memory. *American Psychologist, 36,* 129–148.

112. Ciarrochi, J. V., & Forgas, J. P. (1999). On being tense yet tolerant: The paradoxical effects of trait anxiety and aversive mood on intergroup judgments. *Group Dynamics: Theory, research and Practice, 3,* 227–238.

113. Ciarrochi, J. V., & Forgas, J. P. (in press). The pleasure of possessions: Affect and consumer judgments. *European Journal of Social Psychology, 30,* 631–649.

114. Clore, G. L., & Byrne, D. (1974). The reinforcement affect model of attraction. In T. L. Huston (Ed.), *Foundations of interpersonal attraction* (pp. 143–170). New York: Academic Press.

115. Clore, G. L., Schwarz, N., & Conway, M. (1994). Affective causes and consequences of social information processing. In R. S. Wyer & T. K. Srull (Eds.), *Handbook of social cognition* (2nd ed.). Mahwah, NJ: Erlbaum.

116. Feshbach, S., & Singer, R. D. (1957). The effects of fear arousal and suppression of fear upon social perception. *Journal of Abnormal and Social Psychology, 55,* 283–288.

117. Fielder, K. (2001). Affective influences on social information processing. In J. P. Forgas (Ed.), *The handbook of affect and social cognition* (p. 163–186). Mahwah, NJ: Erlbaum.

118. Forgas, J. P. (1993). On making sense of odd couples: Mood effects on the perception of mismatched relationships. *Personality and Social Psychology Bulletin, 19,* 59–71.

119. Forgas, J. P. (1994). Sad and guilty? Affective influences on the explanation of conflict episodes. *Journal of Personality and Social Psychology, 66,* 56–68.

120. Forgas, J. P. (1995). Mood and judgment: The affect infusion model (AIM). *Psychological Bulletin, 117*(1), 39–66.

121. Forgas, J. P. (1995). Strange couples: Mood effects on judgments and memory about prototypical and atypical targets. *Personality and Social Psychology Bulletin, 21,* 747–765.

122. Forgas, J. P. (1998). On feeling good and getting your way: Mood effects on negotiation strategies and outcomes. *Journal of Personality and Social Psychology, 74,* 565–577.

123. Forgas, J. P. (1998). Asking nicely? Mood effects on responding to more or less polite requests. *Personality and Social Psychology Bulletin, 24,* 173–185.

124. Forgas, J. P. (1998). Happy and mistaken? Mood effects on the fundamental attribution error. *Journal of Personality and Social Psychology, 75,* 318–331.

125. Forgas, J. P. (1999). On feeling good and being rude: Affective influences on language use and request formulations. *Journal of Personality and Social Psychology, 76,* 928–939.

126. Forgas, J. P. (1999). Feeling and speaking: Mood effects on verbal communication strategies. *Personality and Social Psychology Bulletin, 25,* 850–863.

127. Forgas, J. P. (Ed.). (2000). *Feeling and thinking: The role of affect in social cognition.* New York: Cambridge University Press.

128. Forgas, J. P. (2000). *The effects of mood on the accuracy of eyewitness reports of observed social events.* Unpublished manuscript, University of New South Wales, Sydney, Australia.

129. Forgas, J. P., & Bower, G. H. (1987). Mood effects on person perception judgements. *Journal of Personality and Social Psychology, 53*, 53–60.
130. Forgas, J. P., Bower, G. H., & Krantz, S. (1984). The influence of mood on perceptions of social interactions. *Journal of Experimental Social Psychology, 20*, 497–513.
131. Forgas, J. P., Bower, G. H., & Moylan, S. J. (1990). Praise or blame? Affective influences on attributions for achievement. *Journal of Personality and Social Psychology, 59*, 809–818.
132. Forgas, J. P., Ciarrochi, J. V., & Moylan, S. J. (2000). *Affective influences on the production of persuasive messages*. Unpublished manuscript, University of New South Wales, Sydney, Australia.
133. Forgas, J. P., Ciarrochi, J. V., & Moylan, S. J. (2000). Subjective experience and mood regulation: The role of information processing strategies. In H. Bless & J. P. Forgas (Eds.), *The message within: The role of subjective experience in social cognition*. Philadelphia: Psychology Press.
134. Forgas, J. P., & Gunawardena, A. (2000). *Affective influences on spontaneous interpersonal behaviors*. Unpublished manuscript, University of New South Wales, Sydney, Australia.
135. Forgas, J. P., & Moylan, S. J. (1987). After the movies: The effects of transient mood states on social judgments. *Personality and Social Psychology Bulletin, 13*, 478–489.
136. Gilbert, D. T., & Wilson, T. D. (2000). Miswanting: Some problems in the forecasting of future affective states. In: J. P. Forgas (Ed.), *Feeling and thinking: The role of affect in social cognition* (pp. 178–200). New York: Cambridge University Press.
137. Koestler, A. (1978). *Janus: A summing up*. London: Hutchinson.
138. Mayer, J. D. (2001). Emotion, intelligence, and emotional intelligence. In J. P. Forgas (Ed.), *The handbook of affect and social cognition*. Mahwah, NJ: Erlbaum.
139. Moylan, S. J. (2000). *Affective influences on performance evaluation judgments*. Unpublished doctoral thesis, University of New South Wales, Sydney, Australia.
140. Petty, R. E., DeSteno, D., & Rucker, D. (2001). The role of affect in attitude change. In J. P. Forgas (Ed.), *The handbook of affect and social cognition*. Mahwah, NJ: Erlbaum.
141. Razran, G. H. S. (1940). Conditioned response changes in rating and appraising sociopolitical slogans. *Psychological Bulletin, 37*, 481.
142. Schwarz, N. (1990). Feelings as information: Informational and motivational functions of affective states. In E. T. Higgins & R. Sorrentino (Eds.), *Handbook of motivation and cognition: Foundations of social behaviour* (vol. 2, pp. 527–561). New York: Guilford.
143. Schwarz, N., & Clore, G. L. (1988). How do I feel about it? The informative function of affective states. In K. Fiedler & J. P. Forgas (Eds.), *Affect, cognition, and social behavior* (pp. 44–62). Toronto: Hogrefe.
144. Sedikides, C. (1995). Central and peripheral self-conceptions are differentially influenced by mood: Tests of the differential sensitivity hypothesis. *Journal of Personality and Social Psychology, 69*(4), 759–777.
145. Suls, J. (2001). Affect, stress and personality. In J. P. Forgas (Ed.), *Handbook of Affect and Social Cognition*. Mahwah, NJ: Erlbaum.

Chapter 4

146. Bar-On, R. (1997). *Bar-On Emotional Quotient Inventory. Technical manual*. Toronto: Multi-Health Systems, Inc.
147. Bar-On, R. (2000). Emotional and social intelligence: Insights from the Emotional Quotient Inventory (EQ-i). In R. Bar-On & J. D. A. Parker, (Eds.), *Handbook of emotional intelligence*. San Francisco: Jossey-Bass.

148. Beresnevaite, M. (2000). Exploring the benefits of group psychotherapy in reducing alexithymia in coronary heart disease patients: A preliminary study. *Psychotherapy and Psychosomatics, 69,* 117–122.

149. Casper, R. C. (1990). Personality features of women with good outcome from restricting anorexia nervosa. *Psychosomatic Medicine, 52,* 156–170.

150. Costa, P. T., & McCrae, R. R. (1992). *Revised NEO Personality Inventory (NEO PI-R) and NEO Five-Factor Inventory (NEO-FFI) professional handbook.* Odessa, FL: Psychological Assessment Resources.

151. Dawda, D., & Hart, S. D. (2000). Assessing emotional intelligence: Reliability and validity of the Bar-On Emotional Quotient Inventory (EQ-i) in university students. *Personality and Individual Differences, 28,* 797–812.

152. Gardner, H. (1983). *Frames of mind: The theory of multiple intelligences.* New York: Basic Books.

153. Garner, D. M. (1984). *Eating Disorder Inventory.* Odessa, FL: Psychological Assessment Resources.

154. Kooiman, C. G., Spinhoven, Ph., Trijsburg, R. W., & Rooijmans, H. G. M. (1998). Perceived parental attitude, alexithymia and defense style in psychiatric outpatients. *Psychotherapy and Psychosomatics, 67,* 81–87.

155. Lane, R., Sechrest, L., Reidel, R., Weldon, V., Kaszniak, A., & Schwartz, G. (1996). Impaired verbal and nonverbal emotion recognition in alexithymia. *Psychosomatic Medicine, 58,* 203–210.

156. Levine, D., Marziali, E., & Hood, J. (1997). Emotion processing in borderline personality disorders. *Journal of Nervous and Mental Disease, 185,* 240–246.

157. Mayer, J. D., & Salovey, P. (1997). What is emotional intelligence? In P. Salovey & D. J. Sluyter (Eds.), *Emotional development and emotional intelligence: Educational implications* (pp. 3–34). New York: Basic Books.

158. Nemiah J. C., Freyberger, H., & Sifneos, P. E. (1976). Alexithymia: A view of the psychosomatic process. In O. W. Hill (Ed.), *Modern trends in psychosomatic medicine* (vol. 3, pp. 430–439). London: Butterworths.

159. Parker, J. D. A. , Taylor, G. J., & Bagby, R. M. (1998). Alexithymia: Relationship with ego defense and coping styles. *Comprehensive Psychiatry, 39,* 91–98.

160. Parker, J. D. A., Taylor, G. J., & Bagby, R. M. (2001). Relationship between alexithymia and emotional intelligence. *Personality and Individual Differences, 30,* 107–115.

161. Salovey, P., & Mayer, J. D. (1989/90). Emotional intelligence. *Imagination, Cognition, and Personality, 9,* 185–211.

162. Taylor, G. J. (2000). Recent developments in alexithymia theory and research. *Canadian Journal of Psychiatry, 45,* 134–142.

163. Taylor, G. J., & Bagby, R. M. (2000). Overview of the alexithymia construct. In R. Bar-On & J. D. A. Parker (Eds.), *Handbook of emotional intelligence* (pp. 40–67). San Francisco: Jossey-Bass.

164. Taylor, G. J., Bagby, R. M., & Luminet, O. (2000). Assessment of alexithymia: Self-report and observer-rated measures. In R. Bar-On & J. D. A. Parker, (Eds.), *Handbook of emotional intelligence* (pp. 301–319). San Francisco: Jossey-Bass.

165. Taylor, G. J., Bagby, R. M., & Parker, J. D. A. (1997). *Disorders of affect regulation: Alexithymia in medical and psychiatric illness.* Cambridge: Cambridge University Press.

166. Taylor, G. J., Parker, J. D. A., & Bagby, R. M. (1999). Emotional intelligence and the emotional brain: Points of convergence and implications for psychoanalysis. *Journal of the American Academy of Psychoanalysis, 27,* 339–354.

167. Taylor, G. J., Parker, J. D. A., Bagby, R. M., & Bourke, M. P. (1996). Relationships between alexithymia and psychological characteristics associated with eating disorders. *Journal of Psychosomatic Research, 41,* 561–568.

Chapter 5

168. American Psychiatric Association (APA). (1994). *Diagnostic and statistical manual of mental disorders (4th ed.)*. Washington, DC: Author.
169. Bar-On, R. (1988). *The development of a concept of psychological well-being.* Unpublished doctoral dissertation, Rhodes University, South Africa.
170. Bar-On, R. (1997). *The Emotional Quotient Inventory (EQ-i): A test of emotional intelligence.* Toronto, Canada: Multi-Health Systems.
171. Bar-On, R. (1997). *The Emotional Quotient Inventory (EQ-i): Technical manual*. Toronto, Canada: Multi-Health Systems, Inc.
172. Bar-On, R. (2000). Emotional and social intelligence: Insights from the Emotional Quotient Inventory (EQ-i). In R. Bar-On and J. D. A. Parker (Eds.), *Handbook of emotional intelligence*. San Francisco: Jossey-Bass.
173. Bar-On, R., & Parker, J. D. A. (2000). *Handbook of emotional intelligence*. San Francisco: Jossey-Bass.
174. Bar-On, R., & Sitarenios, G. (2000). Occupational EQ profiles. Unpublished manuscript.
175. Bechara, A., Tranel, D., & Damasio, R. (2000). Poor judgment in spite of high intellect: Neurological evidence for emotional intelligence. In R. Bar-On and J. D. A. Parker (Eds.), *Handbook of emotional intelligence*. San Francisco: Jossey-Bass.
176. Cantor, N., & Kihlstrom, J. (1987). *Personality and social intelligence*. Englewood Cliffs, NJ: Erlbaum.
177. Cantor, N., & Kihlstrom, J. (1989). Social intelligence and cognitive assessments of personality. In R. S. Wyer & T. K. Srull (Eds.), *Advances in social cognition* (vol. 2, pp. 1–59). Hillsdale, NJ: Erlbaum.
178. Chapin, F. S. (1942). Preliminary standardization of a social impact scale. *American Sociological Review, 7*, 214–225.
179. Chapin, F. S. (1967). *The Social Insight Test*. Palo Alto, CA: Consulting Psychologists Press.
180. Coan, R. W. (1977). *Hero, artist, sage, or saint? A survey of views on what is variously called mental health, normality, maturity, self-actualization, and human fulfillment*. New York: Columbia University Press.
181. Damm, V. J. (1972). Overall measures of self-actualization derived from the Personal Orientation Inventory: A replication and refinement study. *Educational and Psychological Measurement, 32*, 485–489.
182. Darwin, C. (1872/1965). *The expression of the emotions in man and animals*. Chicago: University of Chicago Press.
183. Dawda, R., & Hart, S. D. (2000). Assessing emotional intelligence: Reliability and validity of the Bar-On Emotional Quotient Inventory (EQ-i) in university students. *Journal of Personality and Individual Differences, 28*, 797–812.
184. Derksen, J., Kramer, I., & Katzko, M. (1999). The reliability and validity of the Dutch version of the EQ-i. Unpublished manuscript.
185. Doll, E. A. (1935). A generic scale of social maturity. *American Journal of Orthopsychiatry, 5*, 180–188.
186. Doll, E. A. (1953). *The measurement of social competence*. Minneapolis: American Guidance Service.
187. Doll, E. A. (1965). *Vineland Social Maturity Scale*. Circle Pines, MN: American Guidance Service.
188. Dupertuis, D. G. (1996). *The EQ-i and MMPI-2 profiles of a clinical sample in Argentina*. Unpublished manuscript.

189. English, H. B., & English, A. C. (Eds.) (1966). *A comprehensive dictionary of psychological and psychoanalytic terms.* New York: David McKay.

190. Fund, S. (2000). *Examining the contribution of emotional intelligence in occupational performance.* Unpublished manuscript.

191. Gardner, H. (1983). *Frames of mind.* New York: Basic Books.

192. Gardner, H. (1993). *Multiple intelligences: The theory and practice.* New York: Basic Books.

193. Goleman, D. (1995). *Emotional intelligence.* New York: Bantam Books.

194. Goleman, D. (1998). *Working with emotional intelligence.* New York: Bantam Books.

195. Heath, D. H. (1983). The maturing person. In R. Walsh & D. H. Shapiro, *Beyond health and normality: Explorations of exceptional psychological well-being.* New York: Van Nostrand Reinhold.

196. Jahoda, M. (1958). *Current concepts of positive mental health.* New York: Basic Books.

197. Kelly, G. A. (1955). *A theory of personality: The psychology of personal constructs.* New York: Norton.

198. Lane, R. D. (2000). Levels of emotional awareness: Neurological, psychological and social perspectives. In R. Bar-On and J. D. A. Parker (Eds.), *Handbook of emotional intelligence.* San Francisco: Jossey-Bass.

199. Lane, R. D., & Schwartz, G. E. (1987). Levels of emotional awareness: A cognitive-developmental theory and its application to psychopathology. *American Journal of Psychiatry, 144,* 133–143.

200. LeDoux, J. (1996). *The emotional brain: The mysterious underpinnings of emotional life.* New York: Simon and Schuster.

201. Leuner, B. (1966). Emotional intelligence and emancipation. *Praxis der Kinderpsychologie und Kinderpsychiatrie, 15,* 196–203.

202. Lindner, R. (1956). *Must you conform?* Boulder, CO: Rinehart.

203. MacLean, P. D. (1949). Psychosomatic disease and the visceral brain: Recent developments bearing on the Papez theory of emotion. *Psychosomatic Medicine, II,* 338–353.

204. Maslow, A. H. (1954). *Motivation and personality.* New York: Harper and Brothers.

205. Maslow, A. H. (1955). Deficiency motivation and growth motivation. In M. R. Jones (Ed.), *Nebraska symposium on motivation.* Lincoln, NE: University of Nebraska Press.

206. Maslow, A. H. (1950). Self-actualizing people: A study of psychology health. *Personality, 1,* 11–34.

207. Maslow, A. H. (1976). *The farther reaches of human nature.* New York: Penguin Books.

208. Mayer, J. D., Caruso, D., & Salovey, P. (2000). Selecting a measure of emotional intelligence: The case for ability scales. In R. Bar-On and J. D. A. Parker (Eds.), *Handbook of emotional intelligence.* San Francisco: Jossey-Bass.

209. Mayer, J. D., Salovey, P., & Caruso, D. (2000). Emotional intelligence as *zeitgeist,* as personality, and as a mental ability. In R. Bar-On and J. D. A. Parker (Eds.), *Handbook of emotional intelligence.* San Francisco: Jossey-Bass.

210. Mayman, M. (1955). *The diagnosis of mental health.* Menninger Foundation, Topeka, KS. Unpublished manuscript.

211. McCallum, M. (1989). *A controlled study of effectiveness and patient suitability for short-term group psychotherapy.* Unpublished doctoral dissertation, McGill University, Montreal, Quebec, Canada.

212. McCallum, M., & Piper, W. E. (2000). Psychological mindedness and emotional intelligence. In R. Bar-On and J. D. A. Parker (Eds.), *Handbook of emotional intelligence.* San Francisco: Jossey-Bass.

213. Møller, C., & Bar-On, R. (2000). *Heart work.* Hillerød, Denmark: TMI.

214. Moss, F. A., & Hunt, T. (1927). Are you socially intelligent? *Scientific American, 137,* 108–110.

215. Moss, F. A., Hunt, T., Omwake, K. T., & Woodward, L. G. (1955). *Manual for the George*

Washington University Series Social Intelligence Test. Washington, DC: Center for Psychological Services.

216. Naglieri, J. A., & Bardos, A. N. (1997). *General Ability Measure for Adults (GAMA).* Tucson, AZ: National Computer Systems (NCS).

217. Nemiah, J. C. (1977). Alexithymia: Theoretical considerations. *Psychotherapy and Psychosomatics, 28,* 199–206.

218. Plake, B. S., & Impara, J. C. (Eds.). (1999). *Supplement to the thirteenth mental measurement yearbook.* Lincoln, NE: Buros Institute for Mental Measurement.

219. Raven, J. C. (1958). *Standard Progressive Matrices.* London: H. K. Lewis & Co. Ltd.

220. Rogers, C. R. (1961). *On becoming a person* (2nd ed.). Boston: Houghton Mifflin.

221. Rotter, J. B. (1966). Generalized expectancies for internal versus external control of reinforcement. *Psychological Monographs, 80,* 1–28.

222. Ruesch, J. (1948). The infantile personality. *Psychosomatic Medicine, 10,* 134–144.

223. Saarni, C. (1990). Emotional competence: How emotions and relationships become integrated. In R. A. Thompson (Ed.), *Socioemotional development. Nebraska symposium on motivation* (vol. 36, pp. 115–182). Lincoln, NE: University of Nebraska Press.

224. Saarni, C. (2000). Emotional competence: A developmental perspective. In R. Bar-On and J. D. A. Parker (Eds.), *Handbook of emotional intelligence.* San Francisco: Jossey-Bass.

225. Salovey, P., & Mayer, J. D. (1990). Emotional intelligence. *Imagination, Cognition, and Personality, 9,* 185–211.

226. Shostrom, E. L. (1964). An inventory for the measurement of self-actualization. *Educational and Psychological Measurement, 24*(2), 207–218.

227. Shostrom, E. L. (1974). *Personality Orientation Inventory: An inventory for the measurement of self-actualization.* San Diego, CA: Educational Industrial Testing Service.

228. Sifneos, P. E. (1967). Clinical observations on some patients suffering from a variety of psychosomatic diseases. *Acta Medicina Psychosomatica, 21,* 133–136.

229. Sternberg, R. (1997). *Successful intelligence.* New York: Plume.

230. Sternberg, R. J. (1985). *Beyond IQ: A triarchic theory of human intelligence.* New York: Cambridge University Press.

231. Strupp, H. H., & Hadley, S. W. (1977). A tripartite model of mental health and therapeutic outcomes: With special reference to negative effects in psychotherapy. *American Psychologist, 32*(3), 187–196.

232. Taylor, G. J. (1977). Alexithymia and the counter-transference. *Psychotherapy and Psychosomatics, 28,* 141–147.

233. Taylor, G. J., Bagby, R. M., & Parker, J. D. A. (1991). The alexithymia construct: A potential paradigm for psychosomatic medicine. *Psychosomatics, 32,* 153–164.

234. Taylor, G. J., Bagby, R. M., & Parker, J. D. A. (1997). *Disorders of affect regulation: Alexithymia in medical and psychiatric illness.* Cambridge, UK: Cambridge University Press.

235. Thorndike, E. L. (1920). Intelligence and its uses. *Harper's Magazine, 140,* 227–235.

236. Thorndike, R. L., & Stein, S. (1937). An evaluation of the attempts to measure social intelligence. *Psychological Bulletin, 34,* 275–284.

237. Wechsler, D. (1940). Nonintellective factors in general intelligence. *Psychological Bulletin, 37,* 444–445.

238. Wechsler, D. (1943). Nonintellective factors in general intelligence. *Journal of Abnormal Social Psychology, 38,* 100–104.

239. Wechsler, D. (1958). *The measurement and appraisal of adult intelligence* (4th ed.). Baltimore, MD: The Williams & Wilkins Company.

240. Zirkel, S. (2000). Social intelligence: The development and maintenance of purposive behavior. In R. Bar-On and J. D. A. Parker (Eds.), *Handbook of emotional intelligence.* San Francisco: Jossey-Bass.

Chapter 6

241. Beach, S., & Fincham, F. (1994). Toward an integrated model of negative affectivity in marriage. In S. Johnson & L. Greenberg (Eds.), *The heart of the matter: Perspectives on emotion in marital therapy* (pp. 227–255). New York: Brunner/Mazel.
242. Brody, L. (1999). *Gender, emotion, and the family.* Cambridge, MA: Harvard University Press.
243. Caspi, A., Elder, G. H., & Bem, D. J. (1987). Moving against the world: Life-course patterns of explosive children. *Developmental Psychology, 23,* 308–313.
244. Carstensen, L., Gottman, J., & Levenson, R. (1995). Emotional behavior in long-term marriage. *Psychology and Aging, 10,* 140–149.
245. Christensen, A., & Heavey, C. L. (1990). Gender and social structure in the demand/withdraw pattern of marital conflict. *Journal of Personality and Social Psychology, 59,* 73–81.
246. Clark, M., Fitness, J., & Brissette, I. (2001). Understanding people's perceptions of relationships is crucial to understanding their emotional lives. In G. J. O. Fletcher & M. Clark (Eds.), *Handbook of social psychology. Vol 2: Interpersonal processes* (Chap.10, pp. 253–278). Oxford, UK: Blackwell Publishers.
247. Dutton, D. G. (1998). *The abusive personality: Violence and control in intimate relationships.* New York: Guilford.
248. Epstein, S. (1998). *Constructive thinking: The key to emotional intelligence.* Westport, CT: Praeger.
249. Fehr, B., & Baldwin, M. (1996). Prototype and script analyses of laypeople's knowledge of anger. In G. J. O. Fletcher & J. Fitness (Eds.), *Knowledge structures in close relationships: A social psychological approach* (pp. 219–245). Mahwah, NJ: Erlbaum.
250. Fitness, J. (2001). Betrayal, rejection, revenge, and forgiveness: An interpersonal script approach. In M. Leary (Ed)., *Interpersonal rejection.* New York: Oxford University Press.
251. Fitness, J. (2000, June). *Emotional intelligence in personal relationships: Cognitive, emotional, and behavioral aspects.* Paper presented at the 2nd Joint Conference of ISSPR and INPR, Brisbane, Australia.
252. Fitness, J. (1996). Emotion knowledge structures in close relationships. In G. J. O. Fletcher & J. Fitness (Eds.), *Knowledge structures in close relationships: A social psychological approach* (pp. 219–245). Mahwah, NJ: Erlbaum.
253. Fitness, J., & Fletcher, G. J. O. (1993). Love, hate, anger, and jealousy in close relationships: A cognitive appraisal and prototype analysis. *Journal of Personality and Social Psychology, 65,* 942–958.
254. Fletcher, G. J. O., & Thomas, G. (1999). Behavior and on-line cognition in marital interaction. *Personal Relationships, 7,* 111–130.
255. Geen, R. (1995). *Human motivation: A social psychological approach.* Pacific Grove, CA: Brooks-Cole.
256. Gottman, J. M. (1994). *What predicts divorce? The relationship between marital processes and marital outcomes.* Hillsdale, NJ: Erlbaum.
257. Huston, T., & Houts, R. (1998). The psychological infrastructure of courtship and marriage: The role of personality and compatibility in romantic relationships. In T. Bradbury (Ed.), *The developmental course of marital dysfunction* (pp. 114–151). New York: Cambridge University Press.
258. Mayer, J. D., & Salovey, P. (1997). What is emotional intelligence? In P. Salovey & D. J. Sluyter (Eds.), *Emotional development and emotional intelligence* (pp. 3–31). New York: Basic Books.
259. Mayer, J. D., Caruso, D., & Salovey, P. (1999). *Emotional intelligence meets traditional standards for an intelligence.* Manuscript submitted for publication.

260. Murray, S., Holmes, J., & Griffin, D. (1996). The benefits of positive illusions: Idealization and the construction of satisfaction in close relationships. *Journal of Personality and Social Psychology, 70,* 79–98.

261. Noller, P., & Ruzzene, M. (1991). Communication in marriage: The influence of affect and cognition. In G. J. O. Fletcher & F. Fincham (Eds.), *Cognition in close relationships* (pp. 203–233). Hillsdale, NJ: Erlbaum.

262. Oatley, K., & Jenkins, J. (1996). *Understanding emotions.* Cambridge, USA: Blackwell Publishers.

263. O'Leary, K. D., & Smith, D. (1991). Marital interactions. *Annual Review of Psychology, 42,* 191–212.

264. Planalp, S., & Fitness, J. (1999). Thinking/feeling about social and personal relationships. *Journal of Social and Personal Relationships, 16,* 731–750.

265. Rusbult, C. E., Bissonnette, V., Arriaga, X. B., & Cox, C. (1998). Accommodation processes during the early years of marriage. In T. Bradbury (Ed.), *The developmental course of marital dysfunction* (pp. 74–113). New York: Cambridge University Press.

266. Salovey, P., Mayer, J. D., Goldman, S. L., Turvey, C., & Palfai, T. P. (1995). Emotional attention, clarity, and repair: Exploring emotional intelligence using the trait meta-mood scale. In J.W. Pennebaker (Ed.), *Emotion, disclosure, and health* (pp. 125–154). Washington, DC: American Psychological Association.

267. Tangney, J. P. (1995). Shame and guilt in interpersonal relationships. In J. P. Tangney & K. Fischer (Eds.), *Self-conscious emotions: The psychology of shame, guilt, embarrassment, and pride* (pp. 114–139). New York: Guilford.

Chapter 7

268. Aldous, J. (1977). Family interaction patterns. *Annual Review of Sociology, 3,* 105–135.

269. Baron-Cohen, S. (1997). *Mindblindness: An essay on autism and theory of mind.* Cambridge, MA: MIT Press.

270. Bissonnette, V. L., Rusbult, C. E., & Kilpatrick, S. D. (1997). Empathic accuracy and marital conflict resolution. In W. Ickes (Ed.), *Empathic accuracy* (pp. 251–281). New York: Guilford.

271. Buss, D. M., Shackelford, T. K., Kirkpatrick, L. A., Choe, J. C., Lim, H. K., Hasegawa, M., Hasegawa, T., & Bennett, K. (1999). Jealousy and the nature of beliefs about infidelity: Tests of competing hypotheses about sex differences in the United States, Korea, and Japan. *Personal Relationships, 6,* 125–150.

272. Colvin, C. R. (1993). Judgable people: Personality, behavior, and competing explanations. *Journal of Personality and Social Psychology, 64,* 861–873.

273. Colvin, C. R., Vogt, D., & Ickes, W. (1997). Why do friends understand each other better than strangers do? In W. Ickes (Ed.), *Empathic accuracy.* New York: Guilford.

274. Davis, M. H., & Kraus, L. A. (1997). Personality and empathic accuracy. In W. Ickes (Ed.), *Empathic accuracy* (pp. 144–168). New York: Guilford.

275. Eisenberg, N., Murphy, B. C., & Shepard, S. (1997). The development of empathic accuracy. In W. Ickes (Ed.), *Empathic accuracy* (pp. 73–116). New York: Guilford.

276. Funder, D. C. (1995). On the accuracy of personality judgment: A realistic approach. *Psychological Review, 102*(4), 652–670.

277. Gaelick, L., Bodenhausen, G., & Wyer, R. S. (1985). Emotional communication in close relationships. *Journal of Personality and Social Psychology, 49,* 1246–1265.

278. Gesn, P. R. (1995). *Shared knowledge between same-sex friends: Measurement and validation.* Unpublished master's thesis, University of Texas at Arlington.

279. Gesn, P.R., & Ickes, W. (1999). The development of meaning contexts for empathic

accuracy: Channel and sequence effects. *Journal of Personality and Social Psychology, 77*, 746–761.

280. Graham, T. (1994). *Gender, relationships, and target differences in empathic accuracy.* Unpublished master's thesis, University of Texas at Arlington.
281. Hancock, M., & Ickes, W. (1996). Empathic accuracy: When does the perceiver–target relationship make a difference? *Journal of Social and Personal Relationships, 13,* 179–199.
282. Hutchison, J., & Ickes, W. (1998). *Length of relationship and empathic accuracy: A cross-sectional analysis.* Unpublished data, University of Texas at Arlington.
283. Ickes, W., & Simpson, J. A. (1997). Managing empathic accuracy in close relationships. In W. Ickes (Ed.), *Empathic accuracy* (pp. 218–250). New York: Guilford.
284. Ickes, W., & Simpson, J. (2001). Motivational aspects of empathic accuracy. In G. J. O. Fletcher & M. S. Clark (Eds.), *Interpersonal Processes: Blackwell Handbook in Social Psychology* (pp.229–249). Oxford, UK: Blackwell.
285. Ickes, W., Buysse, A., Pham, H., Rivers, K., Erickson, J. R., Hancock, M., Kelleher, J., & Gesn, P. R. (2000). On the difficulty of distinguishing "good" and "poor" perceivers: A social relations analysis of empathic accuracy data. *Personal Relationships, 7,* 219–234.
286. Ickes, W., Gesn, P. R., & Graham, T. (2000). Gender differences in empathic accuracy: Differential ability or differential motivation? *Personal Relationships, 7*(1), 95–109.
287. Ickes, W., Hancock, M., Graham, T., Gesn, P. R., & Mortimer, D. C. (1994). (Nonsignificant) individual difference correlates of perceivers' empathic accuracy scores. Unpublished data, University of Texas at Arlington.
288. Ickes, W., Marangoni, C., & Garcia, S. (1997). Studying empathic accuracy in a clinically relevant context. In W. Ickes (Ed.), *Empathic accuracy* (pp. 282–310). New York: Guilford.
289. Ickes, W. (1993). Empathic accuracy. *Journal of Personality, 61,* 587–609.
290. Ickes, W. (Ed.). (1997). Empathic accuracy. New York: Guilford.
291. Ickes, W., Stinson, L., Bissonnette, V., & Garcia, S. (1990). Naturalistic social cognition: Empathic accuracy in mixed-sex dyads. *Journal of Personality and Social Psychology, 59,* 730–742.
292. Karniol, R. (1990). Reading people's minds: A transformation rule model for predicting others' thoughts and feelings. *Advances in Experimental Social Psychology, 23,* 211–247.
293. Kenny, D. A. (1994). *Interpersonal perception: A social relations analysis.* New York: Guilford.
294. Kirchler, E. (1988). Marital happiness and interaction in everyday surroundings: A time-sample diary approach for couples. *Journal of Social and Personal Relationships, 5,* 375–382.
295. Kirchler, E. (1989). Everyday life experiences at home: An interaction diary approach to assess marital relationships. *Journal of Family Psychology, 2,* 311–336.
296. Klein, K. J. K., & Hodges, S. (in press). Gender differences, motivation, and empathic accuracy. *Personality and Social Psychology Bulletin.*
297. Kursh, C. O. (1971). The benefits of poor communication. *Psychoanalytic Review, 58,* 189–208.
298. Levinger, G., & Breedlove, J. (1966). Interpersonal attraction and agreement. *Journal of Personality and Social Psychology, 3,* 367–372.
299. Marangoni, C., Garcia, S., Ickes, W., & Teng, G. (1995). Empathic accuracy in a clinically-relevant setting. *Journal of Personality and Social Psychology, 39,* 1135–1148.
300. Murray, S.L. & Holmes, J. G. (1996). The construction of relationship realities. In J. O. Fletcher (Ed.), *Knowledge structures in close relationships: A social psychological approach* (pp. 91–120). Mahwah, NJ: Lawrence Erlbaum Associates.

301. Noller, P. (1980). Misunderstandings in marital communication: A study of couples' nonverbal communication. *Journal of Personality and Social Psychology, 39,* 1135–1148.
302. Noller, P. (1981). Gender and marital adjustment level differences in decoding messages from spouses and strangers. *Journal of Personality and Social Psychology, 41,* 272–278.
303. Noller, P. (1984). *Nonverbal communication and marital interaction.* Oxford: Pergamon.
304. Noller, P., & Ruzzene, M. (1991). The effects of cognition and affect on marital communication. In G. J. O. Fletcher & F. D. Fincham (Eds.), *Cognition in close relationships* (pp. 203–233). New York: Lawrence Erlbaum Associates.
305. Rausch, H. L., Barry, W. A., Hertel, R. K., & Swain, M. A. (1974). *Communication conflict and marriage.* San Francisco: Jossey-Bass.
306. Roeyers, H., Buysse, A., Ponnet, K., & Pichal, B. (2000). *Advancing advanced mindreading tests: Empathic accuracy in adults with a pervasive developmental disorder.* Manuscript under editorial review.
307. Rothbaum, F., Weisz, J. R., & Snyder, S. S. (1982). Changing the world and changing the self: A two-process model of perceived control. *Journal of Personality and Social Psychology, 42,* 5–37.
308. Salovery, P., Hsee, C. K., & Mayer, J. D. (1993). Emotional intelligence and the self-regulation of affect. In D. M. Wegner (Ed.), *Handbook of mental control* (pp. 58–277). Englewood Cliffs, NJ: Prentice-Hall.
309. Schroder, H. M., Driver, M. J., & Streufert, S. (1967). *Human information processing.* New York: Holt, Rinehart, & Winston.
310. Shapiro, A., & Swensen, C. (1969). Patterns of self-disclosure among married couples. *Journal of Counseling Psychology, 16,* 179–180.
311. Sillars, A. L. (1981). Attributions and interpersonal conflict resolution. In J. H. Harvey, W. J. Ickes, & R. F. Kidd (Eds.), *New directions in attribution research* (vol. 3, pp. 279–305). Hillsdale, NJ: Erlbaum.
312. Sillars, A. L. (1985). Interpersonal perception in relationships. In W. Ickes (Ed.), *Compatible and incompatible relationships* (pp. 277–305). New York: Springer-Verlag.
313. Sillars, A. L., & Scott, M. D. (1983). Interpersonal perception between intimates: An integrative review. *Human Communication Research, 10,* 153–176.
314. Sillars, A. L., & Parry, D. (1982). Stress, cognition, and communication in interpersonal conflicts. *Communication Research, 9,* 201–226.
315. Simpson, J. A., Ickes, W., & Grich, J. (1999). When accuracy hurts: Reactions of anxious-uncertain individuals to a relationship-threatening situation. *Journal of Personality and Social Psychology, 76,* 754–769.
316. Simpson, J. A., Ickes, W., & Blackstone, T. (1995). When the head protects the heart: Empathic accuracy in dating relationships. *Journal of Personality and Social Psychology, 69,* 629–641.
317. Smither, S. (1977). A reconsideration of the developmental study of empathy. *Human Development, 20,* 253–276.
318. Snyder, M. (1987). *Public appearances, private realities: The psychology of self-monitoring.* New York: W. H. Freeman.
319. Stinson, L., & Ickes, W. (1992). Empathic accuracy in the interactions of male friends versus male strangers. *Journal of Personality and Social Psychology, 62,* 787–797.
320. Taft, R. (1955). The ability to judge people. *Psychological Bulletin, 52,* 1–23.
321. Thomas, G., & Fletcher, Garth J. O. (1997). Empathic accuracy in close relationships. In W. Ickes (Ed.), *Empathic accuracy* (pp. 194–217). New York: Guilford.
322. Thomas, G., Fletcher, G. J. O., & Lange, C. (1997). On-line empathic accuracy in marital interaction. *Journal of Personality & Social Psychology, 72*(4), 839–850.
323. Trommsdorff, G., & John, H. (1992). Decoding affective communication in intimate relationships. *European Journal of Social Psychology, 22,* 41–54.

324. Vogt, D. S., & Colvin, C. R. (2000). *The good judge of personality: Theory, correlates, and Cronbachian "artifacts."* Manuscript submitted for publication.

325. Watzlawick, P., Weakland, J., & Fisch, R. (1974). *Principles of problem formation and problem resolution.* New York: Norton.

326. Weary-Bradley, G. (1978). Self-serving biases in the attribution process: A re-examination of the fact or fiction question. *Journal of Personality and Social Psychology, 36,* 56–71.

Chapter 8

327. Abbott, R. D., O'Donnell, J., Hawkins, D., Hill, K. G., Kosterman, R., & Catalano, R. F. (1998). Changing teaching practices to promote achievement and bonding to school. *American Journal of Orthopsychiatry, 68,* 542–552.

328. Battistich, V., Schaps, E., Watson, M., Solomon, D., & Lewis, C. (2000). Effects of the Child Development Project on students' drug use and other problem behaviors. *Journal of Primary Prevention, 21.*

329. Battistich, V., & Solomon, D. (1995, April). Linking teacher change to student change. In E. Schaps (Chair), *Why restructuring must focus on thinking and caring: A model for deep, long term change through staff development.* Symposium conducted at the meeting of the American Educational Research Association, San Francisco.

330. Berman, S. (1990). Educating for social responsibility. *Educational Leadership, 48*(3), 75–80.

331. Bruene-Butler, L., Hampson, J., Elias, M. J., Clabby, J., & Schuyler, T. (1997). The Improving Social Awareness-Social Problem Solving Project. In G. Albee & T. Gullotta (Eds.), *Primary prevention works* (pp. 239–267). Newbury Park, CA: Sage.

332. Cohen, J. (Ed.).(1999). *Educating minds and hearts: Social emotional learning and the passage into adolescence.* New York: Teacher's College Press.

333. Comer, J. P. (1994). Introduction and problem analysis. In N. M. Haynes (Ed.), *School Development Program Research Monograph* (pp. i–vi). New Haven, CT: Yale Child Study Center.

334. Comer, J. P., Haynes, N. M., Joyner, E. T., & Ben-Avie, M. (1996). *Rallying the whole village: The Comer process for reforming education.* New York: Teachers College Press.

335. Dewey, J. (1933). *How we think.* Lexington, MA: Heath.

336. Dewey, J. (1938). *Experience and education.* New York: Macmillan.

337. Elias, M. J., Bruene-Butler, L., Blum, L., & Schuyler, T. (2000). Voices from the field: Identifying and overcoming roadblocks to carrying out programs in social and emotional learning/emotional intelligence. *Journal of Educational and Psychological Consultation, 11*(2), 253–272.

338. Elias, M. J., & Clabby, J. (1992). *Building social problem solving skills: Guidelines from a school-based program.* Morristown, NJ: Center for Child and Family Development (www.EQParenting.com).

339. Elias, M. J., Gara, M. A., Schuyler, T. F., Branden-Muller, L. R., & Sayette, M. A. (1991). The promotion of social competence: Longitudinal study of a preventive school-based program. *American Journal of Orthopsychiatry, 61,* 409–417.

340. Elias, M. J., & Tobias, S. E. (1996). *Social problem solving interventions in the schools.* New York: Guilford.

341. Elias, M. J., Tobias, S. E., & Friedlander, B. S. (1999). *Emotionally intelligent parenting: How to raise a self-disciplined, responsible, and socially skilled child.* New York: Harmony/Random House.

342. Elias, M. J., Tobias, S. E., & Friedlander, B. S. (2000). *Raising emotionally intelligent*

teenagers: Parenting with love, laughter, and limits. New York: Harmony/Random House.

343. Elias, M. J., Zins, J., Weissberg, R. P., & Associates (1997). *Promoting social and emotional learning: Guidelines for educators*. Alexandria, VA: Association for Supervision and Curriculum Development.

344. Felner, R. D., & Adan, A. M. (1988). The school transitional environment project: An ecological intervention and evaluation. In R. H. Price, E. L. Cowen, R. P. Lorion, & J. Ramos-McKay (Eds.), *14 ounces of prevention: A casebook for practioners* (pp. 11–122). Washington, DC: American Psychological Association.

345. Gardner, H. (1993). *Multiple intelligences: The theory in practice*. New York: Basic Books.

346. Goldstein, A. P., Harootunian, B., & Conoley, J. (1994). *Student aggression: Prevention, management, and replacement training*. New York: Guilford.

347. Goleman, D. (1995). *Emotional intelligence*. New York: Bantam Books.

348. Gottfredson, D. C. (1986). An empirical test of school-based environmental and individual interventions to reduce the risk of delinquent behavior. *Criminology, 24*, 705–731.

349. Greenberg, M. T., & Kusche, C. A. (1997). *Improving childrens' emotion regulation and social competence: The effects of the PATHS curriculum*. Paper presented at meeting of Society for Research in Child Development, Washington, D.C.

350. Greenberg, M. T., Kusche, C. A., Cook, E. T., & Quamma, J. P. (1995). Promoting emotional competence in school-aged deaf children: The effects of the PATHS curriculum. *Development and Psychopathology, 7*, 117–136.

351. Hammond, W. R. & Yung, B. R. (1991). Preventing violence in at-risk African-American youth. *Journal of Health Care for the Poor and Underserved, 2*(3), 359–373.

352. Hawkins, J. D., Catalano, R. F., & Associates (1992). *Communities that care: Action for drug abuse prevention*. San Fransisco: Jossey-Bass.

353. Hawkins, J. D. & Weis, J. G. (1985). The social development model: An integrated approach to delinquency prevention. *Journal of Primary Prevention, 6*, 73–97.

354. Henrich, C., Brown, J., & Aber, J. L. (1999). Evaluating the effectiveness of school-based violence prevention: Developmental approaches. *Social Policy Report: Society for Research in Child Development, 13*(3), 1–17.

355. Kelder, S. H., Perry, C. L., & Klepp, K. (1993). Community wide youth exercise promotion: Long term outcomes of the Minnesota heart health program and the class of 1989 study. *Journal of School Health, 63*, 218–223.

356. Kress, J. S., Cimring, B. R., & Elias, M. J. (1997). Community psychology consultation and the transition to institutional ownership and operation of intervention. *Journal of Educational and Psychological Consultation, 8*(2), 231–253.

357. Mayer, J. D., & Salovey, P. (1997). What is emotional intelligence? In J. D. Mayer & P. Salovey (Eds.), *Emotional development and emotional intelligence* (pp. 3–31). New York: Basic Books.

358. National Center for Innovation and Education. (1999). *Lessons for life: How smart schools boost academic, social, and emotional intelligence*. Bloomington, IN: HOPE Foundation (www.communitiesofhope.org).

359. Noguera, P. A. (1995). Preventing and producing violence: A critical analysis of responses to school violence. *Harvard Educational Review, 65*(2), 189–212.

360. Norris, J., & Kress, J. S. (2000). Reframing the standards vs. social and emotional learning debate: A case study. *The Fourth R, 91*(2), 7–10.

361. Pedro-Carroll, J. L., Alpert-Gillis, L. J., & Cowen, E. L. (1992). An evaluation of the efficacy of a preventive intervention for 4th–6th grade urban children of divorce. *Journal of Primary Prevention, 13*, 115–130.

362. Slavin, R. E., Madden, N. A., Dolan, L. J., Wasik, B. A., Ross, S., Smith, L., & Dianda, M. (1995, April). *Success for all: A summary of research*. Paper presented at the meeting of the American Educational Research Association, San Francisco.

363. Sternberg, R. J. (1985). *Beyond IQ*. New York: Cambridge University Press.
364. Tolan, P. H., & Guerra, N. G. (1994). *What works in reducing adolescent violence: An empirical review of the field*. Monograph prepared for the Center for the Study and Prevention of Youth Violence. Boulder: University of Colorado.
365. Weissberg, R. P., & Greenberg, M. T. (1997). School and community competence enhancement and prevention programs. In I. E. Sigel & K. A. Renninger (Eds.), *Handbook of child psychology: Volume 5 child psychology in practice* (5th ed.). New York: Wiley.

Chapter 9

366. Barrick, M. R., & Mount, M. K. (1991). The big five personality dimensions and job performance: A meta-analysis. *Personnel Psychology, 44*, 1–26.
367. Barsade, S. G. (2000). *The ripple effect: Emotional contagion in groups*. Working paper. New Haven, CT: Yale University Press.
368. Bass, B. M. (Ed.). (1981). *Stogdill's handbook of leadership* (2nd Rev.). New York: Free Press.
369. Caldwell, D. F., & Burger, J. M. (1998). Personality characteristic of job applicants and success in screening interviews. *Personnel Psychology, 51*, 119–136.
370. Caruso, D. R., Mayer, J. D., & Salovey, P. (in press). Emotional intelligence and emotional leadership. In R. Riggio & S. Murphy (Eds.), *Multiple intelligences and leadership*. Mahwah, NJ: Erlbaum.
371. Costa, P. T., & McCrae, R .R. (1992). *NEO PI-R professional manual*. Odessa, FL: PAR, Inc.
372. Goleman, D. (1998). *Working with emotional intelligence*. New York: Bantam.
373. Gough, H. C. (1988). *California Psychological Inventory administrator's guide*. Palo Alto, CA: Consulting Psychologists Press.
374. Jordan, P. J., Ashkanasy, N. M., Härtel, C. E. J., & Hooper, G. S. (1999). *Workgroup emotional intelligence: Scale development and relationship to team process effectiveness and goal focus*. Manuscript submitted for publication.
375. Kingsbury, K. E., & Daus, C. S. (2000). *The effects of emotional intelligence on job interview outcomes*. Manuscript submitted for publication.
376. Mayer, J. D., & Salovey, P. (1997). What is emotional intelligence? In P. Salovey & D. Sluyter (Eds.), *Emotional development and emotional intelligence: Implications for educators* (pp. 3–31). New York: Basic Books.
377. Rice, C. L. (1999). *A quantitative study of emotional intelligence and its impact on team performance*. Unpublished master's thesis, Pepperdine University, Malibu, CA.
378. Stein, S., & Book, H. (2000). *The EQ edge*. N. York, ON: Stoddart.
379. Sternberg, R. J. (1997). *Successful intelligence*. New York: Plume.
380. Tett, R. P., Jackson, D. N., & Rothstein, M. (1991). Personality measures as predictors of job performance: A meta-analytic review. *Personnel Psychology, 44*, 703–742.
381. Yukl, G. A. (1981). *Leadership in organizations*. Englewood Cliffs, NJ: Prentice-Hall.

Chapter 10

382. Arkes, H. R., & Blumer, C. (1985). The psychology of sunk cost. *Organizational Behavior and Human Decision Processes, 35*, 124–140.
383. Bahnson, C. B. (1981). Stress and cancer: The state of the art. *Psychosomatics, 22*, 207–220.

384. Benotsch, E. G., Christensen, A. J., & McKelvey, L. (1997). Hostility, social support, and ambulatory cardiovascular activity. *Journal of Behavioral Medicine, 20,* 163–182.

385. Brownley, K. A., Light, K. C., & Anderson, N. B. (1996). Social support and hostility interact to influence clinic, work, and home blood pressure in Black and White men and women. *Psychophysiology, 33,* 434–445.

386. Cameron, L. D., & Nicholls, G. (1998). Expression of stressful experiences through writing: Effects of a self-regulation manipulation for pessimists and optimists. *Health Psychology, 17,* 84–92.

387. Cook, W. W., & Medley, D. M. (1954). Proposed hostility and pharisaic-virtue scales for the MMPI. *Journal of Applied Psychology, 38,* 414–418.

388. Cooper, C. L., & Faragher, E. B. (1992). Coping strategies and breast disorders/cancer. *Psychological Medicine, 22,* 447–455.

389. Cooper, C. L., & Faragher, E. B. (1993). Psychosocial stress and breast cancer: The interrelationship between stress events, coping strategies, and personality. *Psychological Medicine, 23,* 653–662.

390. Derogatis, L. R., Abeloff, M., & Melasaratos, N. (1979). Psychological coping mechanisms and survival time in metastatic breast cancer. *Journal of the American Medical Association, 242,* 1504–1508.

391. Dujovne, V. F., & Houston, B. K. (1991). Hostility-related variables and plasma lipid levels. *Journal of Behavioral Medicine, 14,* 55–56.

392. Faragher, E. B., & Cooper, C. L. (1990). Type A stress prone behavior and breast cancer. *Psychological Medicine, 20,* 663–670.

393. Goldman, S. L., Kraemer, D. T., & Salovey, P. (1996). Beliefs about mood moderate the relationship of stress to illness and symptom reporting. *Journal of Psychosomatic Research, 41,* 115–128.

394. Greenberg, M. A., & Stone, A. A. (1992). Emotional disclosure about traumas and its relation to health: Effects of previous disclosure and trauma severity. *Journal of Personality and Social Psychology, 63,* 75–84.

395. Gross, J. J. (1989). Emotional expression in cancer onset and progression. *Social Science in Medicine, 28,* 1239–1248.

396. Gross, L. (1988). *Art of selling intangibles: How to make your million $ investing other people's money.* New York: Prentice Hall.

397. Kahneman, D., Knetsch, J. L., & Thaler, R. H. (1990). Experimental tests of the endowment effect and the Coase Theorem, *Journal of Political Economy, 98,* 1325–1348.

398. Kahneman, D., Knetsch, J. L., & Thaler, R. H. (1991). The endowment effect, loss aversion, and the status quo bias. *Journal of Economic Perspectives, 5,* 193–206.

399. Kahneman, D., & Tversky, A. (1973). On the psychology of prediction. *Psychological Review, 80,* 237–251.

400. Kahneman, D., & Tversky, A. (1979). Prospect theory: An analysis of decision under risk. *Econometrics, 47,* 263–291.

401. Kahneman, D., & Tversky, A. (1984). Choices, value, and frames. *American Psychologist, 39,* 341–350.

402. Kahneman, D., & Tversky, A. (1991). Loss aversion and riskless choice: A reference dependent model. *Quarterly Journal of Economics, 106,* 1039–1061.

403. Knetsch, J. L., & Sinden, J. A. (1984). Willingness to pay and compensation demanded: Experimental evidence of an unexpected disparity in measures of value. *Quarterly Journal of Economics, 99,* 507–521.

404. Lepore, S. J. (1995). Cynicism, social support, and cardiovascular reactivity. *Health Psychology, 14,* 210–216.

405. Levy, S. M., Herberman, R. B., Maluish, A. M., Schlien, B., & Lippman, M. (1985). Prognostic risk assessment in primary breast cancer by behavioral and immunological parameters. *Health Psychology, 4,* 99–113.

406. Loewenstein, G., & Kahneman, D. (1991). *Explaining the endowment effect.* Unpublished manuscript.

407. Lynch, P. (2000). *One up on Wall Street: How to use what you already know to make money in the market.* Fireside Edition. New York: Simon and Schuster.

408. Matthews, K. A., Owens, J. F., Allen, M. T., & Stoney, C. M. (1992). Do cardiovascular responses to laboratory stress relate to ambulatory blood pressure levels? Yes, in some of the people, some of the time. *Psychosomatic Medicine, 54,* 686–697.

409. Mayer, J. D., & Salovey, P. (1997). What is emotional intelligence? In P. Salovey & D. J. Sluyter (Eds.), *Emotional development and emotional intelligence* (pp. 3–31). New York: Basic Books.

410. McKenna, M. C., Zevon, M. A., Corn, B., & Rounds, J. (1999). Psychosocial factors and the development of breast cancer: A meta-analysis. *Health Psychology, 18,* 520–531.

411. Odean, T. (1998). Are investors reluctant to realize their losses? *The Journal of Finance, 53,* 1775–1798.

412. Pennebaker, J. W. (1997). Writing about emotional experiences as a therapeutic process. *Psychological Science, 8,* 162–166.

413. Pennebaker, J. W., Colder, M., & Sharp, L. K. (1990). Accelerating the coping process. *Journal of Personality and Social Psychology, 58,* 528–537.

414. Pennebaker, J. W., Kiecolt-Glaser, J. K., & Glaser, R. (1988). Disclosure of traumas and immune function: Health implications for psychotherapy. *Journal of Consulting and Clinical Psychology, 56,* 239–245.

415. Petrie, K. J., Booth, R. J., Pennebaker, J. W., Davison, K. P., & Thomas, M. G. (1995). Disclosure of trauma and immune response to a hepatitis B vaccination program. *Journal of Consulting and Clinical Psychology, 63,* 787–792.

416. Salovey, P., & Mayer, J. D. (1990). Emotional intelligence. *Imagination, Cognition, and Personality, 9,* 185–211.

417. Salovey, P., Mayer, J. D., & Caruso, D. (in press). The positive psychology of emotional intelligence. In C. R. Snyder & S. J. Lopez (Eds.), *The handbook of positive psychology.* New York: Oxford University Press.

418. Salovey, P., Woolery, A., & Mayer, J. D. (2000). Emotional intelligence: Conceptualization and measurement. In G. Fletcher & M. Clark (Eds.), *The Blackwell handbook of social psychology: Interpersonal processes* (pp. 279–307). London: Blackwell.

419. Samuelson, W. F., & Zeckhauser, R. (1988). Status quo bias in decision making. *Journal of Risk and Uncertainty, 1,* 7–59.

420. Shefrin, H., & Statman, M. (1985). The disposition to sell winners too early and ride losers too long: Theory and evidence. *The Journal of Finance, 40,* 777–790.

421. Siegman, A. W., & Snow, S. C. (1997). The outward expression of anger, the inward expression of anger, and CVR: The role of vocal expression. *Journal of Behavioral Medicine, 20,* 29–46.

422. Singer, M. (1999, April 26 and May 3). The optimist: Is Ace Greenberg the sanest man on Wall Street? *The New Yorker, 100,* 140–149.

423. Smith, T. W. (1992). Hostility and health: Current status of a psychosomatic hypothesis. *Health Psychology, 11,* 139–150.

424. Smyth, J. M. (1998). Written emotional expression: Effect sizes, outcome types, and moderating variables. *Journal of Consulting and Clinical Psychology, 66,* 174–184.

425. Spiegel, D., Kraemer, H. C., Bloom, J. R., & Gottheil, E. (1989, October 14). Effect of psychosocial treatment on survival of patients with metastatic breast cancer. *The Lancet,* 888–891.

426. Suls, J., & Wan, C. K. (1993). The relationship between trait hostility and cardiovascular reactivity: A quantitative review and analysis. *Psychophysiology, 30,* 1–12.

427. Temoshok, L. (1987). Personality, coping style, emotion, and cancer: Towards an integrative model. *Cancer Surveys, 6*, 545–567.

428. Thaler, R. H. (1980). Toward a positive theory of consumer choice. *Journal of Economic Behavior and Organization, 1*, 39–60.

Chapter 11

429. Bar-On, R. (1997). *The Emotional Quotient Inventory (EQ-I): A test of emotional intelligence.* Toronto, Canada: Multi-Health Systems, Inc.

430. Bar-On, R. (2000). Emotional and social intelligence: Insights from the Emotional Quotient Inventory (EQ-i). In R. Bar-On & J. D. A. Parker (Eds.), *Handbook of emotional intelligence.* San Francisco: Jossey-Bass.

431. Carroll, J. B. (1993). *Human cognitive abilities: A survey of factor-analysis studies.* New York: Cambridge University Press.

432. Ciarrcochi, J., Deane, F., & Anderson, S. (2000). Emotional intelligence moderates the relationship between stress and mental health. Manuscript submitted for publication.

433. Coren, S. (1994). *The intelligence of dogs.* New York: Macmillan.

434. Davies, M., Stankov, L., & Roberts, R. D. (1998). Emotional intelligence: In search of an elusive construct. *Journal of Personality and Social Psychology, 75*, 989–1015.

435. Dawkins, R. (1976). *The selfish gene.* New York: Oxford University Press.

436. Gardner, H. (1983). *Frames of mind: The theory of multiple intelligences.* New York: Basic Books.

437. Goldman, S. L., Kraemer, D. T., & Salovey, P. (1996). Beliefs about mood moderate the relationship of stress to illness and symptom reporting. *Journal of Psychosomatic Research, 41*, 115–128.

438. Goleman, D. (1995). *Emotional intelligence.* New York: Bantam.

439. Goleman, D. (1998). *Working with emotional intelligence.* New York: Bantam.

440. Guilford, J. P. (1967). *The nature of intelligence.* New York: McGraw-Hill.

441. Jensen, A. R. (1998). *The g factor.* Westport, CT: Praeger-Greenwood.

442. Kaufman, A. (2000). Tests of intelligence. In R. J. Sternberg (Ed.), *Handbook of intelligence* (pp. 445–476). New York: Cambridge University Press.

443. Kihlstrom, J. F., & Cantor, N. (2000). Social intelligence. In R. J. Sternberg (Ed.), *Handbook of intelligence* (pp. 359–379). New York: Cambridge University Press.

444. Lane, R. D., Quinlan, D., Schwartz, G., Walker, P., & Zeitlin, S. (1990). The levels of emotional awareness scale: A cognitive-developmental measure of emotion. *Journal of Personality Assessment, 55*, 124–134.

445. Leuner, B. (1966). Emotional intelligence and emancipation. *Praxis der Kinderpsychologie und Kinderpsychiatrie, 15*, 196–203.

446. Mayer, J. D., Caruso, D., & Salovey, P. (1999). Emotional intelligence meets traditional standards for an intelligence. *Intelligence, 27*, 267–298.

447. Mayer, J. D., Salovey, P., & Caruso, D. (2000). Models of emotional intelligence. In R. J. Sternberg (Ed.), *Handbook of intelligence* (pp. 396–420). New York: Cambridge University Press.

448. Nemiah, J. C., Freyberger, H., & Sifneos, P. E. (1976). Alexithymia: A view of the psychosomatic process. In O. W. Hill (Ed.), *Modern trends in psychosomatic medicine* (vol. 3, pp. 430–439). London: Butterworths.

449. Salovey, P., & Mayer, J. D. (1990). Emotional intelligence. *Imagination, Cognition, and Personality, 9*, 185–211.

450. Sternberg, R. J. (1985). *Beyond IQ: A triarchic theory of human intelligence*. New York: Cambridge University Press.

451. Sternberg, R. J. (1993). *Human cognitive abilities: A survey of factor-analytic studies*. New York: Cambridge University Press.

452. Sternberg, R. J. (1997). *Successful intelligence*. New York: Plume.

453. Sternberg, R. J. (1998). *Cupid's arrow*. New York: Cambridge University Press.

454. Sternberg, R. J. (1999). Review of D. Goleman, *Working with emotional intelligence*. *Personnel Psychology, 52,* 780–783.

455. Sternberg, R. J. (Ed.) (2000). *Handbook of intelligence*. New York: Cambridge University Press.

456. Sternberg, R. J., Forsythe, G. B., Hedlund, J., Horvath, J. A., Wagner, R. K., Williams, W. M., Snook, S. A., & Grigorenko, E. L. (2000). *Practical intelligence in everyday life*. New York: Cambridge University Press.

457. Thorndike, E. L. (1920). Intelligence and its use *Harper's Magazine, 140,* 227–235.

458. Thorndike, R. L. (1936). Factor analysis of social and abstract intelligence. *Journal of Educational Psychology, 27,* 231–233.

459. Thorndike, R. L., & Stein, S. (1937). An evaluation of the attempts to measure social intelligence. *Psychological Bulletin, 34,* 275–285.

460. Wagner, R. K. (2000). Practical intelligence. In R. J. Sternberg (Ed.), *Handbook of intelligence* (pp. 380–395). New York: Cambridge University Press.

461. Zentall, T. R. (2000). Animal intelligence. In R. J. Sternberg (Ed.), *Handbook of intelligence* (pp. 197–215). New York: Cambridge University Press.

AUTHOR INDEX

SUBJECT INDEX